Celebration & Renewal

Rites of Passage in Judaism

Celebration

Edited by Rela M. Geffen

&Renewal

Rites of Passage in Judaism

The Jewish

Publication Society

Philadelphia and

Jerusalem

5753 / 1993

The publication of this book was made possible by

a generous gift from LEON J. PERELMAN in tribute to his children

DAVID H. PERELMAN and CYNTHIA STRAUB.

Designed by Rich Hendel
Typeset in Aldus by The Composing
Room of Michigan, Inc.
Printed by Haddon Craftsmen

Library of Congress Cataloging-in-
Publication Data
Celebration & renewal : rites of passage
in Judaism / edited by Rela M. Geffen.
     p.   cm.
Includes bibliographical references and
index.
     Summary: Explains such life-cycle
events as birth, marriage, midlife,
sickness, religious conversion, and
mourning as viewed, experienced, and
treated from a Jewish perspective.
ISBN 0–8276–0422–x
1. Judaism—Customs and practices.
2. Life cycle, Human—Religious
aspects—Judaism.   3. Life change
events—Religious aspects—Judaism.
4. Judaism—20th century.   5.
Judaism—United States.   6. Jewish
way of life.   [1. Judaism—Customs and
practices.]   I. Geffen, Rela M.
II. Title: Celebration and renewal.
BM700.C39   1993
296.4′4—dc20
                              93–12493
                              CIP
                              AC

אל־תטש תורת אמן

משלי א:ח

And do not forsake the Torah *of your mother*

Proverbs 1:8

For my mother, S Y L V I A   M I N T Z   G E F F E N ,

on her ninetieth birthday

Contents

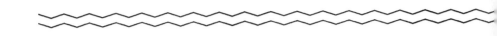

Acknowledgments

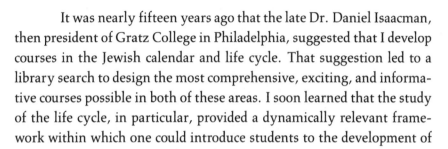

It was nearly fifteen years ago that the late Dr. Daniel Isaacman, then president of Gratz College in Philadelphia, suggested that I develop courses in the Jewish calendar and life cycle. That suggestion led to a library search to design the most comprehensive, exciting, and informative courses possible in both of these areas. I soon learned that the study of the life cycle, in particular, provided a dynamically relevant framework within which one could introduce students to the development of Jewish law and practice. The multigenerational, multidenominational composition of the student body at Gratz College further enriched the learning experience.

The biggest challenge was to find basic texts around which to organize undergraduate, and later graduate, courses. Many of the available books were denominationally oriented mini-encyclopedias or in-depth treatments of individual issues, such as birth control or divorce. In addition, new texts of ceremonies, and responsa were being written each year that I taught the course. Birth ceremonies for girls; organizations to free *agunot* (anchored women); redefinitions of the moment of death; the legitimacy of abortion, on the one hand, and of surrogate mothering, on the other—the 1980s were years during which the study of life's passages and the related Jewish law was a constantly expanding, dynamic experience. And providing students with the tools to prepare for class required the compilation of a constantly expanding ad hoc reader.

In the mid-eighties, the then executive vice-president of the Jewish Publication Society, Mr. Nathan Barnett, was a student in the life cycle course. It was he who first suggested that I create an edited volume that would remedy some of the deficiencies of currently available books, both by being transdenominational in scope and by including subject matter areas not usually covered. I wish to express my thanks to the editorial committee of JPS, under the chairmanship of Chaim Potok, for approving the original proposal; to Sheila F. Segal, for the title *Celebration and Renewal*, for guidance in formulating the structure, and for help in editing early versions of many of the chapters; to Dr. Ellen Frankel, who is able gently but firmly to prod procrastinators while editing with a deft touch; and to Rabbi Michael A. Monson and the staff at JPS for shepherding the book through to publication.

It will rapidly become obvious to the reader that the chapter authors in this volume are an exceptional group. Their breadth of scholarship, dedication to and enthusiasm for this collaborative task, and willingness to rewrite chapters so that the whole would be more coherent made this book possible. Without the technical help and emotional support of Rochelle Cohen at Gratz College, I would never have completed this project. Several people, including graduate students at Gratz and my sister and brother-in-law, Lisa and James Schlesinger, read and critiqued one or more of the chapters. Over the years, scores of students have taught me and each other about the Jewish life cycle as they gave reports in class and exchanged ideas and life experiences. All of these people have enriched this book, but any errors are mine alone.

My sons, Uri Zvi and Amiel Tuvia, were patient with a mother who was sometimes preoccupied with esoteric topics removed from their daily lives. On the other hand, their responses to life cycle events, both happy and sad, during the last four years have convinced me of the importance of writing and teaching about all aspects of life passages from the perspective of the Jewish tradition. The commitment to Jewish family life of my parents, Rabbi Joel S. Geffen, of blessed memory, and Sylvia Mintz Geffen, had a great impact on me. Growing up in their home I learned an appreciation of the rhythm of Jewish life through the calendar and life cycle observances which cannot be duplicated by reading alone. Even so, I hope that this book will be instrumental in expanding the commitments I learned experientially to a broader public. The celebration of my mother's ninetieth birthday this year and her wise attitude toward aging have provided the extended family with a wonderful prism through which a panoply of birth, marriage, divorce, illness, and mourning experiences could be put into perspective. For all of her support and love, I dedicate this book to her.

Philadelphia, 13 August 1992/14 Av 5752

Rela M. Geffen

Celebration & Renewal

Rites of Passage in Judaism

RELA M. GEFFEN

Introduction

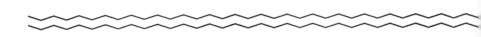

The terms *celebration* and *renewal* reflect Judaism's positive perspective on the unending circle of life from conception through death and back again to life through the continuity of the generations. Even at the close of a period of mourning, one Jew says to another, "Af simchas"—let us come together again at times of joy. Just after a baby boy undergoes the pain of circumcision, the tension in the room is often released in laughter as the person who names the baby, most often the *mohel* (ritual circumciser), wishes his parents the joy of bringing their son to the wedding canopy. What might easily be construed as a ludicrous blessing for an eight-day-old infant actually reflects a communal orientation filled with hope. The ritual belongs not only to the life story of those in the child's immediate family; it also reminds those present of similar ceremonies held at far-off times and places as well as of other birth ceremonies that they themselves have attended. Thus this moment links them to other Jews across space and time, tying their personal history with that of the Jewish people.

The great French sociologist Emile Durkheim wrote about the importance of public ritual life for maintaining and strengthening group norms. He noted, for instance, that many people feel cheated when a bride and groom elope. Look around at a wedding ceremony and you will see couples reliving their own special moments. They may even mouth the words of the wedding formula or of the seven benedictions. It is the ritual familiarity of the ceremony that enhances its power. The very routineness of the passage infuses it with communal and historical meaning for the celebrants, while at the same time reinforcing memories of similar moments in the lives of the congregation. Understanding this aspect of human nature—the need to affirm family continuity within a public context—the rabbis ordained that life's passages be marked in the presence of a quorum, the minimum definition of community. For this reason, circumcision, marriage, and kaddish require the presence of a minyan.

The Fundamentally Democratic Nature of Life Cycle Ritual

In addition to connecting the communal and private histories of spectators and participants, life cycle rituals mark significant life stages experienced by most human beings. These rituals, then, represent the most democratic of ceremonials: they are the great levelers. The rabbis demonstrated their understanding of such universality when they wrote in the Talmud (Mo'ed Katan 27a–b) that rich and poor alike should be buried on the simplest of biers in plain shrouds. Like the Amish code, the rabbinic message conveyed the sense that "plain" is the highest accolade. Thus the rabbis affirmed the right of all members of society publicly to mark life cycle events with honor, regardless of social class, gender or intellectual achievement.

The commandments recited in every morning service from Mishnah Peah 1:1 and Shabbat 127a—that every Jewish community band together to dower poor brides, house travelers, visit the sick, and escort the dead to the grave—exemplify the democratic nature of these rituals. In reality, of course, there was always some differentiation between rich and poor, not in the rituals themselves but in the ceremonies that accompanied them. In late medieval and early modern times, rabbis in some communities even had to invoke sumptuary laws restraining ostentation. Nevertheless, the fundamentally egalitarian nature of life cycle rituals continued, inhering in their universal availability to the community.

Biological Passages and Social Inventions

Some life cycle events, such as birth, puberty, illness, and death, mark passages that are biologically determined, whereas others, such as adolescence, marriage, divorce, and midlife, owe more to social invention. Over time, however, these differentiations may disappear as social convention gains precedence over biological determinism. For example, the fact that the legal status of Bar and Bat Mitzvah originally marked the onset of puberty has become irrelevant to their celebration now; but even so, the attempt by the Reform movement to replace them with Confirmation at age eighteen and later sixteen proved unsuccessful. Within Jewish law these legal marking-off points were in fact always fixed to a certain age regardless of the physical maturity of an individual child (thus a girl reaches majority at age twelve or the appearance of two pubic hairs), suggesting that there was always a sociological as well as a biological definition of reaching the age of responsibility for fulfilling the commandments.

The Question of Universal Passages: The Necessity and Inevitability of Change

Theoretically, all Jews are entitled to celebrate most public ritual ceremonies. Therefore, those who have been single and/or childless and thus unable to participate in those ceremonies and rituals linked to marriage and parenting and for young men, Bar Mitzvah, have themselves felt cheated while often being pitied by the community. Precisely because every Jew felt entitled to participate in such events, those who missed out often suffered a profound sense of deprivation. For women, the absence of rituals surrounding marriage and childbearing, with their accompanying statuses of wife and mother, led to feelings of isolation and loss. Until our own century, the lack of a "coming of age" ceremony for girls such as the Bat Mitzvah must have created some feelings of exclusion. Some men whose thirteenth birthdays were ignored have felt the lack of this ceremony all their lives. Thus we sometimes read of elderly Jewish men staging lavish Bar Mitzvah ceremonies for themselves (Armand Hammer was planning one just before he died).

Today, assumptions about the natural progression and inevitability of life cycle passages, particularly those based on the traditional nuclear family, serve to distance some Jews from the community rather than bringing them closer to it. Many contemporary Jewish families are not conventional in structure and may feel that they do not "fit" into the community with its traditional institutions and rituals. Divorced parents and step-parents may feel uneasy at a Bar or Bat Mitzvah or their children's wedding ceremonies. Never-married singles and single parents may avoid certain communal occasions. All this is further compounded in the case of a mixed marriage or remarriage. Even when a spouse, parent, or step-parent converts to Judaism, the fact that the extended family does not follow suit means that whole sets of relatives, including grandparents or mothers- and fathers-in-law, may not relate to important Jewish rituals.

As one reads through the chapters in this book it will become apparent that life cycle rituals are continually evolving to suit new social roles; if they fail to do so, then over time they cease to be the democratic constants that have always undergirded the Jewish community. Of course, this process requires that the richness of tradition and the historical and familial associations embedded in the rituals be balanced with the need for change. Living as we do in an age of transition, we will probably see many innovations tried but only a few retained as integral to the living tradition.

Perspectives on the Life Cycle and Rites of Passage in this Book

In " 'Be Fruitful and Multiply': Issues Relating to Birth in Judaism," a wide-ranging essay detailing Jewish legal approaches to birth control, abortion, adoption, naming, and the many rituals surrounding the birth of boys and girls, Rabbi David Novak presents several examples of modification, enrichment, or complete innovation in traditional life cycle rituals. Most of the modified or entirely new customs he discusses are linked to the inclusion of women—as mothers whose names are noted in the official Hebrew names of their children; as daughters who are welcomed ceremonially into the covenant of Israel and even as ritual circumcisers.

The chapters on young children by Dr. Steven Brown ("Parents as

Partners of God") and on adolescence by Drs. Shoshana and Melvin Silberman ("From Bar/Bat Mitzvah Through the Teen Years") focus more on the dilemmas of parent-child relationships than on formal rites of passage. Still, they provide some good examples of religious innovations based on Jewish tradition that in many instances have moved beyond a transitional trial stage and are now institutionalized, though in a variety of forms, in American Jewish religious life across the movements. For example, as late as the 1950s and 1960s, most teen-age Jewish girls did not expect to formally mark the legal status of Bat Mitzvah. By the end of the 1980s, however, even in the centrist Orthodox community, many who did not publicly mark their coming of age as Jewish adults felt left out. At the same time, Confirmation, an innovative attempt to create a coming-of-age ceremony later in adolescence, at a time more consonant with norms of adulthood in modern society, appears, after a century of attempted institutionalization, to be losing ground in the Conservative and even the Reform movements. In the meantime, in fact, Bar Mitzvah has been restored, and the innovative Bat Mitzvah ceremony introduced, to most Reform congregations.

Given the impact of America's open society on marital norms in the community, the discussion by Rabbi Stephen Lerner of the history of and process of "choosing Judaism" is crucial for contemporary Jews. Because of individual conviction, but primarily through the stimulus of a loving relationship with a Jew, tens of thousands of adults have converted to Judaism over the last two decades. In addition, the great number of non-Jewish babies adopted by Jewish couples, both owing to infertility problems and for humanitarian reasons, has heightened the need to understand the conversion process for infants and children.

In Jewish marriage, the community's adherence to some customs such as having a wedding canopy (huppah) or breaking a glass at the close of the ceremony are so ingrained that even in the event of an interfaith marriage the Jewish partner often wants to include these rituals in the ceremony. Most Jews, however, are less familiar with the Jewish value concepts governing the relationship between spouses. Rabbi Daniel Gordis's essay "Marriage: Judaism's 'Other' Covenantal Relationship" provides important background about these concepts and their implications for the couple as they embark on their new partnership. Rabbi Gordis explores Jewish marriage as a covenantal bond approximating that between humans and God. As he traces notions of marriage in Judaism from biblical through rabbinic and modern times, it becomes clear that stable, monogamous marriages have traditionally been considered the bedrock of Jewish society and the embodiment of holiness.

As noted earlier, some life cycle stages are more socially than biologically constructed and may vary greatly among cultures and over time. Like adolescence, the stages of midlife and aging have received many definitions through the ages, with the person going through them facing an array of consequences, depending on the cultural and social conditions of his or her community. For instance, as Rabbi Barry Cytron points out in his essay "Midlife: From Understanding to Wisdom," some experts deny that midlife is a stage at all and question whether the "midlife crisis" is an inevitable concomitant of middle age. Moreover, because the life span in earlier centuries was shorter than it is now, one often moved from the stage of childbirth and parenting directly to the status of elder. As a result, Jewish tradition does not have many formal texts or ceremonies linked to this middle-of-life time. Rabbi Cytron's treatment of midlife exemplifies how new rituals develop and traditional ones are redefined, as in the case of adult Bar and Bat Mitzvah ceremonies. He also draws from the traditional metaphors for understanding and finding fulfillment in midlife, at which one assesses one's accomplishments as well as one's contribution to the next generation.

Midlife often brings with it the realization that relationships begun in young adulthood have become weakened. Despite its promarriage and pronatalist position, Judaism has always allowed, if with some dismay, for the failure of human relationships. Thus divorce has always been permitted, though with the important restriction that it be initiated by the husband and granted with his permission. This stricture, despite certain rabbinic leniencies developed over the centuries, has put Jewish women at a considerable disadvantage, which has on occasion grown into full-blown tragedy. In response to this dilemma, the Reform movement has accepted civil divorce granted by the state in lieu of a Jewish divorce (*get*); the Conservative movement, by contrast, has designed a more egalitarian marriage document in which the husband and wife, in advance, name the court as their agent should one partner wish a divorce. In "'The Altar Weeps': Divorce in Jewish Law," Rabbi Irwin Haut traces the development of Jewish divorce law from the biblical and rabbinic periods through contemporary times, exploring key issues still facing traditional Jews both in Israel and in Diaspora Jewish communities.

As one moves through the life cycle, illness may strike, often causing nuclear and extended families to experience extreme stress. Illness strikes not only the aged but the young and middle-aged as well. In his essay "*Bikkur Ḥolim*: Sickness in Jewish Law," Rabbi Nahum Waldman traces biblical, rabbinic, medieval, modern, and contemporary views of illness. He discusses the role of the doctor in healing; whether full disclosure to the patient of the extent of an illness is proper; special obligations when the patients are one's parents; and contemporary issues such as AIDS and life support systems. Along the way we come to appreciate the intricacies of rabbinic law and the extraordinary knowledge and research required of a *posek halakhah* (legal decisor) in contemporary times. Currently at the heart of Jewish legal debate on illness are such topics as the definition of death, the permissibility of transplants, when extraordinary measures should be applied, the propriety of hospice care, initiation and refusal of life support systems, and considerations of passive and active euthanasia.

Even when healthy, aging is difficult to confront for contemporary Americans. Unlike most traditional societies, American culture conveys the idea that age brings obsolescence rather than wisdom. Use of the model of living by mitzvot (commandments) to cope with aging is the subject of Rabbi Dayle Friedman's "The Crown of Glory: Aging in the Jewish Tradition." Pointing to the "graying" of the American Jewish community, she presents traditional Jewish views of aging and suggests a paradigm for applying some of these concepts to enhance the status and quality of life of the Jewish elderly.

Discussions of illness and aging invariably lead to a confrontation with death. Those familiar with Jewish attitudes toward death and with the rites of mourning will be equipped to preserve the dignity of the deceased and to ease their own pain. It is in this spirit that Dr. Judith Hauptman, in "Death and Mourning: A Time for Weeping, A Time for Healing," approaches Jewish attitudes toward bereavement, a process that begins with honoring the dead, then moves the communal focus after burial to comforting the mourner, and finally gently prods the griever through stages of healing back toward the fullness of life. In addition to elucidating traditional principles and laws governing various stages of *aveylut* (mourning), Dr. Hauptman also treats several very contemporary matters such as the status of women as mourners, new rituals related to fetal mourning after miscarriage and stillbirth, and the options of converts after the loss of their non-Jewish parents.

A Final Note to the Reader

The authors whose work is included here represent the broad spectrum of the North American Jewish community: they are Orthodox, Conservative, and Reform rabbis and educators, and academic scholars who teach in public and private universities, colleges of Jewish studies, and denominational seminaries. It is hoped that this work will appeal and find acceptance throughout the English-speaking Jewish community. Each author has provided annotated selections for further study, so that any reader may deepen his or her understanding of particular rites or passages.

There are several ways in which this book may be used by individuals and groups. Chapters on modern passages such as the parenting of young or adolescent children, conversion to Judaism, midlife, and aging will be useful to those experiencing these stages as individuals, and they can also serve as study materials for groups sponsored by synagogues, Jewish community centers, *havurot*, and Jewish family services. Those teaching introductory Judaism classes, especially for Jews by choice, should find all of the essays germane to their curriculum. Finally, it is the editor's hope that students of all religions and ethnic backgrounds, whether studying these materials in university courses on Judaism specifically or as part of courses on world religions, will benefit from comparing the volume's portrayal of the Jewish tradition with their own heritages and life experiences.

Throughout this book, the authors of the various essays examine traditional Jewish sources, laws, and customs and describe a spectrum of contemporary practice. The reader will often find law interspersed with social science and philosophy. Some chapters, such as those on birth, conversion, marriage, divorce, illness, and death, focus more on legal development and the description of rituals, while others, such as those on parenting, midlife, and aging, are more sociological, psychological, and philosophical in emphasis. Yet Judaism's positive way of looking at life as celebration and renewal permeates the whole, reflecting the many voices speaking through this volume.

DAVID NOVAK

"Be Fruitful and Multiply"

Issues Relating to Birth in Judaism

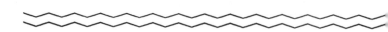

Parenting as a Partnership with God

The unique partnership with God that human procreation involves is perhaps best expressed in a passage in the Talmud which declares that there are three partners in the creation of a human being: God, father, and mother (Kiddushin 30b). This view has many implications.

There is no question that Jewish tradition, starting with the Bible, has been pronatalist. The very first words that God uttered to the new human creatures in the Garden of Eden were "Be fruitful and multiply and fill the earth" (Genesis 1:28). The conception and bearing of children is considered to be the type of commandment that makes humans the partners of God in the process of creation itself. Thus, in a famous passage in the Talmud, one rabbi states that when someone refuses to procreate, it is "as if" that person had shed human blood; in other words, that person has diminished human population by the sin of omission. Another rabbi stated, in this same passage, that it is "as if" that person had diminished the divine image, by not enabling humans, who are in the image of God, to be born (Yevamot 63b).

First, parents are not the absolute creators of their children: they are only their cocreators—God's junior partners, as it were. "Indeed, all lives are Mine: be it the life of the father or the life of the son, they are all Mine" (Ezekiel 18:4). Children are not the simple extension of their human parents. From conception on, the child has certain rights independent of his or her parents. Thus children may not be punished for the crimes of their parents. Neither do parents have a right to abuse their children. This is not only because children are not the property of their parents. In a system that declares as an axiom, "The earth is the Lord's and all that fills it" (Psalm 24:1), there is no such thing as "property" in the sense of human ownership of things, whether animate or inanimate. Everything over which humans have any control is only something lent to them under certain definite conditions. In the case of one's own children, who are themselves considered to be full human persons, parents have fewer privileges and more responsibilities than over anything else in their domain or care. Although children are obligated to both "honor" and "revere" their parents once they reach the age of moral responsibility, that duty is far outweighed by the obligations of parents to their children.

Second, parenthood is not considered a purely natural inclination. Although animals are also blessed with the ability to "be fruitful and multiply," the actual divine commandment is *spoken* to humans only; whereas in the words "let them be fruitful and multiply" (Genesis 1:22) God seems to be speaking *about* animals; in the case of humans "God spoke *to* them" (Genesis 1:28). Being a commandment—a mitzvah— rather than just an inevitable natural inclination means that parenthood must often be accomplished in the face of strong antinatal temptations. We know, for example, that during times of Jewish calamity and destruction some believed that it was pointless, even cruel, to bring children into a world of such unhappiness and persecution, a world that had proved to be a dangerous place for Jews. Such beliefs are common today as well, especially among those convinced that global nuclear destruction is an imminent probability, or that Jewish children are endangered by the persistence of anti-Semitism. Given these understandable fears, which cannot in and of themselves be considered irrational, parenthood for Jews at times has to be a conscious act of faith that God will not allow either the earth or the Jewish people to be destroyed. "There is hope for your future, says the Lord" (Jeremiah 31:16). Jewish parenthood entails a real commitment to the future despite historical evidence to the contrary.

This pronatalist faith is not only deeply grounded in the Bible and Talmud, but it also has been confirmed in our own century by the actions of a particular segment of the Jewish people: Holocaust survivors. If any group of Jews would be justified to despair for the future and refuse to have children, surely these survivors would be so justified. Yet the overwhelming majority regarded themselves as a "saved remnant" (she'erit ha-peleitah) and were determined to build a new Jewish future out of the ashes of their past. As soon as possible the Jewish survivors began to marry and have children. Indeed, many had families larger than those of Jews who had not suffered anything even remotely similar to that trauma. Some of the more articulate survivors have declared that giving birth was their most tangible way of expressing faith that the Jewish people still lives and will continue to live. With their very bodies they made a statement to God, themselves, and the world. Those Jews who have elected to remain childless, however, when marriage and bearing and raising children were biologically and socially possible for them, are sometimes motivated by considerations of personal convenience and comfort, despite the seemingly idealistic rationalizations sometimes offered.

This is an important issue for the entire Jewish people, inasmuch as the American Jewish birthrate, with the notable exception of the most orthodox Jews, is below replacement level. There is much talk these days about overpopulation in the world, yet the Jewish people has not yet overcome the demographic losses of the Holocaust. In 1933 there were some 18 million Jews in the world; now there are about 13 million. Considering that many other peoples have doubled or even tripled their numbers over those same sixty years, and that issues such as high infant mortality hardly affect Jews anymore, increasing the Jewish birthrate has come to be of deep concern for many Jews committed to the survival and growth of their people.

Birth Control

Jewish pronatalism, nevertheless, does not necessarily entail a rejection of family planning. The commandment to be fruitful and multiply is consistent both with spacing children out and with limiting family size. The Mishnah (Yevamot 6.6) contains a debate between the schools of Shammai and of Hillel as to how many children a man must father before he is considered to have fulfilled the obligation to be fruitful and multiply. The school of Shammai is of the opinion that two male children are necessary; the school of Hillel, however, states that one male and one female are needed: that is, a man must minimally replenish humankind as it originated with the first couple—male and female. The law ultimately followed the Hillelite position, although a number of subsequent legal authorities ruled that this was only a minimal standard and that, optimally, every Jewish man should endeavor to father as many children as possible.

At this point, however, we have only half the story. Since the obligation to procreate is considered to be directed only to men, how do women fit in? Obviously, men require women if they are to become fathers. Many authorities, in fact, state that a woman should not prevent procreation by refusing to marry, or by refusing to engage in sexual relations with her husband, or by refusing to conceive. She is considered to be her husband's partner in procreation, and indeed, ultimately God's partner in creation. But because women are not directly commanded to initiate procreation, traditionally they have had more latitude than men in deciding how many children to bear and when to bear them. This situation is not merely a matter of how a biblical commandment is to be interpreted and applied; it also no doubt involves the recognition that women have more at stake in conception, pregnancy, and birth than do men. They have the physical burden and take the physical risks. For this reason, most authorities permit Jewish women to practice birth control as long as it is not by a permanent procedure like sterilization—though even here permanence could be justified if pregnancy and birthing would pose a grave risk to the life or health of a woman.

Traditionally, however, men are not permitted to practice birth control. It is considered a prohibition of "spilling seed," whether it be outside the mouth of the uterus, as when a man uses a condom, or outside the mouth of the vagina, as in coitus interruptus. Needless to say, any sterilization procedure, such as a vasectomy, is strictly proscribed by Jewish law. Although the subject is disputed, many rabbinical authorities would permit a woman to use a diaphragm and spermicide to prevent the man's sperm from entering her uterus and fertilizing an ovum. Even more rabbinical authorities would permit use of the pill, since here no physical barrier separates the male and female bodies. Devices such as the IUD, inasmuch as they seem to be abortifacts, preventing a fertilized ovum from attaching itself to the wall of the uterus, entail the complex moral problem of abortion, which will be discussed in the next section.

In sum, in Judaism, pronatalism and the use of birth control are not seen as mutually exclusive. Although Judaism is clearly pronatalist, birth control is permitted when a woman's own physical and emotional condition and the welfare of her family so warrant. The procreation of human life is the primary value, and concerns for the quality of human life (beginning with that of the woman herself) largely determine now that value is to be implemented.

Abortion

Abortion has become a highly volatile moral issue in which neutrality proves almost impossible. Jews are no exception. Despite much discussion of abortion in the classical and modern Jewish legal and ethical literature, the issue does not lend itself to the often simplistic positions of "pro-life" or "pro-choice" advocates that one hears every day.

The most basic question in any discussion of abortion is whether the fetus, or unborn child (one's very terminology frequently indicates an underlying moral position on the question), is a human person or not. Two differing Jewish views can be identified on this point. On one side are those who see the fetus as "a human within a human" (Sanhedrin 57b, re Genesis 9:6). On the other side are those who regard the child as a human person only after it emerges from the womb (Rashi on Sanhedrin 72b, re Ohalot 7.6); before that, it is simply a part of the mother's body. Yet accepting either of these views as an absolute moral principle from which to deduce the practical rules is inconsistent with the complexity of the issue and, indeed, of the two positions.

According to the first view, it would seem that *any* abortion ought to be prohibited. In fact, however, abortion is not only permitted but mandated when there is a direct threat to the mother. (We will soon examine just what "direct threat" means.) According to the second view, it would seem that *any* abortion ought to be permitted. Yet Jewish legal authorities (*poskim*; sing. *posek*) have always regarded abortion to be an exception, a dispensation from an act generally prohibited, something permitted only because of extenuating circumstances in a particular case. The fact is that most pregnancies are not considered to pose any direct threat to the mother. Thus, within the normative Jewish tradition, there is no permission of *elective* abortion based on a woman's "right" to do with her own body as she (or anyone else) pleases.

Those who accept the first view, that the unborn child is a human person, can still justify the direct-threat-to-the-mother exemption by arguing that in situations where two lives are at stake, the moral obligation is to save the one closest at hand—namely, that of the mother, whose life is always more immediate than that of the unborn child within the recesses of her body. Similarly, those who accept the second view, that the fetus is not a human person, can justify the general prohibition of abortion on the grounds of the proscription of wanton destruction (*bal tashḥit*), which in this case would be self-mutilation. As we saw above, Judaism does not regard anything in the universe as being the *property* of anyone but God. Therefore, one may not destroy anything unless one has been specifically authorized to do so by the Torah for purposes that the Torah regards as acceptable. For example, Jews are authorized to slaughter certain animals, but only in a specified way, and only for the sake of obtaining meat for food or hides to make clothing. (Thus, though vegetarianism is an acceptable Jewish option, it cannot be promoted as a Jewish moral requirement, thereby making the eating of meat immoral.) Jews are also mandated to kill in self-defense, an injunction that has long been used to allow the killing of a fetus that in any way threatens the life of its mother. One is not, however, permitted to kill a fetus for any lesser reason. To do so would be an act of unauthorized mutilation—either self-mutilation or, in the doctor's or another petitioner's case, complicity in self-mutilation, even when done at the mother's request.

So far it would seem that the same practical result emerges whether one holds that the unborn child is a human person or that the fetus is part of its mother's body. But in all legal reasoning about a question of any complexity, practical results are not deduced from one principle alone. Rather, at work is an interplay of several principles. This process is best described by the Talmudic term *pilpul*, meaning "debate" but more often seen as futile hairsplitting. Yet when *pilpul* is carried out responsibly, it is a highly subtle form of legal analysis, one that grounds practical conclusions within the interaction of a variety of principles. And indeed, *pilpul* on this question of abortion does show that some practical differences qualify the two basic views regarding the fetus/unborn child, differences that emerge when the "direct threat" stipulation is specified more precisely.

If the unborn child is regarded as a person, but one whose life can be forfeited for that of the mother because her life is closer at hand than his or hers, then direct threat receives a narrow interpretation, namely, as a threat to the physical life of the mother only. (Indeed, even the source from Ohalot 7.6 mentioned above, which is used by those who argue that the fetus is not a human person, specifically limits the authorization of abortion to cases in which only the dismemberment of the fetus in utero will save the mother from being torn apart by its passage down the birth canal.) In this view, anything less than a direct threat to the mother's life, such as a threat to her overall health or general psychological well-being, would be insufficient to warrant abortion. (It should be noted that this stance would ban virtually all abortions for Jews in the United States, where today less than 2 percent of the abortions performed are for reasons of a direct threat to the mother's life, thanks to a quality of prenatal care unavailable when the rabbinic texts were formulated.)

If the fetus is regarded as part of its mother's body, however, direct threat can gain a broader interpretation. For example, permission for an abortion could then be based on psychiatric considerations such as prepartum depression, especially if there is responsible psychiatric opinion that a continued pregnancy raises the strong probability of suicide in a clinically depressed patient. (Although in fact psychiatric opinion is itself divided on whether abortion in such cases is psychically beneficial or not.) Those who adhere to this view will even authorize an abortion in the case of a fetus that is diagnosed with Tay-Sachs disease, a circumstance of considerable interest inasmuch as Tay-Sachs is an untreatable genetic disease that occurs almost exclusively among Jews. The reasoning in such authorizations, significantly, does not address the hopeless life awaiting the Tay-Sachs fetus once it is born. Rather, authorization is based on the question of maternal well-being: that is, it causes the mother (and the father, though his concerns are not discussed as a reason for abortion in the traditional sources) acute psychic pain to know that the child she is carrying is doomed to such a brief, miserable life. Still, even according to this more liberal view, there has to be some *objective* criterion calling for an abortion, such as clinical depression. Even advocates of this view could not possibly endorse elective abortion as it has been so widely practiced in the United States since the *Roe v. Wade* decision of 1973. From the perspective of halakhah (Jewish law), the burden of proof is clearly on those seeking an abortion, either for themselves or on behalf (and at the request) of someone else.

Although the traditional Jewish position is generally "pro-life," or at any rate anti-abortion, this does not mean that a traditional Jew must actively support the "pro-life" movement as it is constituted politically in American society today. Indeed, one could well question whether the maternal safeguards so much emphasized in Jewish tradition— especially as interpreted by the more liberal current of the faith—would be sufficiently respected if that position became the law of the land. On the other hand, the "pro-choice" stance is clearly inconsistent with the whole thrust of Jewish tradition, for it is based on a notion of human ownership of the human body, an idea that directly contradicts the Jewish dogma that everything belongs to God—men's bodies, women's bodies, anyone's body (Ezekiel 18:4). Rights over any being, including ourselves, are but limited privileges. Divinely decreed duties must always take precedence in the Jewish tradition.

Admittedly, this outlook contravenes the emotional inclinations and political opinions of many Jews today, especially American Jewish liberals. But in traditional Judaism the Torah takes precedence, irrespective of how few Jews accept its teachings, whether on a specific issue or in general. In the case of abortion, there is little doubt that the inclinations and opinions of many Jews have been strongly influenced by the secular culture in which they live. On this question of abortion, especially, traditional Judaism is countercultural.

Naming Children

There is a Hebrew folk saying, recorded in the Bible, to indicate that a person's name can illustrate his or her character: *Kishmo ken hu'*— "Like his name so is he" (1 Samuel 25:25). If, for example, a woman's name is Rinah, meaning "song" (or "joy"), and she is a musical person, one might use this saying to indicate how appropriate her birth name is in retrospect, looking back on her life from the present. Names in the Bible can also be seen to predict at birth what that person's character will subsequently turn out to be. For example, the name of the patriarch Jacob, or Ya'akov, means "usurper"; it describes both how he tried to usurp his bother Esau's prior exit from the womb by grabbing his heel during birth (*Ya'akov* in fact derives from *ekev,* "heel") and how he ultimately usurped Esau as the heir of their father, Isaac, and grandfather Abraham. Similarly, the name of the prophet Samuel, or Shemu'el, means (according to some scholars) "the one about whom God heard me," referring to his theretofore barren mother's prayer for a child. Traditionally, in other words, the name given a child is considered to be a matter of great importance, having considerable influence on the development of that child's character.

Although no codified rules exist to guide parents in the naming of their children, custom has evolved a variety of practices (*minhagim*) commonly accepted by Jews in different localities.

Among Ashkenazim—that is, Jews of Central and Eastern European origin—the custom is to name the child after someone, usually a family member, who has recently died. In most cases this is a grandparent or great-grandparent. The usual explanation for this practice is that the parents hope that in receiving the name of an admired family member the child will emulate in his or her life the virtues of the deceased namesake. To a certain extent, too, it is believed that the soul of the loved one lives on in the child who now bears his or her name. Indeed, learning about the persons for whom they are named is an excellent way for children to identify with the history of their own Jewish families and, by extension, with the history of the whole Jewish people. Some parents even add these personal explanations to the birth ceremonies for their children.

Sephardim—that is, Jews of Iberian or Middle-Eastern origin—usually name their children after a grandparent, either living or dead, and many Sephardic grandparents look forward to being honored with grandchildren who bear their own names while they are still alive to see it. Sephardim are also much more punctilious about naming a boy after a man and a girl after a woman than are most Ashkenazim. In Sephardic families this procedure often has the effect of strengthening trans-

generational ties between grandfathers and grandsons, and between grandmothers and granddaughters.

Frequently, Jewish parents give their child both a Hebrew name and a secular name for use in general society. Sephardim often choose a non-Jewish name whose meaning approximates that of the Hebrew name. Thus, for example, a boy might be called Raḥamim, meaning "compassion" (a name almost exclusively used by Sephardim, by the way), and Clement, based on the Latin *clementia* and meaning virtually the same thing. Among East European Jews, the Hebrew name would be accompanied by a Yiddish one, again often with a similar meaning. Thus the name Dov, meaning "bear" (in this case a name found almost exclusively among Ashkenazim), might be followed by the Yiddish name Ber. Hence, a man would be known as Dov-Ber, both formally and even in ordinary conversation. If a diminutive were to be used, it was usually based on the Yiddish name alone; hence, Dov-Ber would be called Berl as a nickname, or Zev-Wolf would be Velvel.

German-speaking Jews, for the most part, did not attempt to make any connection between the Hebrew and German names given a child. Thus a boy might well be named, for example, Avraham Franz (the latter an especially popular name because of German-speaking Jews' affection and respect for the Austro-Hungarian emperor Franz-Josef, an advocate of equal rights for Jews).

American Jews, most of whom are descended from Ashkenazic immigrants, have generally followed the East European custom of making some connection between the two names given a child at birth, but more often than not the link is a phonic one rather than one based on meaning. Thus, if American Jewish parents name their child Sarah after a grandmother of that name, they are usually only interested in an English name beginning with *s*. So "Sarah," whose English name (if she too lived in America) was likely to have been something like Sadie, now has a granddaughter named after her with a name something like Samantha. In fact, this practice is so widespread that unlearned American Jewish parents may actually ask what is the Hebrew equivalent for a name like Sadie and are surprised to learn that there is no real equivalent but only a phonic similarity to a number of Hebrew names that begin with the Hebrew letter *sin*.

Currently in the United States biblical names are enjoying great popularity, and many American Jews are giving their children Hebrew name that have English equivalents. Thus a child might be given the name Ya'akov after his grandfather and be called Jacob in English—though that namesake might also have been named Ya'akov in Hebrew but have been called something like Jerome in English. Then too, the new Jewish self-awareness occasioned by the successful revival of the Hebrew language in the State of Israel has led to the growing popularity of new Israeli names—Ari, for instance, or Ilana—not only for Israeli children but for American Jewish children as well.

Considering the importance of a name to the overall identity and ideals of a child, many Jews feel that it behooves Jewish parents to select names for their children that will strengthen ties to family and reinforce the historical continuity of the Jewish people.

Adoption

Adoption, in its modern form, is a legal act that nullifies the relationship between biological parents and their offspring and transfers that relationship to others who have contracted to raise that child as their own flesh and blood. In the classical Jewish sources, however, biological ties cannot be so irrevocably canceled, though there certainly is precedent for a child to be raised by someone other than his or her biological parents and to become attached to them. Thus, for example, Moses was brought to Pharaoh's daughter and "became her son" (Exodus 2:10)—which may well have been the ancient Egyptian equivalent of what we know as adoption. Nevertheless, as far as the Jewish sources are concerned, Moses remained the son of Amram and Jochebed of the tribe of Levi and is always included in their genealogy. He was, in short, tied to them by blood.

Emphasis on blood ties did not, however, prevent Jewish tradition from recognizing and even encouraging the practice of raising someone else's child when biological parents were incapable of doing so for physical, emotional, or even financial reasons. The Talmud states that "whoever raises an orphan in his own home, it is accounted to him as if [k'ilu] he had actually sired him" (Sanhedrin 19b). This key statement does not in any way imply that biological parenthood is supplanted. Rather, it

indicates simply that the virtue of parenting can be exercised by persons with children they have neither conceived nor borne themselves. Indeed, they are encouraged to do so, since care of orphans is considered to be something done in imitation of God, who is called "the father of orphans" (Psalms 68:6). Thus substitute parenting, like biological parenting, is an act of partnership with God. Throughout history, Jewish orphans have found loving homes with childless Jewish couples, as well as with Jewish couples who had their own biological children. Furthermore, these "adopted" children were seen as being obligated to treat their "adoptive" parents with the same honor and reverence the Torah mandates for one's biological parents. In Eastern Europe, in fact, it was common for a childless couple who had taken an orphan into their home to refer to this child as their "kaddishl," that is, the one who would mourn their death by saying kaddish (a prayer of praise to God, recited on occasions of mourning) for them. One of the main reasons behind the desire for children is the human need to have the next generation of one's family survive one's own death. In the emotional if not in the full legal sense, therefore, "adopted" children are like biological children.

As regards raising the biological children of someone else, a number of considerations arise from Jewish law that must be taken quite seriously. Most important, enough information about the biological parents should be obtained so that when the adopted child is ready to marry, he or she will not accidentally commit incest by marrying a biological brother or sister or some other forbidden blood relation. For most Jewish adoptive parents, however, this particular consideration is irrelevant, since very few children born of Jewish parents are available for adoption. The acceptance of both birth control and abortion by most Jews, and the growing social tolerance of unwed mothers who choose to raise children by themselves, have meant that Jewish children usually stay within their biological family. Hence, Jews who wish to adopt children almost always have to adopt children born to non-Jewish parents. And in such a case, the most critical question is the religious status of these adopted children. Namely, can children be converted to Judaism? And if so, how?

The classical Jewish sources explicitly recognize the conversion of children to Judaism. As the Talmud puts it, "A minor convert may be immersed by the authorization of a rabbinical court" (Ketubot 11a). This act, of course, involves a legal fiction, in that true conversion is the result

of a responsible decision in which a non-Jew petitions a rabbinical court to become a member of the Jewish people and to accept the kingship of God and the obligations of all of the commandments. Then a rabbinical court must decide whether to take this candidate as a full-fledged convert (*ger tzedek*). Now, in the case of the conversion of a minor, and certainly of an infant, the first step is lacking: minors, by definition, are incapable of making the responsible decision the law assumes to be necessary for valid conversion.

To overcome this impediment, the Talmud introduced a justification based on the principle that one can cause another person to obtain a benefit even without that person's consent. Becoming a Jew is assumed to be such a benefit. Nevertheless, the person so steered may subsequently declare that what the benefactor did on his or her behalf is in fact a liability and not a benefit at all. When this happens, the act of beneficence is declared to be null and void retroactively. Thus the Talmud insists that the non-Jew who is converted as a minor has the right to renounce the conversion when he or she reaches the age of majority (twelve for a girl, thirteen for a boy)—though talmudic interpreters differ as to exactly how and for how long this right may be exercised. From the various opinions, however, it would seem that an adopted child must be informed of his or her origins prior to reaching the age of majority. One's biological origins, in short, may not be ignored.

Generally, children adopted by Jews are converted in infancy. (In cases where conversion was not undertaken early on, it must be done prior to Bar or Bat Mitzvah, or even just prior to marriage—situations calling for great sensitivity on the part of the rabbis involved.) The rite of conversion involves for both boys and girls immersion in a special body of water (*mikvah*) used for various rites, including conversion; beforehand, boys must additionally undergo a religiously conducted circumcision (*brit milah*). The adoptive parents are then usually given a certificate attesting to the conversion of their child and including his or her new Hebrew name. At this time, the rabbinical court (a tribunal of three rabbis) must inform the adoptive parents that the child has the right of renouncing this conversion upon reaching the age of majority. Many rabbis, sensitive to the special emotional situation of adoptive parents and children, suggest that prior to Bar or Bat Mitzvah the parents inform the child that he or she literally has the choice of continuing as a Jew or not, unlike

children born of Jewish parents who, according to Jewish tradition, are Jews whether or not they so choose. When the adopted child makes this decision—or, minimally, does not renounce Judaism—the conversion performed in infancy becomes irrevocable.

Infertility

In a tradition where the bearing and rearing of children is so valued, it is easy to see how infertility can cause great suffering. One of Abraham's most plaintive statements is when he cries out as an old, childless man, "Lord God, what can You give me when I continue to be without off-spring?" (Genesis 15:2). The matriarchs Sarah, Rebecca, and Rachel, as well as the mothers of Samson and Samuel, were all originally infertile and very much depressed by their barren state. Their subsequent ability to conceive and bear children is taken to be the result of the direct intervention of God, a point later emphasized by the Talmud (Ta'anit 2a–b) in commenting on the biblical description of Rachel's conception of Joseph: "And God remembered Rachel, and God listened to her, and He opened her womb" (Genesis 30:22). Indeed, the universal desire for children is considered to be so strong and authentic that Hannah's prayer for a child is stated by the Talmud to be the paradigm for all true prayer (Berakhot 31a–b).

Although according to the traditional sources childlessness calls for divine intervention, limited human intervention is not ruled out. All Jewish legal authorities would certainly permit any reasonably safe surgical procedure that can correct a woman's inability to conceive and carry a pregnancy to term. Medically indicated and approved fertility drugs are also allowed. Only in a case where pregnancy would present an unusual danger to a woman's life or health would conception be contraindicated.

More restrictions, however, apply to the alleviation of male infertility. Generally, the legal authorities permit what is known as AIH—artificial insemination by the husband himself—which may be called for either because some physical or chemical impediment in the woman's vagina inhibits conception through ordinary intercourse or because a man's sperm count is low. In this procedure, semen is taken from the man (preferably in a condom after intercourse rather than by masturbation), possibly concentrated to achieve a higher sperm count, and then mechanically inserted directly into his wife's uterus. Here, as well as in the case of in vitro fertilization—where a woman's ovum is surgically removed, fertilized with her husband's sperm, and then implanted in her uterus for the remainder of the pregnancy—modern medical technology is seen as aiding the normal and accepted practice of sexual intercourse between husband and wife for the sake of conception.

The procedure known as AID—artificial insemination by a donor—is, however, much more controversial. Some legal authorities go so far as to call it adultery, even though the sperm is inserted into the woman's body by mechanical means rather than through sexual intercourse. Other authorities prohibit it on the grounds that it violates the marital union, creating a situation of doubtful paternity and perhaps potential incest between children fathered by the same man. On rare occasions the procedure is reluctantly allowed, where no other means of conception are possible and where the inability to conceive has caused the woman great anguish. In this case the authorities resort to highly arcane Talmudic arguments that their opponents have charged are inappropriate to justify a practice having such serious moral overtones and radical social implications. Hence, when competent medical opinion proposes AID, traditional Jews will seek out equally competent rabbinical opinion to determine whether this procedure is religiously justified.

Surrogate motherhood as a solution for infertility is so new that no detailed rabbinical opinions are available as yet. Yet the option is at best problematic. First, there is the question of polygamy, which for approximately one thousand years has been banned in Judaism. This prohibition, though originally accepted only by Ashkenazic Jews, has since the last century been adopted by virtually all Jews. When fathers do not marry the surrogate mothers of their children, moreover, there is the problem of concubinage, concerning which most Jewish legal authorities have followed Maimonides' prohibition. And if the surrogate mother is already married, adultery would seem to enter the picture as well. Second, if the woman so impregnated is not Jewish, the prohibition of a Jewish man having a non-Jewish wife or concubine is called into question. Third, the only possible biblical precedent for this practice is the warrant ordering a Jewish indentured servant to breed with a non-Jewish slave woman in order to supply the servant's master with more non-

Jewish slaves (Exodus 21:4). The Talmud (Arakhin 29a), however, sees the institution of indentured servitude as being inoperative since the destruction of the First Temple in 586 B.C.E. In any case, to advocate a radical new practice through analogy to slavery (let alone an analogy to prostitution) would be a "defamation of God and the Torah" (*hillul ha-Shem*). It is, namely, a basic criterion in Jewish law that no practices be advocated which imply that the moral standards of Judaism are lower than those of the rest of society (Yevamot 22a; Baba Kama 113b; Sanhedrin 59a).

In addition to these possible legal impediments to using surrogate mothers, serious moral questions arise. For in a time when most Jews agree that the dignity of women needs renewed affirmation (however much they might differ on the practical consequences of that affirmation), it seems difficult to justify a practice in which the body of one woman (usually poorer and less educated than the woman who will finally be the child's "mother") is used to gratify a man (and his wife), with little consideration for the natural tie that exists between a mother and the child she has conceived and borne. A similar problem applies to in vivo fertilization, in which an ovum of one woman, fertilized by her own husband's sperm, is then placed in the uterus of another woman who carries the child to term and delivers it. In these and so many other new questions raised by current medical advances, responsible Jewish approaches require a consideration of important moral issues, from the general perspective of Jewish tradition as well as the more specific one of legal precedents and analogies.

Welcoming the Newborn Child

Over the centuries a number of practices have evolved for welcoming the newborn child, which in very recent times have been added to and modified, especially as regards baby girls. It is the custom among some Jews, for example, to have a modest celebration on the Sabbath evening after the birth of a boy, called *shalom zakhar*—"welcoming a male." Aside from the usual serving of food and drink that is part of every joyous Jewish occasion (*simḥah*), the celebration includes a brief Torah thought (*devar Torah*) appropriate to the occasion and often based on the reading of the Torah to take place the following morning in the syna-

gogue. Nowadays, a growing number of Jews are having a similar celebration upon the birth of a girl, called *simḥat bat*—"the joy of a daughter."

On the eighth day of a boy's life (unless the procedure is postponed for
medical reasons), the rite of circumcision (*brit milah*) is performed. This
is a positive commandment of the Torah, one so important that it is to be
carried out even if the eighth day falls on the Sabbath or Yom Kippur.
The procedure, preferably performed by a religious specialist in circumcision called a *mohel*, consists of three steps: the removal of the foreskin
by cutting with a knife (*milah*), the removal of the membrane covering
the glans (*peri'ah*), and the drawing of the blood from the incision—
called the "blood of the covenant" (*dam berit*)—into the shaft of the
penis (*metzitzah*). The ceremony is preceded by the father's oral designation of the *mohel* as his agent to carry out what the father himself has
been commanded to do. It is concluded by the father, or the father and
the mother together, declaring that this son has now entered the covenant of Abraham, the father of the Jewish people. During the operation,
a revered male member of the family, usually but not necessarily a
grandfather, is honored with holding the baby; he is called the *sandek*.
Other relatives and friends, male and female, may also be honored with
holding the baby before and after the operation.

Rabbinical opinion is unanimous that, optimally, the *brit milah* be
performed by a *mohel* and that the procedure be conducted as a religious
ritual and not just as minor surgery. Since many American Jewish boys
today are circumcised in the hospital as a standard procedure, the question arises as to whether a religious ceremony called *hatafat dam berit*
should be conducted, in which a drop of blood is drawn from the shaft of
the penis as the "blood of the covenant." This ceremony is required
when a boy is born without a foreskin, and when a circumcised gentile
male converts to Judaism. Because rabbinical opinion remains divided on
this issue, any Jewish parents who later regret not having had *brit milah*
for their son, or a Jewish man who discovers that he never entered the
ritual covenant and now wishes to, should consult a competent rabbi for
guidance.

A recent innovation of the Reform movement, and one not without
Talmudic basis, has been to permit women to function in the role of
mohel in *brit milah*. As a result of the growing insistence that women

play a greater role in Jewish ritual, moreover, some mothers now recite a prayer of public thanksgiving and supplication for their son's welfare at the ceremony, or recite the *berakhot* along with their husbands. In earlier Jewish custom (which many still follow), the mother was not present when the circumcision of her son took place, for it was thought to be too great an emotional strain on her in her already weakened physical condition following childbirth.

Following the actual circumcision, the newborn boy is officially named over a goblet of wine, from which the parents and family members and close friends then drink. Often a piece of gauze is dipped into this wine and placed in the baby's mouth during the operation, a gesture of pacification during the somewhat traumatic experience of circumcision. Finally a feast is served in honor of the occasion. This feast is considered a sacred meal (*se'udat mitzvah*), at which special prayers and words of the Torah are to be said.

The procedure for naming a girl is much less formal. The usual practice is for the father to be called to the reading of the Torah in the synagogue (*aliyah*) soon after the birth of his daughter. At that time a brief prayer is read, asking that the mother recover quickly from the rigors of childbirth and invoking God's blessings on the newborn girl and her parents. The prayer for the parents asks specifically that they be privileged to raise their daughter for marriage and a life of good deeds; in many congregations, the prayer now also includes mention of her being raised for a life of Torah learning, something that is stated at the naming of a baby boy. In many non-Orthodox congregations, the mother (sometimes carrying her baby daughter) is called to the Torah with her husband, or even alone, and recites both the *berakhot* for the reading of the Torah and the *berakhah* one is to recite after having successfully come through a dangerous experience.

With the advent of the movement for more participatory rights for Jewish women in public rituals, in liberal congregations a variety of new practices have recently emerged, designed to make the naming of a baby girl an occasion of greater public significance. The ceremony may, for example, be postponed until the mother and child are themselves able to be present in the synagogue, and often the two are called up to the pulpit when the name is announced. Some Jewish parents, influenced no doubt by the movement's emphasis on more intimate prayer settings, have opted to hold the naming ceremonies for their daughters at home, thus making them more like the *brit milah* for boys, which also usually takes place at home. Like the celebration on the first Sabbath of a baby girl's life (a practice now accepted even in many very traditionalist circles), these home ceremonies are frequently called *simhat bat*. On these occasions, the parents themselves, or the rabbi at their request, may devise a service, complete with appropriate prayers and readings, which they and their relatives and friends recite. In some more progressive circles, such innovations as the washing of the baby girl's feet by the parents are now being introduced—though what their staying power will be no one knows.

The final ceremony of welcoming a newborn child is known as *pidyon ha-ben*—"the redemption of the firstborn son." In ancient times, the firstborn son was frequently the family priest, the keeper of the family altar, and the officiant at the rites performed there. Eventually this task was assigned to a particular clan, the descendants of Aaron, called *kohanim* (sing., *kohen*). Because of this substitution, as it were, the Torah mandated that the firstborn son of every Jewish woman (provided she had not previously miscarried, or the firstborn son was not delivered by Caesarean section, and neither parent was the child of a *kohen* or a *levi*) be "redeemed" by paying a *kohen* five shekels as redemption money (Numbers 18:15–16). The ceremony is to take place on the thirty-first day of the baby boy's life, unless that day coincides with the Sabbath or a major Jewish holy day, in which case it is postponed. In contemporary American practice, in fact, it is quite common to have a *pidyon ha-ben* on the first Sunday after the baby's thirty-first day of life so as to enable the largest possible number of relatives and friends to attend.

The ceremony itself consists of the father paying a *kohen* five silver coins—in the United States, silver dollars are typical, though many use special *pidyon ha-ben* coins minted in Israel. The father then states that it is his desire that his son be redeemed, whereupon the *kohen* accepts the redemption coins and blesses the baby with the priestly blessing (*birkat kohanim*) found in the Torah (Numbers 6:24–26). Following the ceremony, a sacred meal (*se'udat mitzvah*) is served.

As in the case of *brit milah*, if the father (or mother) for some reason did not arrange for this ceremony to be held, the firstborn son, upon reaching his majority, must have it done for himself as soon as possible.

In an age when many young people from nonobservant homes have "returned" to traditional Judaism (*ba'alei teshuvah*), the practice of "self-redemption," as it were, is one that further enforces the choice to lead a richer Jewish life.

SUGGESTIONS FOR FURTHER READING

Hayim Halevy Donin, *To Be a Jew* (New York: Basic Books, 1972). A helpful guide to Jewish ritual practice from a moderately Orthodox point of view.

David M. Feldman, *Birth Control in Jewish Law* (New York: NYU Press, 1968). The classic scholarly treatment of the issues of birth control and abortion, written from a moderately traditional point of view.

Michael Gold, *And Hannah Wept* (Philadelphia: Jewish Publication Society, 1988). A moving and learned discussion of the issue of infertility and the options for infertile Jewish couples.

Alfred Kolatch, *The Name Dictionary* (New York: Jonathan David, 1967). A thorough presentation of the wide variety of Jewish names and their meanings.

Michael Strassfeld and Sharon Strassfeld, *The First Jewish Catalog* (Philadelphia: Jewish Publication Society, 1973). An American Jewish best-seller outlining the varied approaches to Jewish ritual in our time; illustrated and written from a generally liberal point of view.

STEVEN M. BROWN

Parents as Partners with God
Parenting Young Children

Parenthood

The Midrash recounts a story about a wealthy group of merchants who embarked on a sea voyage to sell their wares in a far-off port. Aboard the vessel the merchants sought mightily to impress each other with the quality, quantity, and value of their respective goods. When one passenger was asked to describe his particular commodity, he retorted that his merchandise was worth more than any other on board. When asked to display it, he demurred, explaining it was not something one could readily exhibit. The other merchants roundly mocked him.

That night a great storm overwhelmed the ship, which sunk with all its cargo. Luckily, the passengers all made it to shore. As days passed, the rich merchants who had lost everything were reduced to begging in the streets to sustain themselves. One day they noticed walking down the street the passenger who had boasted about having the most valuable merchandise. He was well clothed and looking quite fit.

They inquired how he had managed to avoid their

Translations of classical texts have not been made egalitarian but should be read as such.

own miserable plight. He replied, "I am a teacher of Torah. When I was found after the storm and the local people discovered I was a teacher, they quickly offered me work instructing their children. Thus I am able to support myself because my merchandise didn't go to the bottom of the sea as did yours; it remains eternally with me" (Tanḥuma Truma).

Parents often grapple with the question of what "merchandise" will insure their children a happy and productive life. What resources will best equip them to cope with the vagaries of a rapidly evolving and uncertain world? And if, God forbid, their ship is lost at sea, what will they have left to protect and sustain them when their material supports are gone? The wise Jewish parent realizes that a balance must be sought between enabling children to achieve the good life as it is defined in contemporary culture and teaching them that good living is not to be measured in things but in the quality of relationships and experiences and in service to others. The challenge is enormous: to blend the wisdom of a four-thousand-year-old heritage with insights derived from con-temporary theories of child development and education.

We need to get down to the real basics of parenting. Parents want their children to be happy, healthy, and intelligent; to have opportunities that they themselves might not have had as children and eliminate conflict wherever possible; and to be protected from, or at least be able to cope with, psychological harm and pain, especially the same hurts the parents themselves experienced while growing up. Most of what is done for and to children is motivated by these fundamental desires. The possible consequences, unfortunately, are overprotectiveness, overindulgence, and, ultimately, the creation of totally "me"-centered individuals: in short, these desires, noble though they are, can prevent parents from allowing children to develop the coping mechanisms necessary to func-tion in an imperfect world.

The Good Life

Judaism's view of what constitutes the good life and of how to balance the material and the spiritual has much to contribute to effective parent-ing today. For one thing, the Jewish sense of responsibility for "perfect-ing the world under the sovereignty of the Almighty" can help people effect the changes they want to make in both the intrapersonal and interpersonal spheres of behavior. Similarly, Judaism's emphasis on self-control and discipline, its guidelines for when to say no, can cultivate in adults and children alike the coping mechanisms that all human beings need to operate in a precarious world.

Jewish tradition and practice are rich sources when it comes to the kind of education and training that parents should provide. Parents of young children are charged with two major responsibilities: (1) to select appropriate school experiences and (2) to set an overall tone at a time when their children are most malleable, controllable, and open as well as least subject to rebellion and willful refutation of parental norms and values. Judaism emphasizes the importance of seeking out appropriate schools and teachers, yet it also recognizes that parents cannot be totally objective about their own children. Therefore, parents must look to others to help round out their efforts and give them feedback on what is appropriate for their most precious possessions: their children.

There probably has been no more difficult time in which to parent than the modern age. The enormity of opportunities, pressures, tensions, and responsibilities in an increasingly small world makes it difficult, at best, to create an environment in which parents can fully control what will happen in their young children's lives. Yet we still have many choices, and there is much that Judaism offers to help us make good choices for our children. Parenting is a task that calls one every day, twenty-four hours a day, until children leave the nest. Similarly, Judaism is a religion that takes all of life as its purview, and thus is to be lived every day, twenty-four hours a day. The richness of Jewish living provides an extraordinarily fine guide for parenting.

The notion that one's highest values and most important principles can be expressed in the mundane moments of daily life has been succinctly summarized by Morris Adler in *The World of the Talmud*:

> Religion is not a matter of living on the "peaks" of experience. That is for the saint and the mystic. More fundamentally, religion must mean transposing to a higher level of spiritual awareness and ethical sensitivity the entire plateau of daily living by the generality of men. Idolatry is defeated, not by recognition of its intellectual absurdity

alone, but by a life that expresses itself in service to God. Selfishness and greed are overcome not by professions of a larger view, but by disciplines that direct our energies, our wills, and our actions outward and upward.[1]

Successfully preparing children for the good life—that is, one in which they will find joy and fulfillment as well as enrich the lives of others—results from a myriad of small interactions and events that in turn allow the formation of character, self-image, and quality in relationships.

Responsibility for Education

Jewish tradition recognizes the importance of the earliest memories imprinted on children, especially in their devotion to God, the Jewish people, and Jewish rituals. Perhaps the greatest source of advice for parents in traditional Judaism is the Shulḥan Arukh, the code of Jewish law compiled by Joseph Caro in the sixteenth century.[2] The Shulḥan Arukh covers all areas of Jewish life, from the smallest minutiae of ritualistic observance to huge issues of faith and the world to come. In chapter 165, on the training of children, interesting advice is found, not all of which will be palatable to modern parents, but which challenges one to pause and reflect on parenting approaches and skills:

> It is the duty of parents to train their children in the practice of all the precepts, whether biblical or rabbinic. Each child should be trained in accordance with his intelligence. It is also incumbent upon parents, to guard their children against any forbidden act . . . if words are of no avail, you should chastise them with a rod. But fathers should not strike children mercilessly, as some fools do. They should take special care to train children to tell no lies, but to speak the truth at all times and to shun swearing. The above things are obligatory upon fathers as well as upon teachers.

The agenda here is clear: Parents are responsible for the overall education of their children both at home and at school. They are also charged to recognize the needs and abilities of each child, to be careful not to push them to do things for which they are not ready or in which they lack the capacity to succeed. Though corporal punishment is no longer considered an appropriate method for chastising children, and though even today an occasional slap might be deemed necessary to prevent a child from harming him- or herself, nevertheless, there is still a clear concern lest physical means of control become abuse. The notion of parental consistency is alluded to in the admonition to teach children the ability to separate truth from lies. Sometimes parents use a "white lie" to extricate themselves from an uncomfortable situation, thus setting a poor example that their children may later follow in responding to problematic situations. Obviously, parents are the ultimate role models; they are constantly, in all their actions, modeling what is desirable or undesirable behavior.

The accent of this particular passage on the father's responsibility is of course a traditional point of view, but in fact mothers have always had as much, if not more, to do with the education of their children on a daily basis. Emphasized here is the need for both parents and teachers to attend consistently to the same kinds of values and issues. The link between home and school must be organic and complementary.

Developmental Readiness: Positive Commandments

Another passage helps us better to understand the importance of developmental readiness in shaping the behavior of early childhood experiences:

The time for training a child in the performance of positive commandments depends upon the ability and the understanding of each child. Thus, as soon as the child understands the significance of the Sabbath, it becomes the child's duty to hear the Kiddush, the Havdalah, and the like. The time to train a child to observe the negative commandments, whether biblical or rabbinical, is when he or she understands when told that this thing we are forbidden to do or that food we are forbidden to eat. It is well to train a child to respond "Amen" and other responses at the synagogue. From the time that an infant begins to respond Amen, he has a share in the world to come. It is important that children be trained to behave at the synagogue with awe and reverence. Children who run about to and fro and cause confusion should rather be kept home. (Shulḥan Arukh 165:2)

It helps to remember that this passage was compiled in the sixteenth century: even then parents had problems with bored children running around the synagogue during a long service!

Notice again the tradition's emphatic concern that children be developmentally ready for what is presented to them. It is the parents' responsibility to seek out the appropriate or "teachable" moments in which to expose children to various rituals and religious values. An important distinction, moreover, is made between exposure to the positive and the negative commandments. The positive commandments teach one to *do* certain things, such as observe the holidays, Shabbat, and kashrut or care for the aged. These are the daily rituals and values that are part of the life and breath of a Jewish home, and a child should be asked to perform them as soon as he or she is ready or able. The negative commandments— "Thou shall not steal, covet, or murder"—often have much more philosophical, obscure, or even frightening reasoning behind them. Here, time must be taken for a child to understand what is involved and the reasons behind the forbidden activities.

In other words, it is easiest to teach children to enjoy the positive and exciting aspects of Jewish life and living when they are young. Children are wide-eyed at the various ritual activities and experiences that contribute to the life-style of the Jew. Many of these rituals support basic early-childhood needs for regularity, multisensory experiences, color, and drama. Consider, for example, the building and decoration of a *sukkah*: what better multisensory experience, what more dramatic and exciting possibilities, could one conceive than the building of a portable booth laden with beautiful produce and decorations? The family activity that accompanies the task, with all members participating and making decorations, eating in and enjoying the *sukkah* together, can bring immense joy to a household. It is no wonder that Jewish children in America often look longingly upon their Christian neighbors and the rituals of Christmas, which to them convey a beautiful, warm, intimate family experience. The *sukkah* ritual, however, does serve the child's developmental needs for celebration, intimacy, and building something together; it provides multisensory stimulation as well as concrete satisfaction of the need to express thanks for and appreciation of God's many gifts.

The content of a young child's education is further delineated by the Shulḥan Arukh (165:10):

As soon as a child begins to talk, his father should teach him the verse (Deuteronomy 33:4): "The Torah that Moses has commanded us," etc., and (Deuteronomy 6:4): "Hear O Israel the Lord is our God, the Lord is One." (However, one must be exceedingly careful to make certain that the child is clean while being taught.) They should likewise teach him some other verses little by little until he is fit to attend school. At such a time, his father should engage a teacher who is God fearing, so that he may train the child to be God fearing from its youth. When the child has advanced to the study of scriptures, it is customary to begin to teach him the Siddrah of Vayikra [Lev. 1] containing the laws of sacrifices and purification. For the rabbis, of blessed memory, said: "Let the pure, [the children] come and engage in the study of purity."

Thus is set forth a kind of early-childhood curriculum based on teaching children aurally/orally from a very early age the fundamental verses and daily obligations that underlie all of Jewish tradition. Attention to such environmental details as a student's cleanliness (both for ritual and educational reasons) underscores the tradition's concern with all those elements that are so important to successful educational experiences.

According to Jewish tradition, parents are responsible for equipping children with the tools they will need to function normally, make a living, and enjoy life. Rabbi Judah says: "Anyone who does not teach his son a craft may be regarded as if he is teaching him to steal" (Talmud Kiddushin 29a) It was very clear to the rabbi that a person needed both Torah—spirituality and a clear value system—and *parnasah*—the ability to earn a living. Neither alone is sufficient for a complete and good life.

Obligations Between Parent and Child

The Jewish tradition also delineates parental responsibilities for a child's well-being according to gender roles. For example, "The father should be careful to draw his son away from falsehood" (Sukkah 45b); "It is the father's duty to rebuke his son in order to improve his manner . . . but in a pleasant way and not harshly and he is forbidden to smite his older son" (Otzar Dinim Uminhagim 1); or "The father is responsible to marry off his sons and daughters, and to clothe his daughter as befits her and to provide her with a dowry" (Shulḥan Arukh, Even Ha'Ezer, 71). On the other hand, "The education of young girls is entrusted to the mother and she must educate them in the proper manner . . . to sew and to cook (Otzar Dinim Uminhagim 1). We are also taught that the mother shares responsibility for the education of her children. As it is said, "Hearken my son to the ethics of your father, and do not forsake the Torah of your mother" (Proverbs 1:8).

Today we might disagree with the allocation of these tasks to a particular gender—probably a well-founded reaction—but there can be little objection to the fact that parents must perform various functions to insure the health and happiness of their children. Parents must also agree on which responsibilities will be primary for each of them and which will be shared, so that the child has a strong sense of unity on the parents' parts. In the case of single-parent families or blended families, where the roles are often much more complicated and demanding, the various tasks that need to be performed should at least be evident.

Parents also should be open to learning from their children. The wise parent will incorporate into the family's life-style ideas and activities that enthuse the child or that the child brings to the home from the school. A family that openly accepts a child's contribution to its life will be a richer and stronger one, and in response the child will experience a feeling of ownership of the family's life and activities. Unfortunately, sometimes parents make a decision to give their children some minimal religious education, but then undermine their children's sense of pride and enthusiasm in what they are learning by not allowing aspects of that education into the home. Often this occurs because the parents feel a lack of competence in or knowledge of the given procedure or ritual. Just think of the enthusiasm a child must feel when parents actively embrace his or her contributions toward enriching the family's life as a whole!

Just as the tradition obligates parents to consider carefully their responsibilities toward their children, it also demands that parents educate children in understanding their own responsibilities toward parents and their surrogates, that is, the children's teachers. The Talmud emphasizes that supreme value is placed in honoring parents: "The honor of father and mother is so great that God prizes it more than His own honor, for regarding honor of God it is said: 'Honor the Lord from your wealth' (Proverbs 3:9), if you have wealth you are obliged to do so, and if not you are exempt; but regarding honor of father and mother it is said, 'Honor your father and your mother' (Exodus 20:12), even if you are a beggar" (Talmud Yerushalmi, Peah, 1).

A key factor in Jewish tradition, in other words, involves parents' respecting themselves enough to motivate their children to respect them too. When parents overindulge children, are incapable of saying no to them, or do not demand the quality of language, voice tone, and interpersonal behavior that befits relations between parent and child, adults not only belittle themselves but are poorly preparing their children to deal with their own future parenting responsibilities and interactions with other significant people in their lives. So adamant is the tradition regarding a child's obligation to his parents that it declares: "They asked Rabbi Eleazar: 'How far does the principle of honoring a father and mother extend?' He replied: 'Even if the father should take a purse of money and throw it into the sea in his son's presence, the son should still not reproach him'" (Talmud Kiddishin 32a). Talmud Kiddishin 31a recounts a famous story about what one non-Jew, Dama ben Netina, did in Ashkelon when the sages wanted to purchase from him a precious item worth sixty thousand gold dinars. He repeatedly turned them down, and they assumed that he wanted more money. As they offered him more and more and grew angrier and angrier, the man kept leaving the room. Finally he returned with the merchandise, accepting the original offer as compensation. When the sages asked why he had held out for so long, he replied, "I wasn't holding out for more money at all, but the key to the merchandise was under my father's pillow. Father was sleeping, and I didn't want to disturb him out of respect and honor for him."

In this fast-paced world with increased family tensions and huge lifestyle changes from one generation to the next, the problem of honoring parents becomes increasingly complicated. Many contemporary couples have strong differences with their own parents regarding a philosophy of living. Blended families, divorced and single-parent families, intermarried couples—all these experience exacerbated tensions and pressures in intergenerational relationships. Parents' attitudes toward their own parents, comments made in the home about adult siblings or about grandparents, can influence the perception of young children as to their own responsibilities and attitudes toward their elders. Unfortunately, none of us are perfect role models, and on occasion frustrations with our own parents will be released around our children. Jewish tradition warns that the modeling of correct behavior for children toward parents, and probably toward other significant adults, begins with adults' behavior toward their own parents.

Respect for Teachers

The Jewish tradition looks to the Jewish school as a second home and views teachers as if they had given birth to the children whom they teach: "The world endures only for the sake of the breath of school children" (Talmud Shabbat 119b). In Ethics of the Fathers 1:6, we are reminded to provide ourselves with a teacher and get ourselves a student companion; in other words, the proper peer group is very important in a child's education. Moreover, "He who pays respect to his teacher it is as if he was paying respect to the divine presence" (Talmud Yerushalmi, Eruvin, 5:1).

The tradition is emphatic in reinforcing the respect students should give to teachers: "A student is to carry a torch and walk in front of his teacher [to light the way] . . . to help his teacher dress . . . to help his teacher put on his shoes . . . to stand by his teacher while he sleeps" (Yalkut Shimoni, Beshalakh, 226), "but a student must not bathe with his teacher, but if his teacher needs him, it is permitted" (Pesakhim 51a). These statements imply that teachers should be complete role models for children. The way teachers dress, walk, or talk will influence their students. Conversely, children should be taught to respect teachers for all aspects of their humanity. Mutual respect at home and school requires that children be educated to understand that events are not necessarily all factual, that two people looking at the same incident may interpret it differently. Most educators will strive mightily to solve a problem or resolve a tension if parents make their concerns known in a respectful and reasoned manner. Angry recrimination, accusation, and nastiness understandably make educators defensive and less than willing to solve problems in a manner that will be comforting to the petitioner.

Conflict Resolution

One other dimension is critical to traditional Jewish views of parenting and interpersonal family relationships. An important mitzvah is *shalom bayit,* or domestic tranquillity. Jewish tradition places a high value on respectful and reasonable family relationships and interactions. Of course, no family is free from conflict, just as no two adults always agree when it comes to raising their children. Conflict between parents about what is right for their children, conflict between parents and children as to life-style choices, especially during the teen-age years, can lead to great frustration and tension.

Ironically, one major fear that young Jewish parents have when enrolling their children in formal religious education is that the child may become "too Jewish." Is this related to ambivalence about the values and ritual practices espoused by the institutions? But these very values and practices could result in ethical and moral living, performance of the mitzvot of *tzedakah*—visiting the sick, caring for the poor, comforting the mourner. Even ritual commandments such as practicing kashrut effect a recognition of the sanctity of life and help teach the self-discipline to say no, to understand that everything in the world is not simply for the taking. Any concerned parent would want a youngster to enjoy the beauty of the holy days and Shabbat, the understanding that one day a week a human needs to step back from the world of work and school, relax, be home with the family, and enjoy God's world and the beauty of creation.

Why are some American Jewish parents so uncomfortable with the idea of their children growing more Jewish than they? Could they be afraid that the tradition will drive a wedge between them and their children? Interpreters of the tradition have always understood that there can be great differences of opinion between parents and children. Anticipating conflicts between the precept "Honor your father and mother" and a child's strong embrace of Jewish tradition, Yalkut Mishlei 960 states: "Everything which your father says to you you are obliged to obey. But if he says to you: 'Let us bow down to idols,' you must not obey him, lest you become an apostate." The tradition further admonishes:

A child should not hearken to his father when he tells him to transgress a precept of the Torah, whether it be a positive or a negative command, or even a rabbinical injunction. For it is written (Leviticus 19:3): "Ye shall fear every man his father and his mother, and you shall keep My sabbaths: I am the Lord your God." The keeping of the Sabbath is mentioned in juxtaposition with the fear of father and mother, to mean: "Although I commanded you to fear your father and mother, yet if they tell you to violate the Sabbath, you must not listen to them, and so it is true concerning other precepts, for I am the Lord your God, and both you and your parents are equally bound to honor me, therefore, you must not hearken to them to disregard my word. . . . Thus if a child is told by his father not to speak to or forgive a certain person with whom the child wishes to be reconciled, he should disregard his father's behest, for it is forbidden to hate any Jew, unless he sees him commit a sin. Thus the father tells the child to transgress a command of the Torah (Shulḥan Arukh 143:11).

If the son desires to go to some place to study the Torah, because there he will accomplish more than in his own town, but the father does not consent to it for some reason, he is not bound to listen to him, for the study of Torah is greater than the precept of honoring father and mother . . . if the son desires to marry, and the father does not consent to it, the son is likewise not bound to obey him. (Shulḥan Arukh 143:12)

There is a tremendous amount of psychological and educational wisdom in these passages. At first blush we might react negatively to such strong admonitions that children be taught not to listen to their parents. But in a world of growing anxiety about child abuse, divorce, and enormous intergenerational differences in life-style, the words have tremendous import. It is clear that a parent ethically is forbidden to force a child to break the law, and an aware child has every right to refuse if such a demand is made. On the other hand, many children are sent to Jewish summer camps or to partake of intensive Jewish educational experiences where they learn for the first time about Shabbat and kashrut, only to come home and be told that their desire to keep kosher or observe Shabbat will not be honored and that the child must conform to the family's life-style. An alternative to placing everyone's self-worth at risk and creating enormous confrontations is to seek out a compromise. For example, a child who wishes to keep kosher in a nonkosher home might be allowed not to eat meat and milk together or to substitute flounder for shellfish. A child who wishes to observe aspects of the

Shabbat in a nonobservant family could suspend writing or working with scissors or crayons on Shabbat while still traveling with the family for an outing. Parents, in short, can always find ways of reconciling a child's need to grow in spirituality and commitment with their own life-style choices. Similarly, parents should not dismiss a child's wishes for more intensive Jewish study simply because they did not have the same kind of education and so may fear that such learning would alienate the child from the family.

The need to nurture a child's spirituality and independent sense of values can be applied to situations of family disruption, such as divorce, as well. Parents must be careful not to force their own feelings on an innocent child who likely retains a deep love for both parents. The Shulḥan Arukh's admonition that a child not listen to a parent who tells him not to forgive or reconcile with a certain person is profoundly important in a world of increasing family tensions and often devastating breaks in the nuclear family structure. Likewise, adults should take care not to impose upon children their own frustrations and unfulfilled personal needs. Earlier we spoke about visiting on children the unresolved psychological hurts of the parents' youth. Here is a clear-cut case where parents need to take an attitude toward their children that perhaps ignores what they are experiencing in their own personal lives.

Conflict can also result from unreasonable parental expectations regarding children's behavior. We are cautioned that "a parent is forbidden to place a burdensome yoke upon his children; he must not be too exacting in demanding honor from them, so that he may not cause them to stumble into sin. He should rather overlook their shortcomings and forgive them" (Shulḥan Arukh 144:17). Parents must be flexible enough to understand, to allow children to make mistakes, and not to hold them to standards and expectations beyond their developmental capacity. Parents who wish their child to model a very traditional and observant life-style, for instance, must recognize that the child may be uncomfortable with the restrictions and demands of that tradition and so teach coping skills. They must also give the child options and reasonable responsibilities, such as a say in how long she or he has to sit at the Shabbat dinner table or in synagogue services, or the task of remembering to arrange in advance for a special friend to visit on Shabbat.

Living with Inconsistency

Basic to parenting is the desire to provide children with more positive life experiences than were provided to us as children. The enormous array of extracurricular activities available to children today, taken together with parents' desires for religious training, often leads to complicated choices.

For many parents, the wish to provide the best possible value structure and set of experiences is clear. It is the implementation and the parents' own ambivalence about the interrelationship of the Jewish and secular sides of life that cause conflict. Consistency is often the most difficult issue in Jewish parenting. Many parents feel that because they are not completely observant or knowledgeable in the many facets of the Jewish faith, they are "hypocritical" in choosing what to do for their children; therefore, they reason, it is better to do nothing at all. This "solution" could not be farther from Jewish tradition, common sense, or even psychological developmental truth. None of us is consistent in all behaviors. There is no Jew on earth who can observe all of the mitzvot. Judaism teaches that people constantly grow in performance of mitzvot, and that inability to perform a certain mitzvah does not mean that one should not practice another. The ethical responsibility of parents to give children the best life experiences possible, particularly in their religious upbringing, makes it incumbent on them to seek out beautiful, enriching opportunities for fulfillment. This can, however, be done in a reasonable fashion and keeping the notion of developmental readiness in mind. Let "consistency" be the "hobgoblin" of someone else's worries!

We are taught:

> A thing which is not forbidden in itself, but forbidden because of the sanctity of the day, is not included in the precepts in which a child should be trained. It is, therefore, permissible to give a child food before the kiddush [blessing over wine at the table on festivals and Shabbat] has been recited, although he must be trained to hear the kiddush. It is forbidden, however, to let a child eat outside the *sukkah*; for it is only in the matter of eating before the kiddush, which partakes of the nature of a negative command, that the law has been relaxed, but whenever the violation of a positive command is involved, it is forbidden to let the child transgress it. (Shulḥan Arukh 165:4)

In this case, a child should be taught to eat in the *sukkah* on Sukkot because that is the essence of the mitzvah. In the case of allowing a child a cookie before the kiddush, the tradition understands the impossibility of asking a young child to delay gratification for too long a time. Better that he should be eating the cookie that one is not supposed to eat before the kiddush, thus freeing his mind to hear the prayer and gradually learn it, than that he be denied both the cookie *and* the mental relaxation to learn the blessing.

Though this passage seems to treat a minor aspect of Jewish law and living, it contains a great deal of wisdom about our expectations of young children. As an educator I have often seen parents demand appropriate behavior in certain situations, behavior for which the child simply cannot be held accountable. Similarly, parents may try to do too much in one day and then not be understanding when the child becomes cranky and ungrateful for everything that is going on. Or else parents fail to think ahead to the point when, two or three hours into an outing or "educational" experience, the child will need a nap or snack. Often, in short, appropriate precautions are not taken to insure that the child will benefit from parents' plans and hopes.

Children frequently come to school "overdressed," wearing outfits that are too expensive and of which the parent has forewarned the child to take great care. This dress, in turn, inhibits the child from participating in child-centered activities at school. When a precious blouse or pair of pants is accidentally soiled, the tension felt by the child negates any possible benefit the educational activity might have had. The child is caught among three mitzvot: *Bal tashḥit*—the prohibition against wasteful destruction of property; *Talmud Torah*—the obligation to study and participate in school events; and *Kibud av va-em*—honoring and obeying one's parents. (Though it should be noted that, from another perspective, such ethical conflict resolution among competing "right actions" may indeed be good training for young children.)

Compensating for our own childhood lacks presents parents, and Jewish parents in particular, with another danger; the problem of pushing children to be and do things before they are developmentally ready. Though the Shulḥan Arukh was sensitive to this issue, perhaps the greatest contemporary warning comes in Dr. David Elkind's book *The Hurried Child*, dealing with modern family issues. In dual-career families, for example, children's experiences have to be scheduled around the parents' busy professional lives. Parents may push their young children into various activities, lessons, and events that put enormous strain on them. Too often, parents miseducate by overscheduling, overstressing, and asking children to do too much at too early an age. Some skills, such as piano playing, ice skating, or gymnastics, may be forced on the child at an inappropriate time, only to be rejected later on. In these cases it is too often the parents' interests that are being satisfied, not those of the child.

Knowing how to nurture children through early-childhood experiences, when to make demands and when to hold back, when to hold firm and when to let go, could contribute to making children's religious experiences positive and beautiful. Such sensitivities can be on the level of knowing how long a child should be required to sit at the Shabbat dinner table, and then providing alternatives nearby so that, while playing, the child can hear the singing of Shabbat table songs and *birkat ha-mazon*. Conversely, children should not be included in adult activities where they might interfere with the experiences of others or cause the parents inordinate stress and resentment.

Coping with Imperfection

The third major area of parental responsibility involves teaching children how to cope with a very imperfect world, which necessitates not sparing them from all possible pain or upset. Judaism's legal structure and regulations can help them to learn self-discipline, to say no, to understand that vague ideas of love and appreciation can be expressed through very tangible and specific mitzvot. Judaism is a religion of action. Children must recognize that one's deepest values become manifest in specific deeds.

Parents naturally wish to protect children from stress and upset. A teacher who is not totally loving, kind, and vivacious is condemned as being harsh and uncaring. Disputes between children often lead to interparental debates and telephone wars. Preventing contact with life's tragedies or not emphasizing one's responsibility to help the aged or visit the sick may handicap children in dealing with their future lives. Jewish tradition can help parents teach their children how to cope, by underscoring the fact that educators are to be respected and that children need a variety of experiences with different adult models to help them learn about the many facets, good and bad, of human existence.

The Shulḥan Arukh (165:6) addresses the Jewish idea that although one may lose control, or suffer pain and hardship, coping mechanisms can be developed that lead back to an optimistic and productive view of life:

> If a minor steals anything, he should be forced to return the stolen article if it is still intact; but if it is no longer intact, he is not required to make restitution even after he becomes of age. But to be justified in the sight of Heaven, he should make restitution after reaching the age of majority. Also, if he has committed any other sin in his minority, then when he reaches the age of discernment, it is well that he take upon himself to do a certain thing as penance.

The notion that children be held accountable for their misdeeds is developmentally appropriate, psychologically sound, and certainly consistent with Jewish teachings. While children should be free, loving, and creative spirits, they also need to know that there are limits to appropriate behavior as well as clear consequences to actions. The mitzvah of *teshuvah* (repentance) teaches that through introspection, determination, and a positive attitude we can rise above our basic desires and continue to grow and improve. There is always hope. The Shulḥan Arukh reminds Jews that parents must set limits, whether the child likes it or not. *Above all else, children need to "internalize" such limits so they can develop self-control and self-discipline.* (That is why children become obligated to the mitzvot at age thirteen.) This brings to mind the picture of a young child who was allowed to sit at the dinner table and throw food on the floor. Everyone laughs and tries to clean up the mess, but no one says to the child, "No, you may not do that," and takes the food away. Indulging such behavior does not teach a child to respect either food or other human beings. Rather, teaching a child to discipline antisocial impulses must begin at the youngest age possible.

Lest one think that modern psychology alone has developed new insights into human behavior, a look back at the Jewish tradition puts things into perspective: "A parent should not threaten a child with future punishment. If she/he sees him/her misbehave, she/he should either punish him/her at once, or ignore it. A certain child ran away from school and his father threatened him with punishment. The child thereupon committed suicide. Said the rabbis, of blessed memory, in dealing with a child and a woman, the left hand should repel and the right hand should caress" (Talmud Smachot 2:5–6).

Although the frustrations of parenting are many and children can easily push one to "the brink" in anger and frustration, Jewish tradition teaches that the punishment should fit the crime, and consequences should have clear connections to the action. Many books on effective parenting and discipline have been written with a focus on this issue; the roots of this concern, however, can be found deep in Jewish tradition, which displays an uncanny understanding of human interaction patterns and psychological health.

Parents are willing to tolerate little when it comes to their children experiencing pain or suffering. But perhaps parents and other caring adults do children a great disservice when they are too protective. If children are not allowed to experience some measure of dissonance or disharmony, they will not learn to deal with difficult situations, which are bound to occur. Children in modern society no longer experience death; they rarely have anything to do with the sick or hospitals. The needs of the poor and the homeless are far removed from the environment of most middle-class children. Jewish practice and tradition, however, reject such isolation from reality. Young children need to know that they have responsibility to comfort a sick relative, either by sending a card, telephoning, or, if appropriate, visiting. A knowledge of how Jews respond to death and dying and the ways the community supports the mourner is likewise crucial for youth today. Taking even a young child to a *shivah* home can be a wonderful act of reaffirmation for the mourner, and at the same time teach the child that life for the people he or she knows is not always happy and joyful. When a child is old enough (seven or eight) and has the desire, he or she should be permitted to attend a funeral service and be entitled to grieve a loss.

The ability to say no in a self-disciplined way may be taught through Jewish practice and observance as well. The laws of kashrut, which teach sensitivity for life, identification with the Jewish people, and holiness, also come to teach self-discipline. There are things in the world to which one should say no; there are limits. Very little is there just for the taking. The need to give *tzedakah* (charity) until it hurts, even when it is inconvenient, says that people cannot always watch out only for themselves; even if some sacrifice is required, we have an obligation to render justice to others.

For the observant family, Shabbat is a time when the family says no to the demands of the worldly fight for survival. And when the family says yes to being together, slowing down, declaring an armistice with the daily wars for personal gain, professional and personal success, children experience a way to cope with life's tensions and pressures. This learned ability to say no, to impose limits on the extensive choices and temptations that buffet the family and the child, is perhaps one of Judaism's strongest contributions to mental health and psychological well-being in the modern age.[3]

Final Reflections

Jewish tradition, with its pageantry, value system, discipline, and desire to make the world a better place, can help us as parents and concerned adults to equip children to experience the good life on both the material and spiritual levels. Perhaps the greatest symbol of this good life can be found in the *sukkah*, which is built at a time of year when the weather is changeable, with autumn winds and chill often threatening to undo the most beautiful *sukkah* experience. Yet still Jews leave their well-built homes to dwell in this frail booth that bespeaks God's bounty and gifts. At the same time, its temporary, ramshackle construction is a reminder that ultimately one must rely on things greater than individuals and their material possessions to provide strength, comfort, and value. We recall the merchant who did not lose his wealth in the shipwreck, who knew that material possessions alone do not insure the good life. Rather, it is good living and an understanding of the Source of Blessing that make life beautiful and worthwhile.

With regard to our needs as adults to compensate for psychological hurts we experienced during childhood socialization, Jewish tradition would caution us to take care, as role models, to provide children with more positive experiences than were granted us as children. We should carefully weigh the things we say, and strive not to prejudice children in a way that will close options for them later in life. The way we speak about our parents, treat teachers, and view Jewish growth can broaden or limit children's life-style options. The wise parent is one who learns from children but also actively communicates his or her own values in return.

Finally, Judaism has much to offer in teaching children how to cope. The tradition understands the conflicts that arise in life; beckons us to go out and make the world a better place than we found it; teaches us through ritual and law how to deal with sickness and death, how to fulfill our responsibilities to the poor and the homeless, how to improve relationships with other human beings through introspection and by approaching others for resolution of interpersonal conflict. Finally, it teaches us to say no in a structured way, thus giving us the strength to cope in a world of competing demands and negative challenges. The Jewish tradition in its great wisdom, particularly as the raising of young children is concerned, seeks to concretize in every way possible the spiritual and ethical values that will provide children the means to draw closer to their families, to their people, and to God and attain a sense of belonging and purpose.

NOTES

1. Morris Adler, *The World of the Talmud* (New York: Schocken Press, 1963), p. 64.

2. References to the Shulḥan Arukh in this chapter are from Solomon Ganzfried, *Code of Jewish Law* (New York: Hebrew Publishing Co., 1961).

3. As a side note, it is interesting that one of the advantages of a modern Jewish day-school education is that it helps parents to say both yes and no simultaneously: that is, they can say yes to an intensive and involved Jewish education and no to the problem of peripheralizing one's Jewish learning. Day-school children can pursue all kinds of activities after school and on Sundays. Children in Jewish supplementary schools, in contrast, often have to make very difficult choices between their commitment to a Jewish education and all the other competing activities of youth. Day-school children learn "yes" by going to synagogue on Yom Tov, since they are not missing school and are not making a great sacrifice by saying no to participation in the everyday world. They are saying yes to a four-thousand-year-old tradition that will root them well in future life. Saying no to public school on a Jewish holiday is not as easy; but if a child learns to do so the experience will enable him or her to make even more difficult decisions later in life. Likewise, saying no to the football or Little League practice because one has to go to Hebrew school teaches a child to prioritize, even if at that moment those priorities seem unfair and upsetting.

Although there are no major scholarly treatises on how to be an effective Jewish parent, a number of recent publications are helpful for continued study.

David Elkind's *The Hurried Child* (New York: Addison-Wesley, 1981) is perhaps the best source on the dilemmas faced by modern parents and on how our rapidly changing society affects young children.

For a study of high-achieving parents and their expectations for children, including the consequences of material overindulgence which can diminish children's motivation and sense of self-worth, read Andrea Brooks, *Children of Fast-Track Parents* (New York: Viking Press, 1989).

On developmental readiness, appropriate grade placement in school, and developmentally sound educational practices, see Louise Bates Ames and Joan Ames Chase, *Don't Push Your Pre-Schooler* (New York: Harper & Row, 1980).

For a "creative" Jewish approach to childrearing covering all aspects of education, rites of passage, and the needs of modern families, see Sharon Strassfeld and Kathy Green, *The Jewish Family Book* (New York: Bantam Books, 1981).

Finally, for a more traditional Jewish approach to these areas, consult Hayim Halevy Donin, *Raising a Jewish Child* (New York: Harper & Row, 1977).

MELVIN L. AND SHOSHANA R. SILBERMAN

From Bar/Bat Mitzvah Through the Teen Years

Challenges to Parent and Community

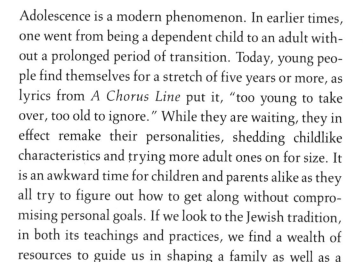

Adolescence is a modern phenomenon. In earlier times, one went from being a dependent child to an adult without a prolonged period of transition. Today, young people find themselves for a stretch of five years or more, as lyrics from *A Chorus Line* put it, "too young to take over, too old to ignore." While they are waiting, they in effect remake their personalities, shedding childlike characteristics and trying more adult ones on for size. It is an awkward time for children and parents alike as they all try to figure out how to get along without compromising personal goals. If we look to the Jewish tradition, in both its teachings and practices, we find a wealth of resources to guide us in shaping a family as well as a communal response to the challenge that adolescence poses.

The Nature of Adolescence

When children enter adolescence, their parents are usually in for a big surprise. Even youngsters who were considerate, accepting, and obedient a short time before may suddenly become surly, defensive, and defiant. To make matters worse, a whole list of rules and expectations that may have been negotiated and accepted during the previous stage of development are now questioned. Not only do adolescents expect more and better reasons for our demands, but they also want to know why they cannot be trusted to make all decisions for themselves. What has happened?

With the onset of puberty, extensive physical changes occur that unsettle children. They lose touch with their own identity as if they were immigrants encountering a new country. The rate of these changes is quite variable; some children grow faster or reach sexual maturity sooner than others. Regardless of the rate of development, however, every adolescent anxiously wonders, "Am I normal?" Adolescents yearn to be normal and inwardly fear they are not; they lose some of the individuality and confidence that marked their earlier years. No longer wholly trusting themselves, they also distrust adults and may even show it on occasion by completely rejecting their elders.

The insecurity of adolescence is reflected not only in their resistance to adults but also in their overwhelming need to gain peer acceptance. Whatever their peers are doing is what the individual teenager feels he or she should do. And whatever ideas, feelings, and experiences a teenager has must be reported and checked out in detail with friends. The peer group gives the conforming adolescent a new sense of security, belonging, and identity. Yet peers can also be intolerant of those who do not conform.

Cognitively speaking, teens indeed have minds of their own. They are now capable of testing their own actions and the actions of others against ethical values and practical criteria. They can point out the holes in one person's argument and expound upon the implications of another's remarks. They can also see various alternatives in a situation and appreciate the consequences of several courses of action. Unfortunately, they are unlikely to use these intellectual powers for purposes of which adults always approve. Rather than being critical of stifling peer group norms or behaving like budding scholars, teenagers much prefer to be critical of their parents.

After the initial adjustment to adolescence, there usually emerges an individual in search of autonomy, personal independence, and the courage to exercise adult rights. The goal at this stage of development is to become prepared financially, psychologically, intellectually, and ethically to leave home and live in the world as a self-reliant adult. The years of nearly total adult guidance, training, and protection are coming to an end. Now home, school, and peers all become a laboratory in which the adolescent tests his or her readiness for independence.

Older adolescents try out their wings in a variety of ways. They may develop intimate relationships outside their family. They may experiment with sex, alcohol, and drugs. They may also assume part-time jobs or make decisions about religious observance that test parental values. Unfortunately, when adolescents try out their wings, they often flop. They come home drunk; they spend their money frivolously; they reject religious practices without thought. The prospect of allowing adolescents the freedom to make their own decisions can be frightening.

Parental Responses to Adolescence

How parents respond to the teenagers in their midst is influenced by many factors. Adolescence is a time of considerable turmoil for most parents. Simultaneous with the conflicts parents experience with their disconcerted children is frequently the stress of dealing with their own aging parents. At the same time, moreover, many parents are assuming demanding responsibilities in their employment careers. And to add to the stress level, even pets obtained when the children were small are now on their last legs and require attention. Because adolescence comes at an especially vulnerable period in parents' lives, it becomes particularly difficult to handle the "closed off" feeling brought on by adolescent silence or rebellion.

Then too, just as adolescents want their first shots at independence, parents want their last shots at influence. Typically, parents hold on to their jobs as protectors and advice givers because they do not feel they have done a good enough job yet. Parents know how tough it is to struggle with schoolwork or gain peer acceptance because they have already been through it. As a result, they pile on anxious and often unsolicited suggestions about how to do most everything.

Of course, parents don't all have the same style with teen-agers. At one extreme are parents who never hesitate to let their teen-agers know "what's wrong with them." The result is generally more silence. As one teen-ager put it to her parents, "I am afraid to tell you who I am because if I tell you who I am, you may not like who I am and it's all I have." At the other extreme are parents who try too hard to obtain their children's approval by doing anything to please or appease them. Such parents are no more trusted by teens than their harsher counterparts. Many parents are not consistently one way or the other but seesaw between harshness and indulgence.

Responses to adolescence are also shaped by the family situation. Some teen-agers still experience the traditional arrangement of a devoted and perhaps intrusive mom who stays at home while a breadwinning and perhaps disconnected dad spends much of his time at work. More likely is a two-parent family with both mom and dad working or simply "on the go" with far less time for the family. A third and not infrequent possibility is a single-parent household in which the parent may rely heavily on the children for companionship.

Whatever the circumstances, virtually all parents find themselves exasperated and frustrated by the actions of their teen-age children. Given these pressures, they are bound to make mistakes: giving only opinions and not asking for or being willing to hear teen-agers' views; deciding things for their teen-ager without having the courtesy to consult them; failing to respect privacy by reading their children's mail, snooping in their rooms, or telling adult friends about their latest travails with the kids; belittling their teen-age offspring when they don't act their age or make mistakes; and complaining that "you never talk to me anymore" rather than firmly expecting communication.

Adolescence in Jewish Families

The experience of adolescence takes on a special character in Jewish families. Most Jewish children enjoy a family that functions as a close-knit unit. Many activities are shared, and support for each other is commonplace. In return for these benefits, children are expected to show a high degree of family loyalty. At the same time, Jewish parents also allow their children considerable independence and self-expression. The combination is rather uncommon among ethnic groups and yields interesting results. On the positive side, there is the potential for producing healthy children who profit from both family support and family permission for autonomous action. For example, Charles Silberman, in his upbeat description of American Jewish life entitled *A Certain People*, states: "Jewish students are far more likely than Gentile students to attend a college away from home and . . . the colleges they choose are farther away." In commenting on the common assumption that Jewish families smother their children, he concludes: "Jewish sons appear to be emotionally freer and more independent of their parents than, say, Italian-Americans, who have a far more powerful sense of obligation."[1] On the negative side, however, is the potential for producing neurotic children who are caught between two conflicting messages: *stay close* and *go off to make something of yourself.* The result, in effect, is "Portnoy's complaint": You're a disappointment if you don't achieve and a disappointment if you don't remain your parent's child.

As Portnoy's contemporaries have aged, things may no longer be exactly the same in today's Jewish families. Jewish families are becoming less close-knit, finding it as difficult as other families to obtain time for joint family activity. Moreover, as third-generation Jewish parents have risen up the socioeconomic ladder, they have found less reason to live through their children's accomplishments. Even so, the dual emphasis on loyalty and autonomy persists, and today's Jewish adolescents, like their parents before them, face life both strengthened and conflicted by these Jewish family values. They continue to be, by and large, high achievers who act confidently and eschew drugs and alcohol. At the same time, they experience considerable academic stress and still feel anxious about disappointing their parents. In fact, many Jewish teen-agers today worry that they will not even match, let alone surpass, their parents' accomplishments.

Today's American teen-agers are the first generation to have lived their entire lives beyond the election of a Catholic president, the black revolution, Vietnam, and the Six-Day War. Because of these watershed events, Arthur Hertzberg, in *The Jews in America*, asserts that Jews, along with other ethnic groups, no longer perceive themselves as outsiders in our society.[2] Although the circumstances may vary from community to community, Jewish teens in the nineties have few feelings of "otherness." As a rule, they can participate in any group in their high school culture without inhibition. This climate exists not only because other groups are far more accepting than ever before of Jewish kids, but also because Jewish kids are far more accepting of themselves. Hence, there is less of a need to stick to one's own kind. In public high schools and in nondenominational private schools, Jewish teen-agers interact freely and frequently with Gentile teens. Their social circles are more integrated than at any other time in the history of the American Jewish community. What this means, of course, is that their commitment to continuing Jewish education, youth group activity, and Jewish summer camping is diminishing. Involvement in these distinctively Jewish spheres can no longer rely so heavily on the need for Jewish socializations. These activities must also speak to the intellectual and emotional needs of today's Jewish teens to win support.

Guidance from Jewish Tradition

Since adolescence can be such a troubling time for Jewish teens, it is natural to ask what guidance traditional sources can offer to inform our responses as parents and as members of the organized Jewish community? At first blush, the answer may seem to be very little. Since adolescence is a relatively new phenomenon, our sages naturally did not treat it directly. However, there are many teachings about the raising and educating of children from which we can glean helpful insights.

There is no better place to begin than with the story of Adam and Eve in the Garden of Eden. Judaism does not view this event as being the original sin and humanity's fall from grace. Instead, it is regarded as a kind of "coming of age." Adam and Eve may have let God down much as do children who disobey fundamental rules of their parents, but in a way they were *expected* to rebel. By eating from the Tree of Knowledge, they courageously challenged authority; thus they could no longer live as carefree children. They were not really punished for their disobedience; instead they were confronted by it, for now they were sent off from childhood and innocence to a life that required the knowledge and awareness they gained from eating the apple. That the Torah does not view these proceedings as a "disgrace" is evident from the very first verse after God's speech casting Adam and Eve from the Garden: "The man named his wife Eve [Ḥava], because she was the mother of all the living" (Genesis 3:20). One message of the story, then, is that parents are not to prolong childhood endlessly.

The story is certainly instructive for our time. Out of educational and economic necessity, young people live at home and are financially dependent on parents for a longer time than ever. This dependence does not require, however, that parents always make life easy at home. If parents constantly provide total financial support, teen-agers may have less desire to get a job. If adults are available for primary relationships, the adolescent may feel less need to seek companionship from peers. Letting adolescents know that we care for them and wish them well is important; we can be there for them, but our support need not mean that we assume responsibility for every problem they face or every mistake they make. It is not our job to type their term papers or write their college essays. Just as God confronted Adam and Eve, parents too must confront their teen-agers with their responsibility to face life without being dependent on others.

The second instructive account in the Torah is God's challenge to Abraham to "go forth from your native land and from your father's house to the land that I will show you" (Genesis 12:1). Abraham is told not only to leave his home but also to begin his journey without even knowing his destination. There could not be a more confronting message here both for adolescents and parents: the job of young people is to someday "leave home," and it is the parents' job to help them do it. That is why the Talmud instructs parents to teach their children two things for the purpose of self-sufficiency: a profession or trade and the knowledge of how to swim!

Another message from Genesis 12 is recognition that parents' values, if they are not worthy, are to be rejected by their offspring (see Steven M. Brown, pp. 42–43). Midrash, for example, tells us that Abraham's father was a maker of idols. It further alleges that Abraham smashed his father's idols at the age of thirteen. What an endorsement of adolescent rebellion! Of course, a parent's values are very often worthy. Perhaps, therefore, one should extend the teaching of Genesis 12 to include the idea that even when parental values are right, a child may need to reject them for a while and return to them as a matter of adult choice.

A third account, the Tower of Babel story, has a similar message: at some point in everyone's life the need for separation and independence outweighs the need for security. All the people on the earth wanted to build the tower "else we shall be scattered all over the world" (Genesis

11:4). The tower would serve as a focal point for keeping people together and a landmark so that no one would get lost. Nonetheless, God "scattered them from there over the face of the whole earth" (Genesis 11:9), not as a punishment but as a challenge to the growing capacity of human beings.

It appears that the high value Jews place on independence and autonomy has its origins in the Torah. That they have heeded the Torah's teachings is evident when one considers the extraordinary physical mobility of Jews not only today but throughout history.

One other biblical message should be noted before going on to rabbinic texts. In perhaps the most direct quotation concerning adolescence, we read in Joel 3:1: "Your old shall dream dreams. Your young shall see visions." Here, it seems, the Bible is saying to youth: do not be constrained by the realities of today; envision how things might be *if everything were possible*. Imagine the inspiration this verse could give today's practical-minded, career-oriented adolescents!

In Genesis Rabbah 63:10, parents are told: "You are responsible for your son till he is thirteen; then say 'Blessed be God who has rid me of responsibility for this [my child].'" This benediction was to be uttered after a Bar (or Bat) Mitzvah's *aliyah* to the Torah as a statement to the child and to the community that the parents were releasing themselves from the need to be parents of a child and henceforth would act as parents of an adolescent. Those responsibilities that have been conferred upon the young person are now in his or her charge. Once again, we see how Judaism teaches parents to relinquish their grip and confront children with the need to build self-reliance and a personal identity.

The insistence on "letting go" is not the only directive, however. Judaism does not teach parents to give up their guidance role entirely. Parents are expected to continue teaching their children, but now special warnings are given. In Pirke Avot (commentary to 3:9) we are told: "He who instructs by personal example rather than mere words, his audience will take his counsel to heart. He who does not practice what he so eloquently preaches, his advice is rejected." We are further advised in Hasidic teachings: "Parents must not so exasperate a child that he cannot constrain himself from rebelling against them" (Sefer Ḥasidim, 13C, 3954, pp. 234–35), and "It is best that a father and son separate if they quarrel with each other, for much pain is caused; and I do not mean only the pain of the father or teacher, but even the pain of the son" (Sefer

Ḥasidim, sec. 343). Finally, the sixteenth-century Shulḥan Arukh (143:12) says: "If the son desires to go to some place to study the Torah, for he thinks that there he will be more successful than in his own town, and the father does not consent to it for some reason, he is not bound to listen to his father, for the study of the Torah is greater than the honoring of parents." These admonitions could apply just as easily to mothers and daughters as well.

As this sampling of Jewish sources suggests, unquestioned obedience to and fear of parental authority is abhorrent to the tradition. The Talmud even cites as evidence the case of a child who committed suicide after a small misdeed because he was mortally afraid of his father. While parents should not overindulge their children, they are cautioned not to be harsh or hypocritical. Above all, youth is a time to be cherished for its freshness and idealism. According to the Talmud, "Youth is a garland of roses" (Talmud Shabbat, 152a).

Jewish Rites of Passage for Adolescents

Traditionally, Bar Mitzvah is a status conferred upon thirteen-year-old boys, indicating that they are no longer minors and can therefore serve as witnesses for legal documents and be counted in a minyan. Moreover, they are now obligated to perform all the mitzvot (commandments) incumbent on an adult male, such as wearing tefillin every morning. Bar Mitzvah is not mentioned among the life cycle events in the Torah. Instead, its practice dates from the Middle Ages.

The ceremony of Bat Mitzvah was introduced in France and Italy and soon spread to other countries. The first recorded Bat Mitzvah in the United States was held in 1922. Today, it is rare to find a community that has not established some means for celebrating a young girl's coming of age as a Bat Mitzvah. Even traditional Jews often mark the event with a ceremony, though one in which girls are not called to the Torah for an *aliyah* and which occurs at age twelve, not thirteen.

Because the modern mind does not view the age of twelve or thirteen as an entrance into adulthood, some voices have called for delaying the event until later in adolescence. However, the long tradition of Bar/Bat Mitzvah at age thirteen is so powerful that delaying it would rob the milestone of its authenticity. Furthermore, the introduction of a Confirmation service in Reform and later in Conservative and Reconstructionist congregations has served to mark a later age for passage into majority. As a result, although the practice of Bar/Bat Mitzvah has endured, for all practical purposes it now marks only the beginning of adolescence, not the beginning of adulthood. Its altered significance today raises many interesting issues.

Clearly, Bar/Bat Mitzvah serves as a dramatic statement to a Jewish young person that "I am no longer just a child." There is hardly a youngster who does not sense from all the surrounding fanfare that he or she is entering a new status in life. However, the precise nature of this new status is unclear to several parties—the youngsters themselves, their parents, and the congregation. While it is true that the Bar/Bat Mitzvah may now be called to the Torah or included in a minyan, most communities give lip service to the status the young person has apparently achieved. Some post–Bar/Bat Mitzvah adolescents are recruited as Torah readers, but beyond that little else seems to change in their participation in synagogue life. Participation in family life may differ somewhat in families that allow teen-agers to influence certain family decisions. In most cases, however, life seems to be largely the same, with perhaps a few more freedoms but rarely more responsibilities.

The cynical view is that Bar/Bat Mitzvah is just a performance, a time when a young person learns ancient skills of cantillation and gives a recital demonstrating competence. (Youngsters with good voices are at a decided advantage in this.) Out of fear of total embarrassment to themselves and their parents, most kids work hard enough to get through it. Yet although, at its worst, a Bar/Bat Mitzvah can be merely a performance, at its best it is meaningful on many levels.

One enthusiastic proponent of Bar/Bat Mitzvah rituals is Rabbi Neil Kurshan, author of the best-selling book *Raising Your Child to Be a Mensch*. Here is what he has to say:

I have often marvelled at the transformation which a Bar or Bat Mitzvah can bring about in the life of a thirteen-year-old, who for the first time leads part of the service, shares in the religious honors reserved for adults, and speaks to all assembled about the significance of the occasion. Contrary to popular impression, the ceremony does not transform a thirteen-year-old into an adult overnight. After the Bar Mitzvah a parent still lives with an adolescent who has to be reminded to clean up his or her room, to do his or her homework, and to help around the house. At its best, however, the Bar Mitzvah demonstrates both to the thirteen-year-old and to all those present that a young person is growing toward adulthood and toward responsibility and obligations to a broader community.

Kurshan goes on to comment that Bar/Bat Mitzvah, despite the relief once it's over, can give young people a great feeling of accomplishment. More than that, it provides a sense of being part of a generational chain. As Kurshan puts it: "At a time in his life when [the youth] is bewildered and maybe even frightened by so many physical and emotional changes taking place within him, he feels connected to a stable tradition."[3]

The hope that Bar/Bat Mitzvah marks an important turning point in a young adolescent's life—rather than just an expensive, exhausting, but otherwise meaningless event—appears to hinge on how it is handled by the family and by the congregation. Everything starts the year or two preceding the event as the young person prepares for the big day. Is this a time for real learning about one's Torah portion or about Judaism in general? Are parents included in the preparation process? Does the practice of Bar/Bat Mitzvah lessons wind up a shouting match between parent and child or a fruitless power struggle? Are any other actions expected of the youngster besides performing at the Bar/Bat Mitzvah ceremony proper? Both the congregation and the parents themselves have a responsibility to think through these questions so that the months and days leading to the final event are not a travesty.

Families are probably best served by pre–Bar/Bat Mitzvah programs that prepare both children and parents for the big day. For example, the program published by the Melton Research Center of the Jewish Theological Seminary of America begins in the sixth grade and takes from fourteen months to two years to complete. The program provides for ongoing interaction between parents and child and involves study, discussion, social action projects, workshops, and field trips. Other family education programs, though shorter in length, can also be worthwhile. In addition, pre–Bar/Bat Mitzvah workshops and support groups exclusively for parents are available. For example, one of the authors of this essay (M.S.) conducted a four-session group for parents on (1) mistakes parents often make around Bar/Bat Mitzvah, (2) how parents should interact with their children as they prepare for their Bar/Bat Mitzvah, (3) family participation in the service, and (4) other possibilities for celebrating the Bar/Bat Mitzvah. Whether or not they are enrolled in such programs or groups, parents can enhance Bar/Bat Mitzvah preparation by studying their child's Torah portion, discussing it and other Jewish topics with their child, going as a family to at least one place of Jewish interest, and perhaps teaching Torah and Haftorah trope to their child (if they know it) or learning it from their child (if they do not).

Special experiences designed exclusively for youngsters during the Bar/Bat Mitzvah year might be provided as well. Rabbi Arthur Green, former president of the Reconstructionist Rabbinical College, suggests taking them, separated by gender, for a few days' retreat in the country to discuss their questions about love and sexuality. With the guidance of sensitive adults, such an acknowledgment of puberty might develop into a serious and anticipated part of Bar/Bat Mitzvah, teaching children that Judaism has something to say about what it means to be a Jewish man or woman on such issues as caring for others and responsible personal behavior.

The Bar/Bat Mitzvah event itself can be a moving and enriching event, or it can be merely one in which everyone goes through the motions and the only value taught is conspicuous consumption. The former possibility is made more likely if some of the following occur: (1) the youngster writes (with some help) his or her own speech or leads a congregational discussion; (2) the parents, without grabbing the spotlight, share some brief remarks on the occasion (this can also be done privately or in writing); (3) the child is urged to give a portion of the gift money to *tzedakah* (charity); and (4) the celebration is modest enough that its meaning is not overshadowed. No doubt achieving all these outcomes requires parental courage and a "neat kid," but not making the effort will insure that nothing of value is gained from the Bar/Bat Mitzvah experience.

Even if the Bar/Bat Mitzvah experience is a good one, what happens afterward? Before Bar/Bat Mitzvah, students spend much of their classroom time gaining Hebrew reading and synagogue skills. Now that this mission has been accomplished, and since teen-agers are capable of serious, abstract thinking, continuation of Jewish education only makes good sense. Adolescents can delve into such important topics as comparing Judaism with other religions, studying about the denominations within modern Judaism, understanding the problems of anti-Semitism, confronting the existence of cults and missionaries, learning how Judaism views biomedical issues, and debating solutions for helping oppressed Jews around the globe and creating a safe peace in the land of Israel. Adolescents can also study classical Jewish texts on a more adult level. Often these studies end with a ceremony called Confirmation.

Confirmation was the first religious innovation made by Reform Judaism. Introduced in 1810 in Kassel, Germany, as an alternative to Bar Mitzvah, it included young women along with young men. The ceremony was usually held for sixteen-year-olds, thus providing a rite of passage for older adolescents.

Unlike Bar/Bat Mitzvah, there is no religious formula for the ceremony. As a rule, students present a cantata or do a presentation of their own creation based on themes such as Freedom and Responsibility; Covenant and Commitment; Where We've Been, Where We're Going. Over the years, many synagogues have utilized the holiday of Shavuot, when Jews celebrate the giving of the Torah and the commitment of the Jewish people to the covenant, as the most appropriate occasion for Confirmation. As the ancient Israelites accepted the Torah at this time of their own free will, confirmants follow in their footsteps by declaring their willingness to continue the traditions of the Jewish people.

Confirmation is practiced today in Reform, Conservative, and Reconstructionist congregations. Rather than replacing Bar/Bat Mitzvah, it has become an additional life cycle event. Besides the study component, it often includes performance of mitzvot such as tutoring younger students, visiting a nursing home, or preparing a holiday program for handicapped students. It differs from Bar/Bat Mitzvah in that it is a group experience rather than an individual one. Bar/Bat Mitzvah features a young adolescent's achievements; Confirmation, at its best, teaches the power and excitement of communal learning and expression. The most successful Confirmation services are those in which the students share their own thoughts and experiences with the congregation instead of using scripted material.

Today we want to involve our students with Jewish learning for as long as possible. Many youngsters can receive high school or college credit in after-school synagogue courses or community study programs. Some may also obtain a certificate allowing them to assist or teach at a religious school. Upon graduation, it is hoped that these programs provide an incentive for students to enroll in Jewish studies courses in college and set the stage for a lifetime pursuit of Jewish learning.

Organized Activity for Jewish Adolescents

The degree to which Jewish adolescents will someday become active in the adult Jewish community depends on one factor more than any other: their involvement in Jewish social circles as teen-agers. In a study by Rela Geffen Monson, *Jewish Campus Life*, the best predictor of later communal involvement was participation in organized activities such as Jewish youth groups, summer camps, tour groups to Israel, and the like.[4] While their continued Jewish education is surely important, as is the quality of the Jewish home life, the quality of the shared group experience will go further in determining just how committed Jewish teen-agers will be later on as adults.

Getting Jewish teen-agers involved in such activities, as we have already noted, is not as easy as it once was. Because Jewish teens mingle freely with non-Jewish teens in their high school cultures, youth groups are less the social havens they used to be. In addition, other competing activities (sports, dance, music) limit Jewish teen-agers' time for youth groups as never before. Of course, the job is not just to get Jewish youth to these activities; they must also be given experiences of substance. That can prove difficult in an age marked by apathy to social and political action. The distressing fact is that as Jewish teen-age interest in organized activity wanes, the communal response is to lower the money and support for the needs of this age group. Youth group leaders are often short-term employees drawn from the ranks of nearby colleges and universities and paid a small amount of money for their services. Although many are enthusiastic young adults who act as positive role models for teen-agers, expecting them to turn around a difficult situation by themselves is clearly unfair and misguided. They need the backup support of a professional youth director.

New Directions for Community and Family

The Jewish community has begun to understand the enormous benefits of providing early-childhood education and quality day care. It has brought young marrieds with young children into organized Jewish life much earlier than heretofore. Similar benefits will accrue from providing top-notch programming for adolescents. Right now, servicing adolescents and their families is an area of great weakness in the Jewish community. Competent, highly trained professionals need to be induced into this area of need. Well-paying positions must be created in the Jewish community so that high school teachers, principals, assistant rabbis, cantors, and other youth professionals with good Jewish backgrounds can combine their current responsibilities with the task of directing high-level youth programs. Moreover, since too often different organizations compete for the same personnel, it is important that these professionals be shared by many synagogues and institutions. Finally, training programs are needed to help the growth and development of youth professionals.

Although some of our past approaches to youth work may still have a place, it is time to rethink how we do things. At a recent national convention of United Synagogue Youth, for example, 1,200 teen-agers spent one day—amid the singing, dancing, banquets, and classes that characterize such gatherings—working in a variety of social action projects in the Philadelphia area. Mitzvah programs created by other organizations have been a new way to channel youthful idealism on an ongoing basis. These activities enhance a growing sense that adolescents can make important contributions in a world that still treats them like children.

New formats may also be useful. Rather than the typical once-a-week meeting, it can make more sense to gather groups of teen-agers for periodic weekend retreats. It is often easier with intensive blocks of time to do the team building that changes a youth group from a collection of teen-agers wanting to be entertained into a cohesive community system, thus allowing a distinctive Jewish peer group to emerge that stands out from the greater peer culture surrounding it.

Letting Go

Parents also must rethink how they do things. First and foremost, they need to view adolescence as a time when it is their job gradually but steadily to transfer power over to their children. Many parents prefer to hold out as long as possible, hoping that their children won't rebel if given only a little independence. As we have seen, that approach is not the one taken by Jewish tradition. With the protracted adolescence of today, it makes more sense for parents to reduce control over teen-agers by a small amount each year of adolescence. To do this wisely, they need continually to examine their priorities and determine which expectations they wish to maintain and which they can give up. At first, for example, young teen-agers can be permitted relatively minor freedoms such as complete choice over whether and what they eat for breakfast; but where they go, when they come home, and how they attend to their household or school responsibilities can still be clearly specified. As time passes, they might be allowed to get a job or have almost exclusive control over the way they keep their bedroom. Year by year, the area of their decision making can increase by whatever degree parents' best judgment and willingness to take risks dictates.

Of course, parents cannot always be sure that teen-agers, when left on their own, will make wise choices. They can err by allowing too much freedom, but they can also err by failing to trust their son's or daughter's capacity to take responsible direction on their own. Parents too often look at their children's past track record and are reluctant to start over again with a clean slate.

As parents slowly phase out their control over children's lives, they can still influence teen-agers by being consistently honest about what they think and feel. Directness, even bluntness, is important to model at this time so that teen-agers have a positive example of how to assert themselves with other people. At the same time, parents need to be careful to avoid intimidation or inducement of guilt (a tall order for Jewish parents!) as they tell teen-agers what's on their minds. It is important that their manner be straightforward and nonmanipulative.

Many parents take just the opposite stance. Knowing that teen-agers are suspicious of adult views, they think the best policy is to keep quiet and leave their children alone. They are right about the difficulties involved in stating opinions to teen-agers, but they make a big mistake in refraining from doing so. Teens still want to know their parents' thoughts and feelings, even if they sulk when parents do speak their minds.

For parents to have more than one-way communication with teen-agers, it is often necessary to make persistent requests to talk things over. Few teen-agers are willing to disclose anything about themselves unless they think their parents expect it. When discussions finally take place, parents should show a genuine interest in what their children have to say. Checking to make sure that intended meanings are being received accurately, acknowledging the validity of the youths' ideas, and empathizing with their feelings all help to gain teen-agers' trust and give them the feeling that communication with parents is worthwhile.

In the final analysis, how well parents communicate with and influence teen-agers depends on their ability *not* to take their rudeness, criticism, and insensitivity personally. Instead, parents could comfort themselves a little with the knowledge that, from a developmental point of view, their children's behavior is perfectly natural and should abate if they let go enough to allow it to happen. Then parents can hope that their children will soon realize that adults are not so boorish as they thought. As Mark Twain quipped, "When I was a boy of fourteen, my father was so ignorant I could hardly stand to have the old man around, but when I got to be twenty-one, I was astonished at how much he had learned in seven years."

As adolescents leave the teen-age years, not only do they become aware that their parents have learned something, but, we hope, they have learned something as well. One of the most important learnings is that each new stage of the life cycle involves struggle and personal responsibility. The Torah's case in point concerns Jacob, who wrestled with an angel before becoming a *mensch* and being renamed *Israel:* one who strives with God. If adolescents have wrestled with themselves and with God, they, too, can enter adulthood, not with complacency but with the goal of striving for self-improvement and for *tikkun olam,* making the world a better place.

1. Charles E. Silberman, *A Certain People* (New York: Summit Books, 1985), p. 142.

2. Arthur Hertzberg, *The Jews in America* (New York: Simon & Schuster, 1989).

3. Neil Kurshan, *Raising Your Child to Be a Mensch* (New York: Atheneum, 1987), pp. 82, 83.

4. Rela Geffen Monson, *Jewish Campus Life* (New York: American Jewish Committee, 1982).

SUGGESTIONS FOR FURTHER READING

Janice P. Alper's *Learning Together: A Sourcebook on Jewish Family Education* (Denver: Alternatives in Religious Education, Inc., 1987) presents fifty chapters featuring models of family education programs and projects that can be implemented at synagogues, centers, camps, and family service agencies.

Neil Kurshan, in *Raising Your Child to Be a Mensch* (New York: Atheneum, 1987), takes a hard look at the toll the "success ethic" may be taking on our children and offers guidance and hope to parents concerned with raising children who are decent, kind, and generous.

A good resource that combines Torah principles and contemporary psychology to teach parents to be loving, confident, and assertive is Miriam Levi, *Effective Jewish Parenting* (Spring Valley, NY: Philip Feldheim, Inc., 1986).

Mel Silberman's *Confident Parenting* (New York: Warner Books, 1988) teaches ways to be both in charge and involved as a parent and gives a four-step program for changing children's behavior.

Sharon Strassfeld and Kathy Green's *The Jewish Family Book* (New York: Bantam Books, 1981) examines issues and concerns of parents throughout the Jewish life cycle.

STEPHEN C. LERNER

Choosing Judaism

Issues Relating to Conversion

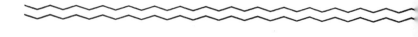

Not so long ago, when an intermarriage occurred, a Jewish family might have sat *shivah* for the renegade. In earlier generations, the commandment of "do not intermarry" was the most important one the Jewish family conveyed to its young. But in our own day, intermarriage is so common that Reform rabbis who refuse to officiate at such weddings may be rejected for attractive pulpits or be subject to serious pressure to reverse their stands. Recently, a Conservative woman expressed outrage that her own marriage to a non-Jew, with a rabbi and minister officiating, would not be recorded in the synagogue bulletin, even though she knew that mixed marriage was considered unacceptable by her movement. What has led to this overwhelming change?

As of 1985, one in two Jews marrying has married a non-Jew, and in 95 percent of cases the partner did not convert to Judaism.[1] This rise of intermarriage threatens the quality and numerical future of the Jewish community, which has already been weakened by the growth of secularization and assimilation, leading many born Jews to regard Judaism as irrelevant to contemporary life. In short, intermarriage has become a major cause of hand-wringing as well as the instigator of sociological and outreach strategies designed to counter the trend.

Although intermarriage is on the rise, there has been some gain owing to the nearly two hundred thousand Gentiles who have elected to convert to Judaism in the past fifty years. Some Jewish groups, especially within the Orthodox movement, routinely turn away prospective converts; nevertheless, more than three thousand non-Jews each year officially attach themselves to Judaism through conversion programs, formal and informal, offered throughout the United States. Conversion is one of the positive realities of contemporary American Jewish life. Those who have become Jews by choice are now found in the ranks of rabbis, Jewish scholars, and synagogue and Jewish communal leaders and have provided a new cadre of proponents of Jewish spirituality and Jewish values. Intermarriage and conversion, then, are two of the central facts of life for American Jews.

The History of Conversion in Judaism

The Bible contains no absolute ban on intermarriage. Both Joseph and Moses, strangers on foreign soil, married local women. The Bible records no criticism of them, for biblical religion was at first a national cult, involving a people with its God in its own place. If one was away from the people Israel and the land of Israel, one was away from God, for it was not yet fully understood that He, in fact, functioned everywhere. Thus, even the prophet Jonah could attempt to flee from God by, so to speak, escaping His sphere. To be sure, one of the great messages of that remarkable book, written late in the First Temple period, is that one cannot elude God.

Similarly, there was no notion of conversion in ancient Israel. If one lived among the Israelites, one might blend into the community by osmosis but not by a formal declaration of faith. Even when Ruth utters that exquisite phrase, "Your people will be my people and your God, my God" (Ruth 1:16), she is telling her beloved mother-in-law, Naomi, that she will follow her from Moab to Naomi's home of Bethlehem in Judah, thus becoming a part of Naomi's people and accepting its deity. If she had meant conversion in our sense of a primary commitment to a religious way, we might have expected Ruth to have pledged her allegiance to Judaism while she was still in Moab rather than when she was already on her way to Judah.

It was probably when the Jews were exiled to Babylon, after the destruction of the First Temple in 586 B.C.E., that a more universalistic view of God and Judaism began to appear. God was thought to be everywhere and, as such, could be worshiped anywhere. A corollary was that anyone could hear God's message and join God's people. Second Isaiah speaks formally of "foreigners who join themselves to the Lord, to minister to Him, to love the name of the Lord and be His servants" (Isaiah 56:6). A nation on its land was replaced by a people with a religious mission, and keeping faith with that mission meant prohibiting intermarriage. Thus, two contrary sides of the coin were imprinted in the Second Temple period: although Jews may not marry unconverted Gentiles, such people may seek to become Jews.

By the beginning of the Common Era, conversion to Judaism was a growing possibility and reality for many in the Roman Empire. Salo W. Baron estimates that as many as 10 percent of the people of that empire were Jews or Jewish sympathizers.[2] In that most creative period of Jewish history, Judaism's vision of one God and its belief in Him as the source of moral and natural order proved attractive to questing pagans. Energetic Jews proudly carried their religious message wherever they went, drawing interested onlookers to Diaspora synagogues.

Both Jewish sources and those hostile to Judaism describe Jewish proselytizing. In the Christian gospel of Matthew (23:15), Jesus is reported to have chastised the Pharisees, the great Jewish teachers of his time, for crossing sea and land to make one convert. The Roman satirist Juvenal mocks Roman parents who themselves became Jewish fellow travelers and then converted their children to Judaism. These people, he proclaims, "despise Roman law but learn and observe and revere Israel's code and from the sacred volume of Moses where the way is not shown to any but true believers, when the uncircumcised are never led to the fountain. . . . Remember the Sabbath day to keep it lazy," Juvenal rails, noting that "the father setting this day apart from life is the cause and the culprit" (Satire 14). Juvenal is just one of the many Roman writers who saw the Jewish incursion into Roman life as unsettling to traditional and honored classical values.

Jewish sources contain many statements lauding conversion and converts. A classic Midrash on Genesis 12:5 that speaks of Abraham and Sarah coming to Canaan with "the souls they had made in Harran" interprets the word *souls* to mean converts—Abraham converts the men and Sarah the women (Sifre Deuteronomy 32 on 6:5). Such non-Jewish biblical figures as Pharaoh's daughter, Bityah, as well as the priest Jethro, the prostitute Rahav, and the prophet Ovadiah, were all understood to have accepted Judaism. The fact that such rabbinic notables as Shemaiah, Avtalyon, and Akiba were reportedly descendants of *gerim* (converts) was recorded rather than suppressed by the sages. Conversion and converts were deemed a source of pride and an indication of Judaism's dynamism.

A well-known story tells of the most beloved and influential Pharisaic teacher, Hillel, who, unlike his contemporary Shammai, was prepared to explain the essence of Judaism to a would-be proselyte who wanted to learn it all as he stood on one foot. Hillel tells him, "What is hateful to you, don't do to others. The rest is commentary. Go and study." The fellow, of course, converts. In a pair of similar legends, Shammai rejected and Hillel drew near two Gentiles who also wanted Judaism on apparently unreasonable terms. In one case, a man wanted to accept only the written and not the oral Torah, and in the other the man wanted to convert in order to be the high priest. In both cases, Hillel instructed the men and they accepted the normative view of Judaism. Some time later, according to legend, after all had converted, the three *gerim* met by chance and declared, "Shammai's ill temper almost drove us from the world, Hillel's gentleness brought us under the wings of the Divine Presence" (Shabbat 31a)—a beautiful phrase for conversion. Clearly, to the rabbis Hillel's sterling qualities brought about a great good: the conversion to Judaism of three men whose initial reasons for seeking instruction were suspect.

Most telling is the inclusion of *gerei ha-tzedek*, righteous converts, in the blessing for the righteous that is part of the *Amidah*, Judaism's central prayer. Along with the pious, the elders, and the learned, proselytes are specifically mentioned, indicating classical Judaism's warm and supportive attitude toward them.

How Things Changed

The three Jewish wars against Rome and the rising competition and eventual triumph of Christianity reduced Judaism's missionary thrust, though the community remained open to converts, if less welcoming. Rabbi Isaac's statement that "one should repulse him [the would-be convert] with the left hand and draw him with the right" (Ruth Rabbah 1:12) mirrored the new reality after 135 C.E., which carried a concern about whether those who joined the Jewish people would remain faithful even in dark times. The Talmud in Yevamot 47a–b describes the new reality:

> We tell a prospective convert in this time: Why do you want to be converted? Do you not see that Am Yisrael is now sick, shoved about, swept and torn, and that troubles ever come upon them? If he says: I know and am unworthy [to share their fate], we receive him, and we tell him some of the light and some of the weighty commandments, and we tell him the sin connected with the leket, shikhah, pe'ah, and poor-tithe. And we tell him the punishment for violating the commandments. We say: Know that before you enter this state, you can eat fat without being punished by excision or violate the Sabbath without being punished by stoning. But now, if you eat fat, you will be punished by excision; if you violate the Sabbath, you will be punished by stoning. And just as we tell him the punishment for violating the commandments, we tell him the reward for obeying them. We say to him: Know that the world to come is made only for the righteous, and Israel in this time is unable to receive either full reward or full punishment. But we do not burden him with too long or too detailed an account. If he then agrees we circumcise him at once. . . . When he is healed, we immerse him at once, and two scholars stand by him and instruct him in some of the light and in some of the weighty commandments. When he has come up from immersion he is like an Israelite in every respect. In the case of a woman, women cause her to sit in the water up to her neck and two scholars stand outside and instruct her in some of the light and some of the weighty commandments.

Even in a time of travail, the openness to converts was remarkable. As long as the prospective ger understood the current plight of the Jews and was prepared to share their trials and tribulations, he or she would be converted.

In fact, in Numbers Rabbah, the great Midrashic collection on the fourth book of the Torah, written when Christianity and Islam had come to dominate Jewish life totally, there appear some of the most beautiful statements about converts. In this great work, converts are as dear if not dearer to God than born Jews. Who can ever doubt Judaism's positive attitude to converts after reading this homily?

The Holy One, blessed be He, greatly loves the proselytes. To what may this be compared? To a king who had a flock which used to go out to the field and come in at even. So it was each day. Once a stag came in with the flock. He associated with the goats and grazed with them. When the flock came in to the fold, he came in with them, when they went out to graze he went out with them. The king was told: "A certain stag has joined the flock and is grazing with them every day. He goes out with them and comes in with them." The king felt an affection for him. When he went out into the field the king gave orders: "Let him have a good pasture, such as he likes; no man shall beat him; be careful with him!" When he came in with the flock also the king would tell them: "Give him a drink"; and he loved him very much. The servants said to him: "Sovereign! You possess so many kids, so many he-goats, you possess so many lambs, and you never caution us about them; yet you give us instructions every day about this stag!" Said the king to them: "The flock have no choice; whether they want to or not it is their nature to graze in the field all day and to come in at even to sleep in the fold. The stags, however, sleep in the wilderness. It is not in their nature to come into places inhabited by man. Shall we then not account it as a merit to this one which has left behind the whole of the vast wilderness, the abode of the beasts, and has come to stay in the courtyard?" In like manner, ought we not be grateful to the proselyte who has left behind him his family and his father's house, has left behind him his people and all the other peoples of the world, and has come and chosen us? Accordingly, He has provided him with special protection, for He exhorted Israel that they shall be very careful in relation to the proselytes so as not to do them harm; and so indeed it says, Love ye therefore the proselyte, etc., (Deut. X, 19) and a proselyte shalt thou not oppress (Ex. XXIII, 9). (Numbers Rabbah 8:2)

In the first millennium of our era, Judaism's attractiveness was indicated by the conversion of kings and large populations. In the first century, the royal family of Adiabene and perhaps much of the population converted to Judaism. Adiabene occupied the territory that had once been Assyria. The royal house proved exemplary. The converts of Adiabene fought alongside other Jews in the war against Rome.

The Khazars, an Asiatic steppe people who conquered south Russia, are the most famous group of converts. Whether the conversion, which occurred in 700 C.E., was motivated primarily by religious belief or by a desire to strike a neutral pose between the Christianity of Byzantium and the Islam of Baghdad, it nevertheless reflected the prestige and respect accorded Judaism. The event continued to electrify Jewry for hundreds of years. Long after the Khazar state had disappeared, the great medieval Sephardic writer, Yehuda HaLevi, used the Khazars' conversion as the backdrop for his great exposition of Judaism, *The Kuzari*.

The heightened anti-Jewish activity and sentiment initiated by the Crusades led to a growing divide between Jews and Gentiles. In such an atmosphere, conversion to Judaism became increasingly inconceivable. People seldom seek to join a hated and feared people. Jews, for their part, turned inward, concentrating on preserving themselves in the face of growing hostility. A virtually total unwillingness to receive *gerim* became the stance of world Jewry.

Forgotten or disregarded was the tremendous missionary activity during the Second Commonwealth, the openness to converts expressed in the *Amidah,* or the host of positive sayings and stories about *gerim* in rabbinic literature. What people did remember was the small number of statements seemingly unfavorable to converts, such as "Converts are as bad to Israel as the tumor, scab, or itch." Judaism had returned to the biblical view which denied that anyone not born into Judaism could be a meaningful Jew.

Modernity and Conversion

The maintenance of hermetically sealed communities continued until the Jews entered modern society with the rise of emancipation and the spirit of enlightenment. As integration replaced separation, and Jews increasingly adopted the mores of their neighbors, they came increasingly to be perceived as eligible mates by their fellow citizens. Today in the United States, marriage of Jew with Gentile is as common as marriage of Jew with Jew. Nor does this surge in intermarriage show any sign of abating.

A major change has taken place in the last generation, however. Whereas previously intermarrying Jews sought to sever their links to Judaism—often by changing their name and concealing all traces of a Jewish past—most Jews who intermarry today are proud of their heritage and seek to maintain some sort of Jewish identification. For some, the Jewish commitment is so strong that they urge the non-Jewish partner to explore Judaism and, they hope, to convert. Within the Conservative, Reform, and Reconstructionist movements there exists today an open and welcoming approach to would-be converts. Whatever ambivalence may once have obtained has largely been dissipated. Many rabbis are involved in one way or another in the guidance of converts by tutoring them or sponsoring special classes and programs designed especially for them.

This atmosphere of outreach does not extend to most of the Orthodox world, however. In many cases, Gentiles approaching Orthodox rabbis are rebuffed in an unfriendly manner or are introduced to study programs of indeterminate length and unreasonable demands. While some Orthodox rabbis will cynically supervise rapid conversions—a malady true of the other movements as well—most such rabbis feel that the best response to the wave of intermarriage is to insist on strict observance and, therefore, to convert only those they feel will practice Orthodoxy.

The Orthodox reluctance to convert has even intensified in some ways. Recently, some of the *mikvaot* (ritual baths) necessary for immersion of converts have been closed to all conversions. Furthermore, Jewish couples seeking to have adopted children converted under Orthodox auspices have had great difficulty in finding rabbis to accommodate their requests, unless the parents promise to observe the tradition as Orthodoxy expounds it. In earlier generations this requirement was less prevalent.

In both Israel and the United States, Orthodox conversions are at least possible. In Israel, special schools for converts exist under the auspices of the Chief Rabbinate, whose attitude is that the land of Israel will make people Jewish and therefore that greater openness to conversion is permissible. However, conversion documents are known to have been issued declaring that a conversion performed in Israel was valid only there and not abroad. In Europe, conversion is difficult to impossible, and, with few alternatives available, many people simply give up and resign themselves to living outside Jewish life.

The most extreme level of resistance is reflected in the Syrian Jewish community, which in the United States is concentrated in Brooklyn and along the New Jersey shore in Deal. In four proclamations (1935, 1946, 1972, and 1984) this community has affirmed and reaffirmed the total exclusion of the convert and his or her Jewish-born partner from the life of the community. The 1946 proclamation declares:

1. Our community will never accept any converts, male or female, for marriage.
2. The rabbi will not perform any religious ceremonies for such couples, i.e., marriages, circumcisions, bar mitzvahs, etc. In fact the Congregation's premises will be barred to them for use of any religious or social nature.
3. The Mesadrim [those in charge] of the Congregation will not accord any honors to the convert or one married to a convert, such as offering him an Aliyah to the Sefer Torah. In addition, the aforesaid person, male or female, will not be allowed to purchase a seat, permanent or for the holidays, in our congregation.
4. After the death of said person, he or she is not to be buried in the cemetery of our community, known as Rodfe Zedek, regardless of financial considerations.[3]

The Syrian community, which is insular even with regard to other Jews, has followed one extreme. A small but growing number of Reform rabbis have followed the opposite route by entering churches and co-officiating with ministers and priests, lending a Jewish aura to marriages that tilt toward Christianity. While the position of these rabbis is manifestly contrary to Jewish law, they argue that their presence shows the Jewish partner that a link to Jewish life and Jewish leadership remains an option. More common is the response of some other Reform and Reconstructionist rabbis who will officiate at quasi-Jewish ceremonies between Jew and Gentile if there is agreement to raise as Jews any children born to the couple.

Another way these contemporary movements have responded to the growing number of intermarriages is to validate the principle of patrilineality. According to this theory, a child born to either a Jewish father or a Jewish mother is presumed to be a Jew, if he or she is raised and educated as a Jew. This implies that the child will celebrate the events of the Jewish life cycle and experience some level of Jewish home life.

This stance flies in the face of Jewish tradition, which from Pharisaic times has recognized only matrilineality as the appropriate determinant of a baby's Jewish status. It is widely posited that the growing acceptance of patrilineality has contributed to the reduced percentage of women converting to Judaism among those who intermarry, because at one time many women converted so that their children would be born Jewish. Moreover, non-Jews married to Jews may become members of Reform synagogues, thus removing another motivation for conversion. The spate of programs, sponsored by Jewish community centers and Jewish family services, designed to reach out to intermarried couples have provided a Jewish rubric for discussions of mixed marriage in the hope that many of the participants will later opt for Judaism. Paradoxically, such programs may also serve to confirm the propriety of the two-religion approach.

Nor has rabbinic officiation at interfaith weddings necessarily changed matters. Drs. Egon Mayer and Amy Avgar found that the presence or absence of a rabbi at such a ceremony had a negligible effect on the subsequent Jewish identification of such couples. They note that, "Whether or not a rabbi was willing to officiate at one's marriage does not appear to have significantly encouraged or deterred the conversion of the non-Jewish partner."[4]

The growing rate of intermarriage and the decline in conversion among mixed couples has led Jewish parents to grasp for straws as well. As long as a rabbi is at a wedding, as long as the grandchildren will be Jewish in some way, they find peace of mind.

A concern for feelings is quite laudable, but Judaism contains clear and necessary standards to secure a Jewish future and maintain a unique and vibrant path. Responding to the very human crisis posed by intermarriage by relaxing Jewish law may risk the development of a new form of syncretism: "*parve*hood"—individuals who or families that, though not fully Jewish, demand full recognition with the Jewish community. Some fear that the traditional and most learned people in the community will be unable to accommodate these quasi-Jews and an irreparable breach will be created. In my view, the community must take steps to encourage Reform and Reconstructionist rabbis (the majority) to join their Conservative and Orthodox colleagues in officiating only at weddings between two Jews. Conversion is a most honorable way for someone to become a Jew. Development of programs encouraging conversion to Judaism should be a major priority of contemporary Jewish life.

A recent study at Brandeis University's Cohen Center for Jewish Studies has confirmed that homes in which conversion has taken place are far more Jewishly identified than mixed-marriage settings. Jews in conversionary homes even report higher levels of some ritual observances than do those in endogamous households.[5]

Encouraging Conversion; or, Converts Make Good Jews

The Jewish community must redouble its efforts to encourage Gentiles to convert when they plan to marry Jews. The programs that exist do work, but they need greater publicity and community support. Outreach and awareness can draw potential converts to rabbis and to classes. The potentially successful "Jew by choice" must approach Judaism with openness and, ideally, enthusiasm if he or she is ever to become a Jew. Judaism is a demanding religion; therefore, the decision to convert cannot be made blithely or without thought.

Jews by choice must say yes to the Jewish belief and value system. They must be willing to change their lives to include Jewish holidays, the Sabbath, synagogue worship and affiliation, prayer, and Jewish study. Some programs require some level of kashrut observance as well. They must, in short, become serious practicing Jews, for only by believing with heart and mind, by experiencing Judaism in their lives, and by identifying religiously and socially with the Jewish community can they incorporate Judaism into their souls. To be a Jew, one must sever any links to a past religion and do so without guilt. In our secularized yet quasi-Christian society, the lure of Christmas can undermine the born Jew and lead him or her into assimilation. This national secularism remains a significant hurdle for converts-to-be, yet most opt for Judaism unequivocally, understanding that the decision to convert is irrevocable.

Once one is in, there is "no way out." Converts should understand that their study of Judaism is linked to a relationship; conversion can take place only if the person has come to *love and live* the Jewish way of life for its own sake.

While there are a small number of potential *gerei ha-tzedek* (righteous converts) who come unattached, the overwhelming number of those converting do so because they are already married to or plan to wed a Jew. Classically, this motivation was seen as less than desirable, but today it is quite clear than an enthusiastic candidate for conversion with a supportive partner has a much greater prospect of following through than a single person, who may find it more difficult to find a niche in the community or to observe the Sabbath in solitude. Thus within the Reform, Conservative, and Reconstructionist communities, it is accepted policy for the Jewish partner to participate in conversion classes as well, to provide support for the Jew by choice, and, most significantly, to deepen his or her own knowledge of and commitment to Jewish living. Nothing is sadder than the would-be convert's losing his or her desire for Jewish living—*shul*, Shabbat, kashrut—because the partner, the born Jew, has belittled these things. What the born Jew, who may have a strong Jewish identity and therefore want a Jewish spouse and Jewish children, often fails to understand is that a convert cannot overnight develop the inbred sense of Jewish identity that the spouse possesses, but must become a Jew gradually through Jewish deeds. After all, the Jew by choice has no Jewish past and cannot summon up nostalgia, or memories of Bubba's blintzes, but gains Jewishness only through ongoing intensive Jewish living.

A Curriculum for Jews by Choice

An appropriate program for conversion requires time. The person must study, integrate values and practices into his or her life, and start to feel at home in the Jewish community. Many recognized programs for conversion range from four months to several years. Nine to twelve months of classes—a cycle of the Jewish year—provide students with the requisites to experience Jewish holidays and to feel comfortable in Jewish settings. There is but one Sabbath each week; one cannot speed up the appreciation of this great day. Holidays occur only at the appropriate time and should be lived, not just studied intellectually. During this period, in sixteen to thirty sessions, depending on the program, the convert and the born Jew will study Judaism's basic beliefs—God, Torah, revelation, Jewish law, Jewish ethics, the notion of peoplehood. They will learn about Shabbat and the holidays of the year, the life cycle from birth to life after death, the liturgy, kashrut, and enough Hebrew to be able to read along in prayer and song. Jewish history and modern Jewish religious and secular movements, especially Zionism, are explored.

Some programs offer large classes for fifteen to forty people. Others provide seminars for six to eight or just tutorials for the couple or individual. Whatever the setting, converts and their partners must have the freedom to discuss issues and ask questions. The teacher should get to know them to gauge their progress and provide caring guidance.

Classes are one part of the program. In addition, students are expected to work closely with sponsoring rabbis of synagogues, which they attend regularly and of which they start to feel a part. Those converts who develop strong ties to synagogues and who make friends in the *shul* community are more likely over the long run to maintain a strong Jewish commitment. Because converts must create Jewish homes and Jewish lives through observances that they have not experienced regularly, it is important that would-be converts visit the homes of committed Jews in the community to share Shabbat and festival meals.

Most converts have a strong faith in God. They are attracted to Judaism's view of the unity of God, who is worshiped without intermediaries; they respond warmly to its emphasis on sanctifying life in this world. By contrast, they have great difficulty comprehending the notion that accepting Judaism involves becoming part of the Jewish people, *Am Yisra'el*, since the notion of peoplehood has no parallel in Christianity. Ironically, it is the sense of *Am Yisra'el* that forms the core, along with childhood family experiences, of the commitment of most Jewish partners. The challenge to the teacher is to move the convert to a broader appreciation of Judaism as a faith lived through a unique people while bringing the Jewish partner to an appreciation of Judaism as a religion, whose starting point is the belief in the Holy One. Then the couple can share the totality that is Judaism.

Not infrequently, the teacher encounters individuals of Jewish origin, raised in Europe or in the United States as Gentiles, who want to return to their ancestral religion for its own sake. Among this special subgroup of converts, the problem of peoplehood or ethnicity is mitigated. When meeting someone Jewish they more fully accept their place with the Jewish people, for, in some way, they already have an attachment to *Am Yisra'el.*

When a convert completes the process of study some sort of final evaluation is in order. It should be done by the teacher and sponsoring rabbi, who evaluate the convert's level of attachment to and knowledge of Judaism. They make a judgment as to whether the convert-to-be has accepted the Jewish beliefs and value system, has adopted the Jewish way of holiness, and has identified with the Jewish people. Then they proceed to the formal, halakhic (legal) conversion.

The Act of Conversion

A male must be circumcised, or if already circumcised, he must be symbolically circumcised by having a drop of blood drawn from the place of circumcision. Clearly, this requirement is a mighty hurdle for many. Even symbolic circumcision, which causes only a split second of physical pain, can, for understandable reasons, put off a would-be convert. This requirement, the historically patriarchal nature of communities, and the fact that only a Jewish mother could create a Jewish child have meant that in the past converts to Judaism were overwhelmingly women. While women still predominate, today an increasing number of men are converting—a larger percentage each year. Some, especially converts from abroad, require circumcision. I believe that the growing number of men converting reflects both the willingness of proud, Jewishly educated women to propose their faith for their partner's consideration and the development of a different sort of man who does not consider his mas-culinity impaired by acceding to his partner's request.

Following, in a man's case, the ritual circumcision (*milah*), a court of three inquires into the candidate's knowledge of and commitment to Judaism; then male and female alike must be immersed in a *mikvah* and accept Judaism's commandments. Only then is a candidate truly Jewish in the eyes of Jewish law.

The Politics of Conversion

The legal and ritual acts described above are not required in the Reform and Reconstructionist movements, which leaves the community with two levels of converts: those who have been converted in accordance with Jewish law and those who have not and whose conversion is therefore suspect. At the same time, an effusion of Orthodox zeal has led to a growing number of instances in which legal conversions have been disqualified because the court comprised non-Orthodox rabbis. Implicit in this disqualification is the notion that non-Orthodox rabbis teach a different Torah from that of Orthodoxy, and that therefore converts accepting a non-Orthodox view of the Torah are not properly Jewish because they have not accepted the proper Torah.[6]

Ironically, the combination of Reform liberalism as expressed in the patrilineal descent decision and Orthodox intransigence is having a negative effect on conversion. Many people are mistakenly convinced that only Orthodox conversions are accepted in Israel (in fact, the Law of Return affirmed by Israel's Supreme Court accepts *any* convert for citizenship). Would-be converts, therefore, often fruitlessly scour the territory for a welcoming Orthodox rabbi. Finding none, they relinquish the goal of conversion, feeling that if it cannot be Orthodox, it might as well not happen.

Conversion of children presents its own set of issues. In many cases, Jewish fathers and non-Jewish mothers have agreed to have their children become Jews with halakhic conversions. Sometimes the father wants the child to have a Jewish imprimatur and no more. When there is a real desire to raise a Jewish child, it is still not clear that a non-Jew, with no knowledge of Judaism, can do the primary job. The notion that a six- or four-hour-a-week Hebrew school program can fill the vacuum of a home devoid of Judaism is flawed. Hence, some rabbis require that prior to the conversion of her child a non-Jewish mother take a course in Judaism along with her husband.

What is gained? If the non-Jewish mother understands something of Judaism, she will be able to participate in the nurturing of her child as a Jew; similarly, the possibility of her separation from and concomitant resentment of this aspect of her child's education is reduced. Moreover, through the educational process, the mother may develop an appreciation of Judaism that leads to her later conversion. Conversions after marriage often lack the sense of compulsion that one can find in brides-to-be—the "I've got to be converted by June 21 at noon because I'm getting married then" syndrome.

It is difficult at the outset to assess whether those whose marriage depends on conversion or who have already set marriage dates are truly sincere. Marriage, however, removes the Damocles sword. Participation in Jewish life, a good marriage with a Jewish partner, and a slow but growing appreciation of matters Jewish often bring a responsible adult to a free and reasoned decision to convert.[7]

Adopting a Non-Jewish Child

Adoption is another area where conversion is important. Some mistakenly suppose that incorporation into a Jewish family is sufficient to Judaize an infant. The fact is, there must be conversion for the child (see David Novak, pp. 23–25)—circumcision for a boy, and immersion in the presence of a proper court of three. Here, too, if one parent is not Jewish, the couple often undertake an introductory program of study of Judaism. The parents then avow that they will build a meaningful Jewish home life and give the child a formal Jewish education. No questions are asked of the child, though a proper gurgle is always welcomed! In these circumstances, the *bet din* (court) is deemed to be conferring a benefit on the child which he or she can affirm or reject only at maturity (twelve for a girl, thirteen for a boy). The Bar or Bat Mitzvah is the public way for youthful *gerim* to reaffirm the decision made for them years before.

The Importance of Support Systems

Conversion involves far more than sitting through a series of classes. During the learning process, and for some time afterward, converts require special attention. Support groups should be established for them and their partners to deal both with the problems they expect to have and with those that they are astounded to encounter.

Gerei ha-tzedek are often troubled that their parents are unhappy with their decisions. The parents may understandably feel betrayed or abandoned by their beloved child's decision; if devout Christians, they may even feel that their child's chosen path leads to the loss of salvation. Sometimes the child is surprised at the intensity of the parental sentiments or by an upwelling of anti-Semitism that they never suspected. More disconcerting to the potential convert is the lack of support or even active antagonism that the in-laws might convey, though this occurs less often than before. Furthermore, there can be the biting and sarcastic remarks of Jewish friends who, tragically, are as likely to view conversion as absurd as praiseworthy. This reality makes synagogue participation all the more crucial to the conversionary couple, because the synagogue will provide them with peers who can enthusiastically support their decision. Support groups allow converts to talk about the pain of giving up Christmas, the issue of Israel, the reality of anti-Semitism, and the difficulty of feeling at home in Jewish life, where lox, latkes, Yiddish expressions, and the Jewish heart seem to count more than faith and mitzvot.

A host of other programs can play a significant role in building Jewish commitment, from weekend retreats to walking tours of Jewish neighborhoods to holiday workshops to Shabbat meals. In converting someone to Judaism, more than knowledge is imparted. The beauties of Jewish life and the magic of a people's history and dreams must be shared.

Conclusion

Intermarriage is here to stay and growing. Unless the Jewish community en masse formulates an Amish-like posture, intermarriage is not likely to be eliminated. Of course, intensive Jewish education in youth—day schools and *yeshivot* and deep Jewish living, Shabbat, kashrut, prayer, and community, all infused by an abiding faith in a living God—will make a tremendous difference in creating the kind of Jew who is not likely to consider intermarriage. Yet short of messianic times, the most intensive and effective programs to gain proselytes should be furthered.

Rabbis and other Jewish professionals who make outreach for conversion their specialty must be supported. The cooperation of all parts of the Jewish religious community should be sought to develop programs that all can accept. This will involve compromises on many sides, but religious leaders must be willing to put aside particular interests for the greater communal good.

Ironically, the intermarriage crisis has rekindled an appreciation of the propriety and desirability of conversion after centuries of its denigration. When talking to converts about the wonders of Judaism, Jews also talk to themselves. As Judaism has again become an *or le-goyim*, a light to the nations, it has also brought a new light and spirit to all Jews.

NOTES

1. See the *1990 National Jewish Population Survey* published in the summer of 1991 by the Council of Jewish Federations. The disturbing findings reveal that while the rate of intermarriage has increased sharply, the rate of conversion to Judaism has declined.

2. Salo W. Baron, *A Social and Religious History of the Jews*, 18 vols., 2d ed. (Philadelphia: Jewish Publication Society, 1952), 1:167–79.

3. See the texts of the bans in S. Zevulun Lieberman, "A Sephardic Ban on Converts," in *The Conversion Crisis*, ed. Emanuel Feldman and Joel B. Wolowelsky (Hoboken, NJ: Ktav/Rabbinical Council of America, 1990) pp. 49–52.

4. Egon Mayer and Amy Avgar, *Conversion among the Intermarried* (New York: Petschek National Jewish Family Center, American Jewish Committee, 1987), p. 33.

5. S. B. Fishman, et al., *Intermarriage and American Jews Today: New Findings and Policy Implications* (Waltham, MA: Cohen Center for Modern Jewish Studies, Brandeis University, 1990), p. 25.

6. As Jacob I. Schochet (*Who Is a Jew* [New York: Shofar Association, 1987], p. 30) puts it, "This refusal by the 'orthodox' to acknowledge the legitimacy of the non-Orthodox is not an ad personam bias, nor a political judgment against an organization. It is, rather, the refusal on principle to accept a philosophy and a way of life that contradict the foundations of Torah life, of Jewish tradition." That such an argument is frequently merely a pretext for delegitimatizing non-Orthodox rabbis is underscored by the fact that some leading Orthodox rabbis have suddenly arranged for the conversion of people who have not studied the "correct" Torah, in that they were taught by Conservative rabbis.

7. Although most of those who convert after marriage do so during the first decade of married life, I have converted people after thirty-seven and forty-four years of marriage to Jewish partners.

SUGGESTIONS FOR FURTHER READING

Bernard Bamberger, *Proselytism in the Talmudic Period* (New York: Ktav, [1939] 1968), is a fine study of rabbinic attitudes to conversion, showing the overwhelmingly positive response converts received in the Talmudic period. It is paralleled by William G. Braude's *Jewish Proselyting in the First Five Centuries of the Common Era* (Providence, R.I.: Brown University Press, 1940).

A fascinating autobiography of a Roman Catholic priest who converted to Judaism can be found in Abraham Carmel, *So Strange My Path* (New York: Bloch, 1964).

David Max Eichhorn, ed., *Conversion to Judaism: A History and Analysis* (New York: Ktav, 1965) presents a history of conversion from biblical times to the present, plus an examination of conversion from various perspectives. The book is the work of many hands and includes reflections of Jews by choice as well.

Emanuel Feldman and Joel B. Wolowelsky, *The Conversion Crisis* (Hoboken: Ktav/Rabbinical Council of America, 1990) is a collection of essays from *Tradition,* modern Orthodoxy's journal, which shows the wide range of attitudes to conversion within the Orthodox world.

A solid introduction to Judaism, Conservative-style, directed especially at converts, is obtainable in Simcha Kling, *Embracing Judaism* (New York: Rabbinical Assembly, 1987).

The director of the Reform outreach program, Lydia Kukoff, gives an introduction to the issues facing converts in *Choosing Judaism* (New York: Union of American Hebrew Congregations, 1981).

Julius Lester, *Lovesong: Becoming a Jew* (New York: Henry Holt, 1988), is the moving memoir of a black professor/activist once distrusted by the Jewish community who returns to the religion of his Jewish great-great-grandfather.

Joseph R. Rosenbloom, *Conversion to Judaism: From Biblical Times to the Present* (Cincinnati: Hebrew Union College, 1978) presents another comprehensive study of conversion in Jewish history.

Susan Weidman Schneider, *Intermarriage: The Challenge of Living with Differences between Christians and Jews* (New York: Free Press, 1989) is a first-rate study of intermarriage with an excellent chapter on conversion to Judaism.

Devorah Wigoder's *Hope Is My House* (Englewood Cliffs: Prentice-Hall, 1966) tells the story of a woman who converted in America and has spent the rest of her life as a Jew in Israel.

DANIEL H. GORDIS

Marriage

Judaism's "Other" Covenantal Relationship

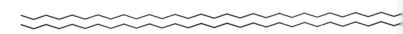

Marriage as a Reflection of a World Order

Over the course of Jewish history, the ways in which Jews have understood their relationship with God—their covenant—have changed dramatically. But at least until modern times, few Jews even attempted a theory of Jewish life that did not have covenant at its core; as a result, the customs and practices of traditional Judaism have always sought to provide both individual Jews and Jewish communities with concrete ways of expressing their relationship with God. One of the most significant insights of traditional Judaism has been its contention that a relationship cannot exist in a vacuum. Just as one could not successfully sustain a relationship of love with another human being without expressing that love in numerous observable ways, so too does the Jew's relationship with God require concrete expression.

That expression takes many forms in Jewish life. Traditional Judaism regulates virtually every element of human life, including diet, clothing, relations with others, and speech, all with an eye toward dedicating every moment of human life to an awareness and appreciation of the Jew's relationship, or covenant, with God.

The tradition has sought to infuse into virtually each dimension of human life a sense of *Kedushah*, or holiness. But in addition to its insight that a relationship with God could be expressed in seemingly mundane aspects of human life, Jewish tradition also claimed that a relationship with God, a Being no human being can fully grasp, could be better appreciated by seeking to create a parallel human model—a relationship between two human beings.

This human relationship, fashioned in the shadow, or image, of one's relationship to God, would both further the classic Jewish goal of investing human life with sanctity and serve as a model of how Jews might think about their infinitely more subtle covenant with God. In Jewish thought, the relationship most approximating that between human beings and God is the marital relationship between a man and a woman. An exploration of the Jewish traditions surrounding weddings and married life will reveal not only the significance of the various elements of the rituals themselves, but also the fundamental religious and theological claims that lie "behind the scenes" of the Jewish conception of marriage.

The analogy between the marital relationship and the covenantal relationship is almost as old as classical Judaism itself. As early as the eighth century B.C.E., the biblical prophet Hosea used the image of a marriage torn asunder to describe God's vexation with a people who had abandoned their part of the covenant. Through Hosea, God turns to the People Israel and issues a combined demand and warning:

> Rebuke your mother [=your nation], rebuke her—
> For she is not My wife
> And I am not her husband—
> And let her put away her harlotry from her face
> And her adultery from between her breasts.
> Else will I strip her naked
> And leave her as on the day she was born:
> And I will make her like a wilderness,
> Render her like desert land,
> And let her die of thirst. (Hosea 2:4–5)[1]

The analogy between human marriage and a Divine covenant was not limited to moments when a relationship had been violated.[2] Sometime around the first century C.E., the rabbinic sages began to allegorize the

Song of Songs as an expression of God's love for the Jewish people. Despite some of the rather sensual images of this poetry, the allegorical view of the book has achieved near canonical status. Finally, it is no accident that when Jews welcome the Sabbath on Friday evening, the liturgy refers to that unique and spiritually reenergizing day as the "Sabbath Bride."

The rabbis suggested their sense that ideal human love reflected Divine love with such comments as, "If a man and wife are worthy, the Divine Presence is with them,"[3] and "Whoever marries a worthy wife is kissed by Elijah and loved by the Holy One."[4]

Where did the relationship between God and human beings begin? God would not have created humanity, claims the tradition, unless it were God's wish that some human-Divine relationship develop from that act.[5] As a result of this conception, the notion of covenant receives much attention in the Jewish wedding ceremony, and the specific act of creation is directly addressed in its customs and liturgy. The Jewish wedding also expresses the traditional belief that the world was created with a purpose. Because the tradition expects that the perfection that marked the Garden of Eden will one day be restored to human lives in the form of a messianic era, the wedding tradition also reflects a concern with messianic ideas.

Another element of the Jewish conception of marriage is the notion that this distinctive human relationship also represents one of the most significant means by which *Kedushah* is injected into the lives of communities and individuals. It is significant that the rabbinic term for Jewish marriage is *kiddushin,* etymologically related to the term for sanctity.[6] It is also no accident that Maimonides, in the *Mishneh Torah,* his classic code of Jewish law, includes the laws pertaining to marriage not in the section on women, but in matters related to holiness. Ultimately, Jewish tradition claims, it is in a relationship in which two human beings recognize each other as creations in God's image and treat each other as such that true sanctity begins to pervade the world. Some scholars have described Judaism as a continuing process of bringing the world to a state of perfection.[7] To the extent that this characterization is accurate, marriage represents a starting point from which sanctification can be extended beyond the married couple to family, community, the Jewish people, and ultimately the entire world.

A third major characteristic of Judaism's reflections on marriage is the conception that marriage is the natural state for adults. Not only is marriage a reflection of a cosmic relationship with God and a mechanism for furthering Judaism's goal of sanctifying the human world, but it is also traditionally seen as a means of perfecting human beings who would otherwise be in some way incomplete.

This notion of marriage as the "natural state" for human adults has its origins in Judaism's biblical roots. The second chapter of the book of Genesis describes God's concern over Adam's lone existence in the world and portrays God as saying, "It is not good for man to be alone; I will make a fitting helper for him" (Genesis 2:18).[8] A few verses later, the text states rather matter-of-factly that "a man leaves his father and mother and clings to his wife, so that they become one flesh" (Genesis 2:24). Indeed, this union of male and female is requisite, according to the Bible, so that human beings may fulfill the first command addressed to them in the first creation story, "be fertile and increase, fill the earth and master it" (Genesis 1:18).[9]

Later biblical works echo this perspective, perhaps most notably with Ecclesiastes' counsel: "Enjoy happiness with a woman you love all the fleeting days of life that have been granted to you under the sun—all your fleeting days. For that alone is what you can get out of life." Marriage as a natural state for human beings is expressed most clearly in the rabbinic tradition, which is replete with such aphorisms as "A wife-less man exists without joy, without blessing or boon"[10] and "It is better to live one's life with another than alone."[11] The Babylonian Talmud records a statement of the sage Samuel that the purpose of marriage extends beyond the need for biological preservation of the human species: "Even if a man [already] has a number of sons, it is forbidden for him to live without a wife, as it is written [in Genesis 2:18], 'it is not good for man to be alone.'"[12] The Jerusalem Talmud, echoing the conception that human marriage mirrors the cosmic relationship between God and human beings, claims, "A man cannot live without a woman, a woman cannot live without a man, and the two of them cannot live without the presence of God."[13] The Zohar, the classic Jewish mystical text of the thirteenth century, asserts, "A man without a wife is only half a person."[14] The rabbinic view of marriage is also emphasized by the Talmud's chastisement of Ben Azzai, the one talmudic authority who consciously avoided marriage.[15] The rabbis even permitted the sale of a Torah scroll, an act forbidden in virtually all other cases of financial need, in order that a man or a poor woman could marry.[16]

There can be no question, then, that the Jewish tradition has always conceived of marriage as a crucial dimension of human life. We have noted three aspects of its centrality in Jewish life: (1) as a reflection of the covenantal relationship between God and Jews; (2) as a crucial means of imbuing human societies with sanctity; and (3) as the natural and appropriate state for human beings. With this theoretical foundation, we turn our attention to a brief history of the institution of Jewish marriage.

Some Biblical Roots of Jewish Marriage

Most of modern Jewish life is the product not of biblical law and tradition but of the rabbinic experience and texts from the first century B.C.E. through the fifth or sixth century C.E. While the majority of Jewish marriage rituals do emerge from the rabbinic period, some of the basic elements of Jewish marriage are as ancient as the Bible itself.

THE BIBLICAL PRECEDENT FOR MONOGAMY AND FAMILY

Despite the fact that Jewish marriage did not become exclusively monogamous until the Middle Ages with the decree of Rabbenu Gershom (ca. 960–1028),[17] the Bible describes even the earliest forms of Jewish marriage as being essentially monogamous. Though some prominent biblical characters did have more than one wife or a wife and a concubine, these celebrated examples seem to have been exceptions to the rule. Of course, monogamy as a way of life became even more pervasive during the rabbinic period, in which it was clearly the normative Jewish model. The Bible's implicit endorsement of monogamy, the theoretical permissibility of polygamy notwithstanding, emerges not only from the biblical descriptions of the lives of many significant biblical characters, but from suggestions in poetic texts such as the Song of Songs as well. The Bible also foreshadows later Judaism's stress on children and the family. In the biblical mindset, childbearing was considered a blessing, and the absence of children a serious misfortune.[18] Although divorce was permitted, it was apparently not common and was certainly not considered ideal.[19]

The Bible provides us with virtually no information about the wedding ceremony itself. While the rabbis, as mentioned above, referred to the act of marrying with the verb *kiddesh* (to sanctify or set aside), the Torah refers to the act as "taking" (*lakah*). The marriage of Moses' parents is described with the verb "to take,"[20] and in the book of Deuteronomy the institution is described in more general terms with the simple declarative "a man takes a wife and possesses her" (Deuteronomy 24:1). Although the text of the Torah provides us with virtually no indication of what this "taking" involved, simple reason, supported by stories such as those about Jacob and Leah, suggests that some sort of celebration must have taken place (Genesis 29:22–28). There is also evidence that public exhibition of evidence of the bride's virginity (most commonly the blood-stained sheet) was part of the ritual,[21] a custom perpetuated in only a few extremely religious Jewish communities today.

THE *SHADKHAN* AS A BIBLICAL INSTITUTION

The Bible also provides the origin of the Jewish institution of the *shadkhan*, or the matchmaker. The most famous use of the *shadkhan* in the Bible concerns the servant Eliezer, whom Abraham sent on a journey to find a wife for his son, Isaac (Genesis 24:1–67). Although the systematic use of a matchmaker was abrogated in the Western European communities of the eighteenth century, the institution continues in many Sephardic communities to this day.[22] In fact, the Jewish matchmaker has become a favorite character of modern stage and film. *Fiddler on the Roof*, Broadway's recreation of the Eastern European shtetl, and *Crossing Delancey*, a recent Hollywood product about life on the Jewish Lower East Side of Manhattan, both feature a matchmaker in central and memorable roles. Finally, one could argue that Jewish computer dating services, commonly found in metropolitan American Jewish communities, represent no more than the resurrection of this essentially biblical tradition in a technologically more modern form.[23]

The institution of the *shadkhan*, in its various forms, reflects a serious concern in Jewish life for the appropriateness of a prospective mate for a Jewish man or woman. In essence, the *shadkhan* also implies a basic mistrust of the romantic impulse, or at least a belief that more than romance is necessary to make a marriage viable. Concern for the appropriateness of a spouse is first voiced in the Torah by Abraham to Eliezer with this demand: "and I will make you swear by the Lord, the God of heaven and the God of the earth, that you will not take a wife for my son from the daughters of the Canaanites among whom I dwell, but will go to the land of my birth and get a wife for my son Isaac" (Genesis 24:4). Indeed, this concern has pervaded Jewish communities since the biblical period. The Mishnah[24] describes the festivities that took place in Jerusalem on the fifteenth day of the month of Av and on the afternoon of Yom Kippur, the most sacred day of the Jewish calendar year, when unmarried Jewish young women, dressed in borrowed white garments, would "go out and dance in the vineyards." What did the women say? "Fellow, look around and see—choose what you want! Don't look for beauty, look for family: 'Charm is deceitful and beauty is vain, but a woman who fears the Lord will be praised.' (Proverbs 31:30)"[25] Later, in the rabbinic period, Rav, one of the foremost sages of his time, included among those who married impetuously and who deserved punishment those who marry without premarital matchmaking arrangements.[26]

This attempt to temper the romantic impulse, however, in no way went so far as to deny the legitimacy of the role of love in marriage. The biblical story of Jacob toiling for fourteen years in order to marry the woman he loved (Genesis 29) and the poignant images of the Song of Songs attest to the centrality of love in a significant relationship between a man and a woman. Even the Talmud recognized that personal taste plays a crucial role in the viability of such relationships and so warned that "it is forbidden for a man to marry a woman until he sees her."[27] The legitimacy of love even made its way into later legal responsa. Joseph ben Solomon Colon (ca. 1420–1480), an Italian expert on Jewish law, was known for his opposition to the arbitrary use of power. When asked whether a man could marry a woman he loved over the objections of his parents, Colon replied that if the woman were suitable for the man in respect to her values and religious orientation, the father could not refuse permission to his son to marry her.[28] Colon's attempt to insist on both the cerebral qualities that make a marriage and the legitimacy of love seems to capture the potentially conflicting, but never mutually exclusive, views of the Jewish tradition as to the ideal components of a marriage.

The Torah's concern with the appropriateness of a spouse as well as its realism about the potential for failure in marriage reflects the tradition's awareness that marital relationships demand something both beyond love and beyond the cerebral. The sages of the midrash[29] described that element as God's contribution to the relationship, and told the following well-known but still timeless parable to make their point.

A Roman matron asked Rabbi Yossi in how many days God had created the world. When he replied, "Six," she responded, "And what does God do now?" When Rabbi Yossi told her that God is busy making marriages, saying "This man to that woman, this woman to that man," the Roman matron exclaimed, "That is all? I can do that!" Rabbi Yossi observed, "It may be easy for you, but for God it is as difficult as the parting of the Red Sea." . . . What did the matron do? She married one thousand male slaves to one thousand female slaves, all in one night. The next morning these slaves came to her, one with a wound, one with an eye that had been put out, each couple with its own tale of misery. . . . The matron sent for Rabbi Yossi and said, "Rabbi, your Torah is truth, and it is beautiful and praiseworthy. You spoke well in all you said."[30]

BIBLICAL LAW REGARDING PROHIBITED MARRIAGES

The final element of modern Jewish marriage with roots in biblical Judaism is the series of restrictions upon whom one may and may not marry. As much as Jewish tradition values both observable characteristics such as family, personal qualities, and moral structure, and as much as it gives credence to the role of love in selecting a mate, biblical law is known for its enumeration of categories of people that certain Jews may not marry.

Marriages prohibited in Jewish law fall into two categories: those that are void despite any ceremony that may have been performed,[31] and those that, though impermissible at the outset, can be validated by performance of a legitimate ceremony.[32] Clearly, the first category involves much more serious violations of sexual and communal taboos than the second.

Marriages that are flat-out prohibited, and therefore void even after the fact, are generally divided into (1) incestuous unions, (2) union with a woman who is already married to another man, and (3) union with a non-Jewish woman. The first group, incestuous marriage, is covered in great detail in Leviticus 18: prohibited are, among other relationships, marriages between parents and children or grandchildren; between brothers and sisters, even if they share only one parent; marriage with step-parents or step-siblings; with a wife's sister if the wife is still alive (this prohibition obviously assumes the permissibility of polygamous marriage); and with a son- or daughter-in-law. The prohibition against marrying a woman already married is also expressly biblical (Leviticus 20:10). The *Shulḥan Arukh*, the code of Jewish law, also lists a series of other more distant relationships that are also prohibited.[33]

The final category of marriages in the "prohibited and void" category is perhaps the most controversial today, for it is the classification that forbids marriage between Jews and non-Jews. With the political, economic, and social emancipation of the Jews in Europe over the past few centuries, the Jewish migrations to America, and the consequent integration of Jews into virtually all professional and social walks of life, Jews and non-Jews interact, work together, and meet socially in ways virtually unprecedented in Jewish life. It is only natural that such meetings and relationships often result in couples who wish to be married. Various branches of modern Judaism have responded to this challenge in differing fashions.

The two more traditional branches, Orthodox and Conservative Judaism, do not recognize mixed marriages as legitimate, and rabbis of these movements do not perform interfaith ceremonies. This position is predicated not only on the explicit prohibition of such marriages in the legal sources,[34] but also on the more sociological contention that a home in which the married parties do not share the same religious worldview cannot be a home permeated by the values and traditions of Jewish life. Concerns about transmitting a coherent religious message to children when the parents do not share the same religion is also of paramount importance in the continuing objections of Conservative and Orthodox Judaism to mixed marriage.

The Reform movement, however, which does not consider ritual Jewish law legally binding in the modern period, recognizes mixed marriage and permits its rabbis to legitimize such unions. As a result, mixed marriages performed by a rabbi are no longer rare in the United States.

Some Reform rabbis will also co-officiate with priests, ministers, or other clergy in a wedding ceremony. Those who are unwilling to do so will often request of the couple a commitment that their children be raised as Jews.[35] Of course, many interfaith couples elect to be married civilly and avoid religious ceremonies altogether.

The second set of prohibited marriages, those that are prohibited but potentially valid, are less objectionable because they do not constitute *gilui arayot* (roughly translated as "incest") as defined by the Torah. Thus, while the tradition urges Jews not to marry people in these categories, those marriages that do take place are valid after the fact. For example, a woman who willingly had an adulterous affair is, strictly speaking, forbidden to both her husband and the other man with whom she had sexual intercourse.[36] Similarly, although it is considered a righteous act to remarry one's divorced wife, one may not do so if the woman has been sexually involved with someone else in the interim (Deuteronomy 24:4). Other "prohibited but valid" marriages include those between priests and divorcées or converts,[37] or between a *mamzer* (a child born of an adulterous relationship) and anyone but another *mamzer*.

Subsequent to the rabbinic period, rabbinic enactments expanded the list of these prohibited marriages. The rabbis added stipulations that after a divorce or the death of a husband, a woman should not marry for ninety days (so that issues of paternity could be easily clarified), and that a pregnant or nursing woman should not marry until the child had reached the age of two years (for fear that another pregnancy or an additional child to nurse would harm the health of the first child).[38] Of course, after the prohibition of polygamy by Rabbenu Gershom, marriage to a second wife was also prohibited.

Although these marriages are technically valid after the fact and, unlike the first category (which leads to absolutely no change in the personal status of the parties involved), continue in effect unless terminated by divorce or death,[39] many traditional communities consistently attempted to pressure such couples into terminating the union by divorce, and within relatively short order.

Today, the Reform movement has abandoned these restrictions, with the obvious exception of polygamy, which in any case is prohibited by the laws of the United States and most other nations. Although Orthodox communities continue to adhere to the rulings, there are occasions in all but the most observant groups in which marriages such as these do occasionally take place. It is in the Conservative community, however, where the most discussion of these restrictions has occurred, specifically the ones prohibiting marriages of priests (that is, descendants of the *kohanim*) with divorcées or converts. In the past several decades, Conservative rabbis have voted to permit such unions, largely because they reject the assumption that a convert must have been sexually licentious before her conversion[40] and because divorce no longer implies morally inappropriate behavior in a woman. The diminished ritual and liturgical importance of the priest today, who without an active temple cult in Jerusalem performs only a few minor roles in the synagogue, has also contributed to these new rulings. Aside from its reconsideration of the prohibitions related to priests, though, Conservative Judaism still abides by the other restrictions enumerated here.

As we have seen, a few of the salient characteristics of the modern Jewish institution of marriage do emerge from the biblical period. The emphasis on monogamy, some precedent for a wedding rite and celebration, the notion that the selection of a partner is a tremendous responsibility that should not always be left to the couple alone, and Judaism's limitations on who may marry whom all emerge from various texts in the Bible. Yet to those who have even a vague familiarity with the modern Jewish wedding ceremony, it is clear that much in the way the Jewish community currently celebrates marriage must have developed after the close of the biblical period. Indeed, Jewish marriage as it exists today is essentially a rabbinic institution. Let us therefore turn to an examination of today's rites and their significance.

The Modern Jewish Wedding Ceremony

The Jewish wedding ceremony is an intricate array of rituals, customs, and liturgical elements. Because one of the central insights of biblical and rabbinic Judaism was that sanctity in human life could be best achieved by *legislating* behavior in those areas of human life with potential for sanctification, the traditional elements of the marriage ceremony are legally mandated by Jewish law. The rabbis even remarked that "anyone who is not knowledgeable about the legal details of divorce and marriage should not become involved with them."[41] As we shall see, virtually every detail of the wedding ceremony has been addressed in the classic Jewish legal sources.

CUSTOMS PRIOR TO THE WEDDING DAY

The elaborate series of marriage customs begins before the wedding day itself. In most traditional communities, and in some more liberal settings as well, it is customary for the groom to be called to the Torah at a synagogue service before the wedding, usually, but not always, on the Saturday morning before his wedding. In Conservative and Reform communities in which this practice is observed, the bride may also be called to the Torah. Typically, the rabbi of the congregation will also recite a blessing in honor of the couple about to be married. This ceremony is known by its Yiddish name, *aufruf*, meaning "to be called up."

Aside from the preparation of the myriad details for the wedding, the other major ritual that takes place before the wedding day is the immersion of a traditional bride in a *mikvah* after her last menstrual period before the wedding. [42] If a parent of either the bride or groom has died, it is also customary in some communities to visit the grave of that parent before the wedding day. In other communities, a brief memorial prayer is recited before the public wedding ceremony, rather than at graveside.

THE WEDDING DAY ITSELF

Although the wedding day ultimately culminates with tremendous joy and celebration, it begins on a rather solemn note, in that a wedding represents not only a physical and emotional union between two people but also an attempt on their part to mirror the relationship between God and humanity. Indeed, the wedding day shares many qualities with the most sacred day of the year, Yom Kippur. Many reasons for these parallels have been suggested, but the most cogent one is that both days begin a new epoch in a person's life, and every Jew naturally seeks to enter these new periods in a state of cleansed spirit and conscience. Certain German communities used to stress this connection with a custom, performed under the wedding canopy, in which the bride and groom gave each other as gifts the shrouds in which they would one day be buried.

The parallels between the wedding day and Yom Kippur are expressed most clearly in the tradition that the bride and groom fast on the day of the wedding until the ceremony is concluded. Although this custom developed rather late, having originated in medieval Germany, it is now observed in traditional communities throughout the world. However, Jewish legal sources stipulate that on certain days, such as the celebration of the beginning of a new Jewish month, the couple should not fast.[43] The couple is also excused from fasting if it is a hardship for them. In many Reform and Conservative communities, as a result, the custom of fasting on the wedding day has fallen into disuse.

Other parallels between the wedding day and Yom Kippur include the wearing of white (since the bride traditionally wears a white gown, and in more observant communities the groom wears a white *kittel*, or robe, as well) and the recitation by the couple of the traditional confession before the start of the wedding ceremony. This confession, known as the *viddui*, is recited numerous times in the liturgy of Yom Kippur as well as on one's deathbed.

THE *KETUBBAH*—TRADITIONAL TEXTS AND INNOVATIONS

Strictly speaking, a legitimate Jewish wedding has two fundamental requirements: first, both parties must enter the marriage voluntarily and willingly; second, their marriage must be accompanied by a *ketubbah*. The term *ketubbah*, which comes from the Hebrew verb "to write," refers to the traditional marriage document, in use since rabbinic times. The traditional *ketubbah* stipulates the obligations that the husband takes on vis-à-vis his bride during marriage, as well as his financial obligations in the case of divorce.

Over the course of marriage, the husband traditionally has three primary obligations to his wife: he must provide her with food, clothing, and sexual satisfaction. Food and clothing, of course, represent the basic economic necessities of life, and the clear implication of the traditional *ketubbah* text is that the husband will effectively provide for his wife's economic well-being. In the case of divorce, the *ketubbah* requires the husband to pay the wife a sum of money, which is dependent on her marital history prior to the current marriage.[44]

Because the traditional *ketubbah* text assumes that it is the husband who will provide for the wife, this document has come under attack by those seeking greater equality between men and women. Before briefly addressing the substance of this critique and the suggestions for making the ceremony more egalitarian, a word about the original intentions of the *ketubbah* is in order. Though clearly the respective roles of the bride and groom as stated in the *ketubbah* are not equal, it must be stressed that, far from being an intentionally misogynous document, the *ketubbah* was originally created to protect women from being simply discarded by their husbands with no provision for their economic welfare. To that extent, the *ketubbah*, despite its dated perception of social reality, was not a tool of repression, but actually a liberating document for women. The *ketubbah* was considered so basic to a just marital relationship, in fact, that the Talmud commented that the fundamental distinction between a wife and a concubine was that a wife had to be given a *ketubbah*, while a concubine did not. [45] The rabbis further stipulated that a man was forbidden from living with his wife, even for one hour, without a *ketubbah*. [46]

These comments on the history and intent of the *ketubbah* do not satisfy most couples who wish to equalize their roles in marriage. These couples, as well as many rabbis and feminist thinkers, point to several distinct difficulties with the traditional *ketubbah* text: (1) the lack of mutuality, given the dramatically changed social and economic circumstances of women today; (2) the reference in the document to the woman's previous marital status—and specifically to the usual use of the term *betultah*, or "virgin," as it is commonly translated, to refer to a previously unmarried woman[47]—with no mention made of the man's marital or sexual history;[48] and finally, (3) the one-sided focus on financial issues.

The two most obvious solutions to these objections are to do away with the *ketubbah* altogether, or to revise it. While the Orthodox community continues to use only the standard text, practices in the other movements vary. Some Reform rabbis have simply dispensed with a *ketubbah*, and many Reform and liberally inclined Conservative rabbis also use nontraditional texts, pointing out that no single *ketubbah* text was ever adopted universally by all Jewish communities. Research into ancient *ketubbot* has shown, for example, that some traditional communities avoided making any reference to the bride's marital or sexual history,[49] while others used terms such as *penita* (unmarried), thus avoiding the issue of virginity.

Similarly, although Maimonides claims that a nonvirgin must be identified as such by use of the term *be'ultah* (married woman), other equally significant sources deny this. In the Talmud, Rabbi Meir suggests that the classification of the bride ought not depend on her physical virginity but on whether her societal attractiveness has been affected in any way.[50] And Rabbi David Hoffmann, the leading light of German Orthodoxy at the end of the nineteenth century, urges that if a woman is not a virgin, no term be used to designate her.[51] Some communities also sought to include in the ketubbah some mention of nonfinancial elements of the marriage; one ancient ketubbah has been located in which the groom declares his bride to be not simply "my wife" but "my friend and my wife in covenant" (ha-veirati ve-eshet beriti).

Today, many liberally inclined Jews who still elect to use a ketubbah make much more significant changes in the text, usually omitting virtually all financial elements of the document and ensuring that obligations be assumed by both partners.[52] Those who choose to use nontraditional marriage documents often do so fully cognizant that they thereby depart radically from tradition and that no halakhically sanctioning community stands behind these new texts. Rather than emulating the public nature of the traditional text, these tend to be rather private documents, expressing the feelings and commitments of the couple rather than the communal nature of the institution of marriage that is implied by use of the traditional text.

Proponents of these new texts further argue that even if more traditional communities reject the legitimacy of creative ketubbot, that rejection will have no bearing on a couple's marital status. Because Jewish law effectively recognizes common-law marriage,[53] even the most traditional communities, they assert, need to recognize these arrangements as marriage, even if a ketubbah is not included. The argument for the new marriage documents, despite their lack of universal acceptance, has been voiced most eloquently by Rabbi Daniel Leifer:

Those who think that they can achieve major halakhic change within the existing Jewish community will perhaps be disappointed by my perspective. I believe, however, that those who are struggling to change Orthodox halakhah and/or the minds of the traditional Orthodox decision makers are wasting their time and energy. It is my conviction that change is affected through the creation of new alternative and rival Jewish rituals and halakhic forms which will ultimately affect and bring about change in the traditional forms and the traditional community.[54]

Before concluding our discussion of the *ketubbah*, mention of another common emendation to the traditional text is in order. This emendation addresses the ever-vexing ethical problem of the *agunah*, the Jewish woman whose husband refuses to grant her a religious divorce. In response to this agonizing dilemma, the Conservative movement began widespread use of an additional clause written by the eminent Talmudic scholar Dr. Saul Lieberman. The "Lieberman clause," as it is known, stipulates that the bride and groom agree that their lives will be conducted according to Jewish law and that, in the event of a divorce, they agree to follow the dictates of a given *bet din* (Jewish court). Thus, if the husband refuses to issue a *get* (a traditional Jewish writ of divorce), the *bet din* will order the husband to do so; if he refuses, the theory goes, his wife can petition a secular court to compel the husband to issue a *get* or else find him in breach of a contract, namely, the *ketubbah* he signed at the time of his marriage.[55]

The Reform movement has not adopted any parallels to the Lieberman clause, because that movement does not require a *get* for the dissolution of divorce. In the Orthodox community, where the problem of the *agunah* is unfortunately a serious one, no emendations to the *ketubbah* have as yet been employed in search of a solution.

KABBALAT KINYAN AND BEDEKIN

Just prior to the wedding ceremony itself, the groom (and, in liberal communities, the bride as well) is asked to indicate his acceptance of the terms of the *ketubbah*, a ceremony known as *kabbalat kinyan*. Indeed, the closing lines of the traditional text state, "We have acquired from [the groom] and [the bride] appropriate authority by means of a legally valid instrument to transact all that is written and discussed above, and everything is in force and established." The groom (and sometimes bride) indicates his acceptance by pulling a handkerchief out of the hand of the officiating rabbi; then, in testimony to their having witnessed that act of acceptance, two witnesses sign the document.

Traditionally, the only signatures on the *ketubbah* were those of the witnesses, who had to be observant Jewish men over the age of thirteen who were not related to the bride or groom. In some liberal communities today, women are also permitted to sign the *ketubbah*. In communities where most lay people are not observant, but the rabbi still considers it important that the signatories of the *ketubbah* be observant Jews, it has become customary for the rabbi and cantor to sign the document.[56] In many non-Orthodox communities, it is now accepted practice for the bride and groom to sign the *ketubbah* as well.

Following the signing of the *ketubbah*, which may be accompanied by a brief *devar Torah*, or discussion of a word of Torah, comes a ceremony known as the *bedekin*. Based on the biblical tradition in which Rachel was surreptitiously substituted for her older sister, Leah, the rite calls for the groom himself to place the veil over the bride's head and to recite the blessing given to Rebecca before she left her own home, "O sister! May you grow into thousands of myriads" (Genesis 24:60). In some communities, other members of the family may also offer blessings for the bride and groom, either taken from traditional texts or created for that special occasion. This may well be the first time the groom sees his bride dressed in her gown, prepared to marry him. It is not surprising, therefore, that the moment of the *bedekin* is often extremely emotional; it, more than anything else, is the signal that the wedding is about to begin.

THE TIME AND PLACE OF THE CEREMONY

From the perspective of Jewish law, a wedding ceremony may be performed virtually anywhere. The most common venues are synagogues, hotels, and homes, but any aesthetically pleasing spot is acceptable. Some communities prefer to perform weddings outside under the stars, in symbolic statement of the hope that the couple will participate in God's blessing to Abraham: "I will bestow My blessing upon you and make your descendants as numerous as the stars of heaven and the sands of the seashore" (Genesis 22:17).[57]

The time of the ceremony is governed somewhat more strictly by Jewish law. Because of the need to sign the *ketubbah*, traditional Jewish communities do not hold weddings on the Sabbath or festivals (Rosh Hashanah, Yom Kippur, Sukkot, Shemini Azeret, Simḥat Torah, Passover, and Shavuot).[58] Nor are weddings permitted on the intermediate days of Sukkot and Passover, because of a rabbinic tradition that two separate joys should not be mixed: each should be celebrated in its own right.[59] The tradition also prohibits weddings during periods of collective Jewish mourning—that is, during the seven weeks between Passover and Shavuot, and the three weeks between the seventeenth day of the month of Tammuz and the ninth day of the month of Av.[60] Most Reform communities, and a few liberal Conservative communities, do not adhere strictly to these limitations.

Otherwise, the ceremony may be held at any time, on any day of the week. Though Sundays are usually most convenient, it is an ancient tradition to hold the ceremony on Tuesday, because it was on that day during creation that God said, "It is good," not once, but twice (Genesis 1:10, 12). This tradition of holding weddings on a Tuesday to mirror this element of the creation story illustrates the point made at the outset of this chapter regarding the centrality of the theme of creation in the Jewish marriage ceremony. We will return to this theme again below.

THE PROCESSIONAL AND THE ḤUPPAH

The wedding ceremony itself takes place under a canopy called the ḥuppah. The canopy may be made of virtually anything, though it is usually cloth and often is a prayer shawl (tallit) that the bride has given to the groom or that belongs to a member of the bride's or groom's family. The ḥuppah has many levels of meaning: it symbolizes the home that the bride and groom will establish together, as well as the home to which the groom used to bring his bride in ancient times. In other interpretations, the ḥuppah also symbolizes the bedchamber of the newly married couple.[61]

Although use of the ḥuppah was not universal in medieval Europe,[62] it is a very old custom. Indeed, the Talmud describes how in earlier times the father of the groom would build the ḥuppah in preparation for his son's marriage,[63] often using such valuable materials as gold or scarlet cloth.[64] In France, a unique custom developed in which the groom imitated the protective actions of Boaz as described in the book of Ruth. That text tells that when Ruth lay beside Boaz on the threshing floor, she said to him, "Spread your robe over your handmaid, for you are a redeeming kinsman" (Ruth 3:9). Thus arose the practice in the French Jewish community in which the groom placed a prayer shawl over the head of his bride, symbolically inaugurating his responsibility to protect her.

Today, the *huppah* is part of virtually all Jewish weddings. The practice of standing under the canopy, however, rests on more than mere custom. Because Jewish law actually called for the bride to be brought to the home of the groom, it is traditional for the groom to arrive at the *huppah* before the bride in the processional and to wait for her, thus anticipating the moment at which he will usher her into his home.[65] The tradition of the *huppah* also suggests the themes of creation and messianism, for, according to the Talmud, God created ten *huppot* for Adam and Eve, and will do the same for the righteous in messianic times.[66]

The processional, a part of virtually every Jewish and Christian wedding in the United States, does not have halakhic status. Thus, the tradition has nothing to say about which members of the bridal party march in when, with the exception of how the bride and groom arrive at the wedding canopy. Because the groom awaits his bride under the *huppah*, it is traditional for the groom to be ushered in (usually by his parents) first. If the groom wears a *kittel* during the ceremony, he usually dons it at this point. Once the bride (usually escorted by her parents) has walked most of the way to the *huppah*, the groom walks to her, and the two symbolically enter their "home" together.

Before the liturgical section of the ceremony begins, it is customary in traditional communities for the bride to walk around the groom several times. The purpose of walking around the groom is to suggest the degree to which their lives will be intertwined. The number seven (though such a common biblical and rabbinic number hardly requires explanation) is derived from the fact that the phrase "and when a man takes a wife" appears in seven different biblical verses. In some communities, the tradition calls for the bride to circle the groom only three times. In more egalitarian approaches, couples usually disregard this tradition, or the groom may circle the bride after she has circled him.

ERUSIN: THE FIRST OF THE TWO CEREMONIES

The Jewish wedding ceremony comprises two major sections: *erusin* (betrothal) and *nisu'in* (marriage). When the bride and groom have reached the *huppah*, the *erusin* ceremony begins. It is a simple ceremony, marked by two blessings recited by the presiding rabbi, who holds a cup of wine. The first blessing, over wine, is one said at almost all joyous occasions. The second blessing is unique to this occasion and reads as follows:

> Blessed are You, Lord our God, Master of the Universe, Who has sanctified us with His commandments, and commanded us regarding forbidden unions, and Who forbad betrothed women to us, and permitted to us those married to us by *huppah* and *kiddushin*. Praised are You, Lord, Who sanctifies His people Israel with *huppah* and *kiddushin*.[67]

After the completion of the second blessing, the rabbi gives the cup of wine to the groom, who drinks of it; the cup is then presented to the bride, who drinks from the same cup, symbolizing their commitment to sharing their lives from that moment on.

Several crucial themes of the Jewish wedding are expressed in the seemingly simple language of these few lines of this second blessing. First, the liturgical language points to older customs, for in earlier times the Jewish wedding took place in stages over the course of an entire year. At the first ceremony, *erusin*, the couple were reserved for each other and were forbidden to have relationships with anyone else. But it was not until approximately a year later, at the *nisu'in* ceremony, that they were permitted to consummate their relationship sexually and that the bride moved into the groom's home. The language of the second blessing, "who forbad betrothed women to us, and permitted to us those married to us by *huppah* and *kiddushin*," reflects this earlier practice, and apparently served in ancient times as a warning to the couple not to cohabit until the completion of the second ceremony.

Another perhaps more subtle theme emerges from this blessing as well. The language clearly enunciates the central Jewish tenet that marriage is not a private affair but one that affects and involves the entire community. It is not only the couple who are sanctified by their marriage; the sanctification touches the entire people Israel. Why? The marriage of a man and woman tells the community that it has the capacity to survive. Marriage reflects the first union between Adam and Eve, who set not a private stage, but a stage for the playing out of all of human history. Marriage is ultimately a reflection of the survivability of the covenant, and God's covenant with humanity was made not individually, but collectively. All of this, and more, emerges from the simple words of this blessing.

At this point in the traditional ceremony, the groom performs the specific act that formalizes the marriage. Today it is customary for the groom to place a ring on the index finger of his bride's right hand and to recite in Hebrew a phrase that means, "Behold, by this ring you are consecrated to me as my wife according to the laws of Moses and Israel." Once again, the words "according to the laws of Moses and Israel" suggest the themes of covenant and community, central throughout the ceremony.

This phrasing, now standard in virtually all Jewish communities, was not the only one suggested by the tradition, however. Other known versions include "Behold, you are *reserved* to me . . ."[68] and "according to the laws of Moses and the *Jews*."[69] Instead of a ring, it used to be permissible for the groom to give the bride a detailed deed, and he could then recite the phrase "Behold, you are consecrated to me with the deed. . . ." As long as the bride accepted the deed with the intention of becoming his wife, the marriage was valid.[70] Even the act of sexual intercourse was at one point a valid means of marrying a woman. In front of two halakhically acceptable witnesses, a man could say to a woman, "Behold, you are consecrated to me with this [following] act of sexual intercourse according to the laws of Moses and Israel," whereupon he took her to a private place to consummate their union.[71] Although this process led to a valid marriage, for obvious reasons the sages of the Talmud condemned it, calling it prostitution; they insisted that anyone who employed this method of *kiddushin* should be flogged.[72]

In earlier times, too, various items, including fruits and a prayer book,[73] could be used to symbolize the betrothal, though today a ring is the most common token. Even so, the nature of that ring is still regulated by Jewish law. It must belong to the groom, and it has to have at least some value, since it substitutes for money that might also have been given to the bride. Tradition requires that the ring not have gems on it, which would make its value difficult for the bride to assess. Similarly, while the ring may be decorated, the decorations should not be cut out of the ring, for the circularity and solidity of the metal suggest the permanence of the relationship now being created.

In recent decades, the wife's role during the ring ceremony has been much discussed. Should she remain silent and relatively passive, as was the case in the traditional ceremony and continues to be the practice in Orthodox circles, or can she also "betroth" her future husband in some sense? From the strict point of view of Jewish law, the bride cannot betroth the husband; traditional communities, therefore, do not permit the woman to say to the groom, "Behold, you are consecrated to me. . . ." But it is not uncommon, particularly in Conservative circles, for the bride to say something to the groom, usually quoting a biblical verse that speaks of love, relationship, or commitment. In such cases, the bride may also present the groom with a ring, for as the Talmud explains, it is permissible for the bride to give the groom gifts under the *huppah*.

In liberal Conservative and Reform communities, the concern is less for the strict requirements of Jewish law than for egalitarian treatment of both men and women. In those communities, it is common that the woman places a ring on the man's finger and recites exactly what he said to her (with the necessary grammatical changes). Some modern Orthodox men, whose communities do not sanction double-ring ceremonies, elect to wear a wedding band after the ceremony, there being no serious traditional objection to this practice.

One additional halakhic issue raised by today's ceremonies deserves mention. We have already noted that because the ring represents an item of value that the groom gives to the bride, Jewish law requires that it belong to him. Many couples, however, wish to use a ring that has been in the family for generations, perhaps a grandmother's wedding band or some other similarly meaningful heirloom. But if the family member wants the ring back after the ceremony, is this permissible? Can the groom betroth the bride with a ring that is not actually his? The rather surprising answer is yes. Because of the general halakhic principle that "a gift given with the condition that it be returned *is* considered a gift,"[74] Jewish law recognizes the ring as belonging to the groom for the duration of the ceremony, and the marriage is valid.

After the ring ceremony, the *ketubbah* is read aloud, marking the division between the formerly separated elements of the marriage ritual. In traditional communities, the entire document is read in the original Aramaic; at most Conservative weddings, the opening and closing sections of the original Aramaic are read, followed by an English translation or paraphrase. The *ketubbah* is then given by the officiating rabbi to the bride, since, at least in the traditional texts, the document enumerates the promises the groom makes to the bride and so becomes her property.

NISU'IN: THE SECOND OF THE TWO CEREMONIES

Immediately following the reading of the *ketubbah*, the second ceremony begins. This ceremony involves the recitation of seven blessings and hence is commonly referred to as the *Sheva Berakhot*. The text of the liturgy is as follows:

1. Praised are You, O Lord our God, King of the Universe, Creator of the fruit of the vine.
2. Praised are You, O Lord our God, King of the Universe, Who created all things for Your glory.
3. Praised are You, O Lord our God, King of the Universe, Creator of man.
4. Praised are You, O Lord our God, King of the Universe, Who created man and woman in Your image, fashioning woman from man as his mate, that together they might perpetuate life. Praised are You, O Lord, Creator of man.
5. May Zion rejoice as her children are restored to her in joy. Praised are You, O Lord, Who causes Zion to rejoice at her children's return.
6. Grant perfect joy to these loving companions, as You did to the first man and woman in the Garden of Eden. Praised are You, O Lord, who grants the joy of bride and groom.
7. Praised are You, O Lord our God, King of the Universe, who created joy and gladness, bride and groom, mirth, song, delight and rejoicing, love and harmony, peace and companionship. O Lord our God, may there even be heard in the cities of Judah and in the streets of Jerusalem voices of joy and gladness, voices of bride and groom, the jubilant voices of those joined in marriage under the bridal canopy, the voices of young people feasting and singing. Praised are You, O Lord, Who causes the groom to rejoice with his bride.[75]

During the recitation of these blessings, as was the case in the first ceremony, the rabbi holds a cup of wine aloft. And once again, upon completion of the blessings, groom and bride drink from the cup.

The most striking characteristic of the blessings is that, with the exception of the last one, they focus not on love, but on the theme of creation. In addition to referring to God as "Creator of the fruit of the vine" in the omnipresent blessing over wine, the liturgy refers to God as creator of all things, creator of man, creator of man and woman, and creator of the peace of the Garden of Eden. The theme of creation plays several significant roles in the ceremony. First, it relates to the Jewish conception of marriage as a natural state and suggests that, by marrying, the couple now enters this appropriate condition. Second, it suggests that the marriage furthers God's process of creation, furthering a project the tradition sees as yet unfulfilled.

Rashi, the classic medieval commentator on the Talmud, offers an alternate explanation for the blessings.[76] He suggests that the second benediction is in honor not of the couple, but of all those assembled at the ceremony. The third is in honor of the creation of Adam. The next three refer specifically to the couple being married. And the last is in honor of all Jews everywhere, including, of course, the couple themselves.

One element of the blessings that cannot be denied is that they refer to grooms and brides, men and women, beyond time. Obviously, one element of this "era beyond time" is the Garden of Eden, cited specifically in the liturgy. But in mentioning creation, the liturgy subtly suggests the tradition's commitment to the notion of *purposeful* creation, and alludes to the future era when God's purpose for humankind will be realized. Jacob Neusner has suggested that the couple represents not only Adam and Eve in the Garden of Eden, but also young men and women in a rebuilt Jerusalem, redeemed in the messianic era.[77] In both representations, the couple exists beyond time and history, in a direct relationship with God and the people Israel.

The seven blessings are repeated once after the ceremony, at the festive meal that follows. There, the grace after meals is recited using one cup of wine, and the *Sheva Berakhot* using another. Upon completion of the blessings for the second time, the two cups of wine are mixed into a third, and husband and wife now drink from the third cup. The blessings are then recited every day for the next seven days, as long as at least one person is present at each meal who was not present before. On the Sabbath, the Sabbath Bride "herself" is considered the new "person."

If the rabbi speaks at the ceremony, he or she usually does so after the seven blessings. But it is not unusual for more than one person to address the couple under the *ḥuppah,* at any of several points during the ceremony. Some rabbis also elect to offer a separate blessing for the couple, often the tripartite "Priestly Blessing" (Numbers 6:24–26). Such matters are not regulated by tradition.

The next, and final, ritual element of the ceremony is the shattering of a glass. Traditionally, it is the groom who shatters the glass with his foot, though in some more modern communities groom and bride both do so. Most traditional commentators explain this custom as having originated with incidents recorded in the Talmud in which Mar, the son of Ravina, and Rav Ashi deliberately smashed costly glass at their sons' weddings to put a stop to the raucous dancing and celebrating.[78] Modern explanations have focused on a more solemn theme, claiming that the broken glass reminds Jews assembled at a joyous occasion of the Temples and recalling those individuals, Jew and non-Jew alike, who do not have the freedom to celebrate either religiously or publicly. A more mystical explanation of the ceremony is that the glass represents the couple and that just as the glass, when it is broken, enters a state from which it will never emerge, it is the hope of the community that this couple will never emerge from their married state. Finally, one modern source suggests:

> Beneath its articulated Jewish historical meaning (remembrance of the destruction of the Temple), this act has symbolic sexual-anthropological meaning. It is an obvious representation of the sexual consummation of the marriage by the breaking of the hymen. It also is an act of noise-making employed to chase away demons that might attack the couple as they pass through that liminal period between unmarried and married status.[79]

This evaluation of the tradition of breaking the glass is extraordinarily novel. Whether these anthropological factors actually played a role in the origins of the ceremony is difficult to say.

Following the breaking of the glass and, usually, the recessional, it is customary for the new husband and wife to retire to a private setting for a short while before greeting the assembled. This period of time, known as *yiḥud,* was formerly the moment at which the marriage was consummated. Though that practice is extraordinarily rare nowadays, traditional Jewish law still requires a period of *yiḥud.*[80] Especially given the frenetic pace of many modern weddings, this private time, during which husband and wife can speak briefly, break their fast, and relax before being "besieged" by the assembled, retains its importance.

With *yihud*, the ceremony is completed; it is followed in traditional settings by the festive meal, including the grace after meals and the repetition of the *Sheva Berakhot*. These festivities are as much a part of the tradition as the ceremony itself. The Talmud discusses the tradition of dancing before the bride, and presents a scholarly debate over whether the amount of dancing is dependent on the bride's physical beauty.[81] The anticipated conclusion, that all brides are equally beautiful, reflects the tradition's commitment to the notion that all human beings are created in God's image, and that all marriages further the continuing process of creation and of perfecting God's world. The same talmudic section also states that scholars participated in the merriment, pushing it to new limits. Judah ben Hai is said to have danced before the bride with a myrtle branch, and the sages even had to rebuke Samuel ben Rav Isaac for dancing while juggling. Rav Aha, in another "shocking" incident, is said to have danced with the bride on his shoulders.[82]

Today, especially in traditional circles, it is customary to add to the merriment of dancing by wearing masks, lifting the bride and groom aloft on chairs—basically, inventing ever new ways of fulfilling the commandment of being *mesameah hatan ve-kallah*, of adding to the joy of the bride and groom.

Marriage and Sexuality in the Jewish Tradition

Jewish tradition recognizes sexuality as a fundamental human drive. As with many other dimensions of human life, such as food, clothing, and speech, the tradition has consistently sought to sanctify sexuality by placing upon traditional Jews certain strictures regarding their sexual activity.[83] The most basic of these restrictions are shared by many cultures. Polygamy (since Rabbenu Gershom) and adultery are forbidden, as are the incestuous relationships discussed earlier in this chapter. But nothing about these limitations should be taken to mean that sexuality is seen as wrong or even a "necessary evil"; rather, Jewish tradition recognizes it as perhaps the most powerful form of communication, and many of the regulations of Jewish law promote, rather than repress, sexual expression between mutually committed partners.

JEWISH TRADITION'S POSITIVE ORIENTATION TOWARD SEXUALITY

As mentioned in the discussion of the *ketubbah* above, a woman has a right to sexual satisfaction in marriage. Though the houses of Shammai and Hillel debate the amount of time a recalcitrant husband may take to mend his ways, Shammai's view of two weeks is ultimately rejected in favor of the Hillelite position of one week.[84] Both groups agree that the husband's failure to meet the deadline is automatic grounds for divorce.

The mere existence of an entire body of Jewish law on modesty is indicative of the rabbis' awareness that body language is a potent and all-pervasive means of communication in human society. They were sensitive to the fact that the two most commonly used verbs in the tradition to refer to sexual intercourse were *lishkav* (to lie with) and *la-da'at* (to know). The former implies not only a sexual union, but also a connection with one's partner; this element of sexuality is highlighted even more clearly by the second verb. The sages' commitment to the deeply communicative nature of sexuality is expressed clearly in the talmudic dictum, "One should not drink from this glass, and cast his eyes upon another."[85] The subtle sexual overtones of the adage are commonly interpreted to mean that the sages frowned on a man's having sexual intercourse with one woman while thinking of another.

The talmudic sages' positive attitude toward sexuality emerges most clearly from the amusing tale in which a disciple asked his teacher to instruct him in sexual technique. When the teacher refused, the disciple is alleged to have hidden under his master's bed. The student attempted to justify his audacity to his teacher by saying, "It is Torah, and I need to learn."[86]

Finally, a medieval prayer, ascribed to Naḥmanides (1194–1270), an extraordinarily strict legal authority, but most probably written later, indicates that the link between religiosity and healthy sexuality continued beyond the Talmudic period. The prayer reads:

O Lord my God and God of my fathers, ground of all the universes, for the sake of Your great and holy name alluded to in the verse "the Lord has remembered us, He will bless, He will bless the House of Israel, He will bless the House of Aaron," may it be Your will that You emanate from Your spirit of power unto me and give me might and strength in my organs and my body that I might regularly fulfill the commandment pertaining to my sexual cycle; that there be not found in my organs, body or passion any weakness or slackness, that there be no forcing, unseemly thought, confusion of mind, or weakening of power to prevent me from fulfilling my desire with my wife. Rather, now and forever, let my passion be ready for me without fail or slackness of organ, at any time that I should desire. *Amen selah.*[87]

EXTRAMARITAL AND PREMARITAL SEXUALITY

Judaism's attitude to extramarital sexuality is that of the wider Judeo-Christian tradition. Although the Jewish legal sources on adultery use that term only in the case of a married woman who has intercourse with a man other than her husband,[88] the expectation today, especially since the ban on polygamy, is that married men will also restrict their sexual activity to their wives.

Much less clear in the legal tradition, however—and much more debated in modern liberal circles—is Judaism's attitude to premarital sex. All rabbinic texts clearly assume, but most do not state, that marriage is the only appropriate setting for sexuality. Either as a result of this expectation or in order to make the expectation easier to comply with, the rabbinic tradition urged early marriage for both men and women. An instructive, though probably historically inaccurate, account in rabbinic literature claims that Jews would marry off their sons at twelve years of age and their grandsons again at twelve; hence, at the age of twenty-six a man could already be a grandfather.[89] The suggestion in *Ethics of the Fathers* that men should be married by eighteen seems much more realistic,[90] as does the Talmudic claim that if a man reaches the age of twenty and is not married, then God curses him.[91] Similar pressures were exerted on the parents of young girls. Commenting on the verse "Do not profane your daughter by making her a whore" (Leviticus 19:29), Rabbi Akiba is said to have explained, "This refers to a father who defers marrying off his daughter until she reaches the age of majority [i.e., twelve]."[92]

Traditional authorities have sought to maintain the traditional ban on premarital sex. Norman Lamm, a well-known Orthodox spokesman on the subject, summarizes his position as follows:

> In the Jewish view, it is insufficient to affirm that the act must have meaning: it must also have value. For Judaism, the value in human sexuality comes only when the relationship involves two people who have committed themselves to one another and have made that commitment in a binding covenant recognized by God and society. The act of sexual union, the deepest personal statement that any human being can make, must be reserved for the moment of total oneness.[43]

Yet despite the rabbis' clear expectations regarding sexuality and marriage and the equally forceful claims of those such as Lamm, no verse in the Bible or statement in the Mishnah or Talmud contains any specific prohibition of premarital sex. Even the strict Naḥmanides wrote to a student saying:

> Casual intercourse is prohibited to the Jews only on authority of Rabbi Eliezer ben Jacob's statement that except for such a prohibition, it might happen that a brother would marry his sister, or a father, his daughter. Of such a state the Torah speaks when it says, "and the earth will be filled with immorality."[94]

This rather weak justification for the ban highlights the degree to which compelling legal sources are astonishingly lacking in the traditional literature. A specific halakhic prohibition on premarital sex is found for the first time in a classic Jewish legal source in Maimonides' *Mishneh Torah*.[95]

As a result of this absence of direct legal prohibition, and because changing societal values and institutions have forced a delay in marriage until a person's twenties or thirties, many liberal authorities argue that a ban on premarital sex is neither realistic nor necessary. Modern liberal Jewish thinkers have sought new ethical standards for judging whether a given setting for sexual expression is appropriate, usually defining a spectrum that ranges between completely casual sex outside any ongoing relationship on one end and marriage on the other.[96] For some, a relationship based on trust and mutual commitment is a sufficient prerequisite for a legitimate sexual relationship.

One of the most vociferously debated sexual issues in the Jewish community today is that of homosexuality. A complete discussion of the topic would demand much more space than is available here, but the broad strokes of the argument can be easily described. Traditional camps, citing classic legal sources, argue that homosexual sexual activity (not homosexual inclinations, which are not discussed) is prohibited in the strongest possible terms in the Bible; indeed, it is called an "abomination," a term reserved for a very few crimes, including child sacrifice. They cite primarily Leviticus 18:22, which reads: "Do not lie with a male as one lies with a woman; it is an abomination."[97] As justification for their continued reliance on the biblical tradition, these thinkers offer their general legal philosophy, as well as arguments related to the sanctity of the family, the obligation to rear children, and Judaism's needs to hold out against the moral turpitude of much of modern society.

Liberal thinkers approach the matter very differently. Because they have a laxer attitude toward Jewish law generally, they see the biblical stipulations as not posing much of a problem. Furthermore, these rabbis and critics point to evidence which suggests that homosexuality is not the product of a person's individual choice but the result of a complex host of biological and social factors. In support of their position, they pose the following ethical dilemma: "If it is true that a person does not choose to be a homosexual, and that such a person has no choice but to engage in homosexual acts or to remain celibate for life, how can Jewish tradition reasonably claim that God would prefer celibacy?" While traditionalists claim, legitimately, that liberals have not been able to base their position on the legal sources, liberals also rightly point out that the traditionalist position would be ethically very weak if, in fact, people were *created* homosexual or heterosexual. The debate will no doubt continue for some time, and will likely turn in the next generation or two on many factors, including changing patterns of sexual behavior in the Jewish community and increased scientific understanding of the phenomenon of homosexuality.[98]

In the meantime, virtually all elements of the Jewish community insist that rejection of the legitimacy of homosexual activity does not imply rejection of the homosexual person. Orthodox and Reform thinkers alike have stated that religious communities should reach out to homosexuals with caring and kindness and urge them to participate in a full and vibrant Jewish life. Whether such an attempt is realistic if at the same time the legitimacy of a person's sexual orientation is denied is, like virtually every other element of the issue, hotly debated.

THE JEWISH CYCLE OF MARITAL SEXUALITY

As part of its continuous and creative pursuit of means to sanctify virtually every dimension of human life, Jewish tradition has developed restrictions not only on nonmarital, premarital, and extramarital sexual behavior but on marital sexuality as well. The tradition essentially claims that while marriage offers the strengths of commitment and dependability, it also carries the risks of routinization and boredom. Traditional Judaism's response to this risk of routinization is known in some circles as *tohorat ha-mishpaḥah*, or "family purity." The following section will touch only briefly on this extraordinarily complicated tradition.

Historically, the system predates even the rabbinic materials on the subject, and has its origins in biblical legislation related to menstrual women. Twice in the book of Leviticus, the Torah warns against sexual intercourse with a menstruating woman. "Do not come near a woman during her period of uncleanness to uncover her nakedness" (Leviticus 18:19) is followed two chapters later by a more explicit admonition: "If a man lies with a woman in her infirmity and uncovers her nakedness, he has laid bare her flow and she has exposed her blood flow; both of them shall be cut off from among their people" (Leviticus 20:18).

The Torah stipulates that "when a woman has a discharge . . . she shall remain in her impurity seven days; whoever touches her shall be unclean" (Leviticus 15:19). The sages of the Talmud, however, extended this period by requiring seven "clean days" *after* a woman has ceased menstruating before she could resume sexual intercourse. Though the Torah describes no actual rite that should be performed before resuming sex, the rabbinic tradition developed the now well-entrenched custom that a woman visit a *mikvah* (ritual bath) on the evening of the seventh "clean" day and immerse herself, while unclothed, during which time she also recites a special blessing for the occasion.

Medieval sources restricted contact with a menstrual woman even further, providing ammunition for the feminists and other critics of the tradition who argue that the entire system erected to address *niddah* (impurity, or menstruation specifically) represents a blood taboo and that the genuine issue is anything but "family purity." These groups urge that the restrictions be dropped altogether, since we now understand menstruation to be a perfectly natural, and in fact necessary, human function; the practices associated with *niddah*, these critics maintain, only reinforce misogynous attitudes toward women's bodies. Indeed, the practice of abstention followed by purification has been all but completely abandoned in Reform circles, and in Conservative communities it is primarily the younger rabbis who support a shift back to some form of the observance.[99]

Surprising though it may seem, however, some feminists have begun to endorse the tradition as well. These advocates essentially agree with the modern Orthodox idea that interruption of a married couple's sexual life is necessary to insure the continued sense of anticipation and sanctity that characterize sexuality at its best.[100] But another, more creative feminist position claims that because menstruation represents the "loss" of a potential, and because sexuality represents life in all its potential, a temporary withdrawal of husband from wife enacts a symbolic mourning for the loss of that potential. In the words of one noted feminist author on the subject:

> *Tumah* [=impurity] is the result of our confrontation with the fact of our own mortality. It is the going down into darkness. *Taharah* [=purification in the *mikvah*] is the result of our reaffirmation of our own mortality. It is the reentry into light. Tumah is evil or frightening only when there is no further life. Otherwise, tumah is simply part of the human cycle. . . . To be reborn, one must reenter this *womb* and "drown" in living water.[101]

Other feminists, of course, reject this explanation as an apologetic attempt to conform feminist thinking to Jewish law. In the Conservative community, some couples address the issue by having both the wife and the husband visit the *mikvah* (there are separate *mikvah* facilities for men and women in most cities with major Jewish populations) on the day that they will resume sexual intercourse. By and large, however, the custom is observed only in the Orthodox community.

Back to the Covenant

Over the course of fifteen hundred years, the Jewish tradition has developed an ornate and sophisticated set of rituals and liturgies for marriage. It is the purpose of these customs not only to perform the simple task of ushering a couple into the state of matrimony but also, and perhaps even more importantly, to do so while stating for the couple and the entire Jewish community the crucial nexus that exists between marriage and other basic tenets of Jewish faith.

The sages hoped that these ceremonies would convey to the couple the need to maintain the conventional element of their relationship in the years beyond their wedding, and would encourage men to make much use of affectionate language and other means of establishing intimacy in the relationship.[102] They claimed that "one who loves his wife more than himself, about him did Scripture state, 'You will know that all is well in your tent'" (Job 5:24).[103] In general, the sages' admonitions about relationships between spouses center on the theme of *derekh eretz*, or common decency and appropriateness.

Given the tradition's view of the cosmic and Godly nature of marriage, it is perhaps fitting that the rabbis chose as the verse to be recited when one dons phylacteries, another symbol of the Jew's relationship with God, these poignant words of the prophet Hosea:

> And I will espouse you forever:
> I will espouse you with righteousness and justice,
> And with goodness and mercy,
> And I will espouse you with faithfulness,
> Then you shall be devoted to the Lord. (Hosea 2:21–22)

NOTES

1. Unless otherwise noted, all biblical quotations in this chapter are taken from *The Tanakh—The Holy Scriptures: The New JPS Translation According*

to the *Traditional Hebrew Text* (Philadelphia: Jewish Publication Society, 1988).

2. See, in addition, the marital images in Jeremiah 2:2 and Isaiah 50:4–7.

3. B.T. Sotah 17a. Unless otherwise noted, translations of rabbinic texts in this chapter are those of the author.

4. Derekh 'Eretz Rabbah 5.

5. While this view is implicit in the text itself, it is also discussed more forthrightly in many rabbinic sources. See, for example, Rashi's commentary on Genesis 1:1.

6. On a more legal plane, the use of the term *kiddushin* may be seen as analogous to the Temple-based institution of *hekdesh*, in which something of value was set aside for ritual use at the Temple and could not be "defiled" by use for any other purpose. Similarly, in the traditional rabbinic conception of marriage, a woman is "set aside," or consecrated to her husband, and is forbidden to engage in a sexual relationship with anyone else as long as she is married. Cf. B.T. Kiddushin 2a–b.

7. See Irving Greenberg, *The Jewish Way* (New York: Summit Books, 1988), for a current and thoughtful expression of this thesis.

8. The obvious androcentric perspective of this verse is a subject that deserves much discussion, but space here does not permit that. This chapter will address certain elements of the feminist critique of Jewish tradition in general and Jewish marriage in particular, but again, it cannot do justice to this crucial topic in such a limited space.

9. Biblical scholars, both traditional and modern, have located two creation stories in Genesis. Most modern scholars agree that the second narrative begins in the second half of verse 2:4. For a brilliant homiletic interpretation of the different perspectives of these two stories, see Joseph B. Soloveitchik, "The Lonely Man of Faith," *Tradition*, 7, no. 2 (Summer 1965): 5–67. For a more critical discussion of this issue, see E. A. Speiser, *The Anchor Bible: Genesis* (New York: Doubleday, 1964), pp. 3–21.

10. B.T. Yevamot 62a.

11. B.T. Yevamot 118b. The original Aramaic here, *tav le-meitva tan du, mi-le-meitav armelu*, necessitates the rather free translation found in the text.

12. B.T. Yevamot 61b.

13. J.T. Berakhot 9:1.

14. Cited in Maurice Lamm, *The Jewish Way in Love and Marriage* (San Francisco: Harper & Row, 1979), p. 119.

15. B.T. Yevamot 63b.

16. Cf., *inter alia*, J.T. Bikkurim 3:6; B.T. Megillah 27a; B.T. Bava Batra 151a.

17. There are still certain elements of the Jewish community, particularly in Northern Africa, that have not adopted Rabbenu Gershom's position and will

permit polygamous relationships. Their numbers, however, are extremely small.

18. Numerous examples could be cited, but for two of the most famous, consider Sarah's desire to provide Abraham with children through her maidservant, Hagar (Genesis 16:1–4), and Hannah's almost primal prayer at Shiloh for a child (I Samuel 1:4–20). For a thoughtful and accessible discussion of infertility in the Jewish tradition, see Michael Gold, *And Hannah Wept* (Philadelphia: Jewish Publication Society, 1988).

19. For the issue of divorce in the Torah, see Deuteronomy 24:1–4. For a more complete discussion of divorce in the Jewish tradition, see, in this volume, Irwin H. Haut, "The Altar Weeps."

20. The JPS translation reads "married," but this obscures the specific verb employed in the text.

21. Though this is nowhere explicitly stated, it is suggested by Deuteronomy 22:13–22. For other legislation in the Torah that clearly implies the significance attached to virginity, see Exodus 22:15–16, Levitus 21:13ff., and Deuteronomy 22:23–29. In the rabbinic period, the significance of virginity continued, though rabbinic sources make it clear that at issue is not an intact hymen, but the women's marital and conscious sexual history. In rabbinic law, a woman has the right to claim that she is still a virgin because her hymen was ruptured in an injury (Mishnah Ketubbot 1:7). Interestingly, if a woman was betrothed but the marriage never consummated, she was legally classified as a nonvirgin for the purpose of future marriages (Mishnah Ketubbot 1:2, 4), and a child less than three years of age who had had intercourse was still considered a virgin (Mishnah Niddah 5:4).

22. Jews throughout the world are typically divided into two primary groups, Ashkenazim and Sephardim. Ashkenazim descend primarily from European Jewish communities, while Sephardim trace their roots to North Africa, Spain, and Yemen. The two groups are distinguished today by different customs and traditions in some religious matters, by slightly differing liturgies, and by very different cultural and ethnic practices.

23. For a nontechnical discussion of the status of modern "matchmakers" in Jewish communities, see Judith Colp, "The New *Shadchens*," *Moment Magazine* 15, no. 3 (June 1990): 46ff.

24. The Mishnah is effectively the first rabbinic code of Jewish law. Compiled by Rabbi Judah the Prince in approximately 220 C.E., it is the basis of what later became the Talmud.

25. This translation is taken from Jacob Neusner, *The Mishnah: A New Translation* (New Haven: Yale University Press, 1988).

26. B.T. Kiddushin 12b. Codes of Jewish law later incorporated this position as legal. Cf. Sh.Ar. Even ha-Ezer 26:4.

27. B.T. Kiddushin 29b.

28. Maharik, *Shoresh*, 164.

29. The term *midrash* refers to the genre of Jewish literature, predominantly from the rabbinic period, which tells stories based on or otherwise expounds on earlier sources, most commonly biblical texts.

30. The tale is loosely paraphrased. It is found in numerous locations in rabbinic literature, including Genesis Rabbah 68 and Leviticus Rabbah 8.

31. The rabbinic term for such marriages is *ein kiddushin tofesin*, which, roughly translated, means "the marriage does not take hold."

32. Rabbinic texts refers to these marriages as those in which *kiddushin tofesin*, or "the marriage takes hold."

33. Sh.Ar. Even ha-Ezer 15.

34. The original biblical prohibition is usually located in Deuteronomy 7:3. This position is reflected in the Talmud in B.T. Avodah Zarah 36b and the codes in Sh.Ar. Even ha-Ezer 16:1. Because the marriage is considered void, no change in the personal status of the Jew involved takes place with such a marriage (cf. B.T. Kiddushin 68b; B.T. Yevamot 45a; and the codes *ad loc.*).

35. The religious status of these children is a tremendously complicated matter which this chapter cannot address in detail. Although Jewish law does not recognize intermarriage as marriage at all, even traditional Jewish law does not see children of such unions as illegitimate, since according to Jewish law illegitimacy results only from adulterous relationships; it does not apply to children conceived in the absence of a binding marriage. However, in cases where the woman in the marriage is not Jewish, traditional Jewish law (again, recognized by both the Conservative and Orthodox movements in Judaism) considers the child non-Jewish, since a child's religion is dependent on the mother's faith.

Reform Judaism, which accepts intermarriage, ultimately found that it could not adhere to this standard, for how could it permit a marriage but then insist that the resulting children were not Jewish? As a result, in the mid-1980s, the Reform movement debated and ultimately passed a resolution on "Patrilineal Descent," which effectively argued that in an intermarriage, a child would be considered Jewish regardless of which parent was the Jewish partner.

This position, rejected by the Conservative and Orthodox movements, has also proved controversial in the Reform community as well. Many Reform rabbis believe that such a position is likely to cause an irrevocable split in the Jewish community, since now some elements of the community will recognize such children as Jewish and others will not. While many Reform rabbis do recognize the decision on patrilineality, significant numbers do not. Many seasoned observers of the modern American Jewish community seem to agree that the issue is, as yet, unresolved.

36. B.T. Sotah 27b; Sh.Ar. Even ha-Ezer 11:1, 178:17.

37. The prohibition of marrying a priest (any Jew who has the status of *kohen* today) to a convert actually stems from an antecedent prohibition not mentioned in the text, that of marrying a priest to a *zonah*, or sexually licentious woman. Though space here does not permit a discussion of the details of this law, halakhah generally classified a convert over the age of three as a sexually licentious woman because of suspicious sexual practices of non-Jewish communities in rabbinic times. For obvious reasons, the Reform and Conservative communities have either abandoned or struggled with this ruling.

38. Sh.Ar. Even ha-Ezer 13:1, 11–14.

39. Sh.Ar. Even ha-Ezer 15:1, 18; 44:7.

40. See note 37 for a brief clarification.

41. B.T. Kiddushin 6a. The translation is rather colloquial.

42. The significance of this custom is discussed more fully in the section on family purity below.

43. Sh.Ar. Oraḥ Ḥayyim 573.

44. The traditional text calls for a settlement of two hundred *zuz* for a previously unmarried woman, referred to as a "virgin" in the text, and one hundred *zuz* for all other women (cf. Mishnah Ketubbot 1:2; Sh.Ar. Even ha-Ezer 66:6; and Maimonides' Mishneh Torah Hilkhot Yibbum 4:34). If he wished, the husband was allowed to increase the amount of money stipulated in the *ketubbah*, but he was not permitted to decrease it in any way.

45. Mishnah Ketubbot 5:2.

46. B.T. Ketubbot 7a.

47. The term *betulah*, however, need not mean virgin. It can, in fact, depending on context, mean "previously unmarried woman." The sociological reality of the period, in which sex was predominantly limited to the domain of marriage, explained the conflation of the two meanings.

48. For an attempt to address this issue within the constraints of traditional halakhah, see Joel Roth and Daniel Gordis, "Textual Tradition and Sociological Reality: Their Tension in the Marriage Contract," in *Proceedings of the Rabbinical Assembly Committee on Jewish Law and Standards 1980–1985* (New York: Rabbinical Assembly, 1988).

49. This and the following examples are taken from Mordechai Friedman, *Jewish Marriage in Palestine* (New York: JTSA, 1980), 1:116–117, and accompanying notes.

50. J.T. Ketubbot, 25b.

51. David Z. Hoffmann, *Melamed Le-Ho'il* (three vols. in one) (New York: A. L. Frenekel, 1954), 3:23.

52. For some samples of such innovation texts, see Daniel Leifer, "On Writing New *Ketubbot*," in *The Jewish Woman: New Perspectives*, ed. Elizabeth Koltun (New York: Schocken Books, 1978), pp. 59–61. See also discussion in

Michael Strassfeld and Sharon Strassfeld, *The Jewish Catalogue*, 3 vols. (Philadelphia: Jewish Publication Society, 1973–1980).

53. Leifer, "On Writing New *Ketubbot*," p. 53. This position in Jewish law, not universally accepted, but also certainly not the position of a small minority, is predicated not on an approval of civil or legal marriages, but on the supposition that no man would intend his intercourse with a woman to be purely licentious but would intend it to formalize a marriage. Cf. B.T. Yevamot 107a; and commentary of the Tosafot *ad loc.*

54. Leifer, "On Writing New *Ketubbot*," p. 54.

55. For a more complete discussion of the problem of the *agunah*, the characteristics of a *get*, and the Lieberman clause, see Haut, "The Altar Weeps," in this volume.

56. Interestingly, an Orthodox authority, Rabbi Eliezer Berkovitz, in *Not in Heaven* (New York: Ktav, 1983), pp. 94–95, has recently suggested that the requirement that witnesses be observant Jews be waived, because the social and religious implications of their decisions are wholly different from what they were in the formative stages of rabbinic Judaism.

57. Cf. Isserles's commentary to Sh.Ar. Even ha-Ezer 61:1.

58. Based on the biblical tradition, which reads, in the creation story, "it was night, and it was day . . . ," the Jewish day begins and ends at the setting of the sun. Thus, traditional Jews do not perform marriages between sundown on Friday night until sunset on Saturday night, though ceremonies later on Saturday evening are permissible.

59. Cf. B.T. Mo'ed Kattan 8b; and Sh.Ar. Even ha-Ezer 64:6.

60. Cf. Sh.Ar. Oraḥ Ḥayyim 493:1, 551:2. The seven weeks between Passover and Shavuot are interrupted by several days in which weddings are permitted, most notably the two times that Rosh Hodesh, or the celebration of a new month, occurs during that period, and Lag be-Omer, the thirty-third day of the month of Omer.

61. Cf. Genesis Rabbah 4:4. For a more general usage of the term *ḥuppah* (referring to marriage in general), cf. Mishnah Avot 5:21.

62. Note, for example, that Isserles's commentary to Sh.Ar. Yoreh De'ah 391 and Even ha-Ezer 55:1 considers it a novel custom.

63. Cf. Genesis Rabbah 28:6; B.T. Berakhot 25b; B.T. Sanhedrin 108a.

64. Cf. B.T. Sotah 49b; J.T. Sotah 9:16.

65. Cf. Psalms 19:6, Maimonides' Hilkhot Ishut 10:1; Ran to Ketubbot 2a; Beit Shemu'el 55, no. 4.

66. B.T. Bava Batra 75a.

67. This chapter makes a careful attempt to avoid gender-specific language when referring to God. In translations of original texts and prayers, however, the rendering is intentionally literal.

68. Tosefta Ketubbot 4:9. See full citation and discussion in *Encyclopedia Judaica*, "Marriage," 11:1047.

69. T. J. Ketubbot 4:8. See full citation and discussion in *Encyclopedia Judaica*, "Marriage," 11:1047.

70. B.T. Kiddushin 9a; Sh.Ar. Even ha-Ezer 32:1, 4.

71. B.T. Kiddushin 12b; Maimonides' Hilkhot Ishut 3:21; Sh.Ar. Even ha-Ezer 26:4, 33:1.

72. B.T. Kiddushin 12b; Maimonides' Hilkhot Ishut 3:21; Sh.Ar. Even ha-Ezer 26:4, 33:1.

73. Cf. Responsa of Solomon ben Abraham Adreth, *She'eolot u-Teshuvot (Responsa of Rashba)* (Benei Berak: Sifriyati, 1981), p. 83; and discussion in Isaac Klein, *A Guide to Jewish Religious Practice* (New York: JTSA, 1979), p. 403.

74. The Hebrew rendition of the phrase is *matanah al menat le-hahazir shemah matanah.* Cf., *inter alia*, B.T. Sukkah 41b.

75. Translation taken from Jules Harlow, *A Rabbi's Manual* (New York: Rabbinical Assembly, 1965), p. 45.

76. Rashi on B.T. Ketubbot 7b–8a, s.v. *"Mai mevarekh."*

77. Jacob Neusner, "Coming Together," in *The Way of Torah: An Introduction to Judaism* (Encino, Calif.: Dickenson, 1974), pp. 15–17. See also the excellent discussion in Leifer, "On Writing New *Ketubbot*," p. 56.

78. B.T. Berakhot 31a.

79. Leifer, "On Writing New *Ketubbot*," p. 55.

80. Cf., *inter alia*, B.T. Ketubbot 54b, 56a; Maimonides' Hilkhot Ishut 10:1–2, Isserles to Sh.Ar. Even ha-Ezer 55:1, 61:1; Sh.Ar. Even ha-Ezer 55:2.

81. B.T. Ketubbot 17a; cf. also Rashi *ad loc.*

82. Cf. B.T. Ketubbot 16b–17a.

83. Readers interested in more comprehensive discussions of Judaism and sexuality are referred to Louis Epstein's *Sex Laws and Customs in Judaism* (New York: Bloch, 1948) and *The Jewish Marriage Contract* (New York: Jewish Theological Seminary, 1927), both of which are highly detailed, though somewhat apologetic works. See also Robert Gordis, *Love and Sex: A Modern Jewish Perspective* (New York: Farrar, Straus & Giroux, 1978).

84. Mishnah Yevamot 5:6; Mishnah Eduyot 4:10. The first source contains the well-known listing of which categories of men were obliged to have sex with what frequency.

85. B.T. Nedarim 20b.

86. The Hebrew phrase is *torah hi, ve-lil'mod ani tzarikh.* Cf. B.T. Berakhot 62a.

87. Cited in Eugene B. Borowitz, *Choosing a Sex Ethic: A Jewish Inquiry* (New York: Schocken Books, 1969), p. 164.

88. Cf., *inter alia*, Exodus 20:13; Deuteronomy 5:17; B.T. Makkot 7a; and B.T. Sanhedrin 41a.

89. Lamentations Rabbah 1:1.

90. Mishnah Avot 5:21.

91. B.T. Kiddushin 29b–30a.

92. B.T. Sanhedrin 76a–b.

93. Lamm, *Jewish Way in Love and Marriage*, p. 31.

94. Hayim David Chavel, *Kitvei Rabenu Moshe ben Maimon* (Jerusalem: Mossad HaRav Kook, 1963), 1:381–382; cited and translated in Borowitz, *Choosing a Sex Ethic*, p. 45.

95. Maimonides' Hilkhot Ishut, preface and 1:4.

96. See Borowitz, *Choosing a Sex Ethic*, for the fullest exploration of this issue.

97. The JPS translation uses "abhorrence." "Abomination" is used here because it is the much more common and familiar translation. While the verse clearly refers only to male homosexuality, lesbian practices were later outlawed by the sages of the Talmud. The Torah itself contains no mention of female homosexuality.

98. For a concise summary of views on homosexuality that reflects the plurality of positions within the Jewish community, see *Judaism Magazine*'s special issue devoted to that subject, vol. 32, no. 4 (Fall 1983). For a more recent and extraordinarily thoughtful (though by no means unassailable) position, see Bradly Shavit Artson, "Judaism and Homosexuality," *Tikkun* 3, no. 2 (March–April 1988): 52ff.

99. It is not accidental, for example, that Robert Gordis, a major spokesman for the Conservative movement, did not even mention the custom in his book *Love and Sex*.

100. For the best popular presentation of this view in print, see Norman Lamm, *A Hedge of Roses: Jewish Insights into Marriage and Married Life* (New York: Feldheim, 1966).

101. Rachel Adler, "Tumah and Taharah: Ends and Beginnings," in Koltun (ed.), *The Jewish Woman*, p. 64.

102. B.T. Bava Metzia 59a.

103. To be sure, rabbinic literature is replete with rather sarcastic and biting comments on the difficulty of marriage, but the brilliance of the sages stemmed from their ability to be realists about human beings, human nature, and human relationships while at the same time believing that the potential for humanity was best captured by the biblical and rabbinic claims that human beings are created in the image of God. For a wide selection of rabbinic maxims on the subject of marriage, see Judah David Eisenstein's *Otzaor Ma'amarei Hazal* (available only in Hebrew) (New York: G. N. Y., Z. Solis, 1947), and Reuben

Alcalay's *Basic Encyclopedia of Jewish Proverbs* (New York: Hartmore House, 1973), s.v. "Marriage."

SUGGESTIONS FOR FURTHER READING

Eugene Borowitz, *Choosing a Sex Ethic: A Jewish Inquiry* (New York: Schocken Books, 1969); though somewhat dated, is nonetheless an informative and thoughtful examination of the liberal critique of traditional Jewish perspectives on premarital sex. Excellent notes and references.

David Feldman, *Marital Relations, Birth Control, and Abortion in Jewish Law* (New York: Schocken Books, 1978), is a very technical but copious and complete discussion of the halakhic (Jewish legal) attitudes to birth control, abortion, and sexuality. The classic treatise on the subject, it may prove difficult for the lay reader.

Robert Gordis, *Love and Sex: A Modern Jewish Perspective* (New York: Farrar, Straus & Giroux, 1978), is a good example of the Conservative movement's attempt to remain faithful to the Jewish moral and legal traditions while also addressing the ethical critiques of modernity. See also an earlier work by the same author, *Sex and the Family in the Jewish Tradition* (New York: Burning Bush Press, 1967).

Isaac Klein, *A Guide to Jewish Religious Practice* (New York: Jewish Theological Seminary of America, 1979), is the standard reference work on Jewish law by a very traditional Conservative rabbi. Though not all Hebrew terms are translated, the work is very accessible to the lay reader, and contains several chapters on marriage and family purity. The rest of the volume addresses the other elements of the Jewish life cycle, the yearly calendar cycle, and dietary laws.

Maurice Lamm, *The Jewish Way in Love and Marriage* (San Francisco: Harper & Row, 1979) provides an excellent look at and intelligent argument for the modern Orthodox perspective on marriage, with a detailed discussion of all the elements of the wedding ceremony, from a well-known Orthodox rabbi.

Norman Lamm, *A Hedge of Roses: Jewish Insights into Marriage and Married Life* (New York: Feldheim, 1966), is the classic modern Orthodox treatise defending the laws of "family purity." It does not reflect the feminist argument stated in this chapter, but summarizes the more usual explanations in an easily readable format.

Michael Strassfeld and Sharon Strassfeld, eds., *The Jewish Catalog*, 3 vols. (Philadelphia: Jewish Publication Society, 1973–1980), is a popular set of volumes representing the *havurah* movement's approach to Jewish tradition. A development resulting largely from 1960s social forces, the *havurah* phenomenon reflected in many senses the passion of Orthodoxy, the commitment to some form of tradition and critical study of text of the Conservative movement, and, often, politics commonly associated with the Reform movement. See index in vol. 3 for references to weddings (vol. 1), *tumah* and *tohorah* (vol. 1) and *ketubbah* (vols. 1 and 2).

BARRY D. CYTRON

Midlife

From Understanding to Wisdom

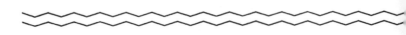

Introduction: Defining Midlife

"I can't define it, but I know it when I see it."

That was the well-crafted phrase offered by Justice Potter Stewart when the U.S. Supreme Court was deliberating the meaning of obscenity.[1] With slight modification, those words could easily apply to the way many feel about midlife. Perhaps it is the difficulty in anticipating and defining this phase of life that accounts for the potent emotional language frequently used to describe its onset. Americans regularly speak of a midlife "crisis," while the French call it, with equal passion, *l'après-midi,* "afternoon."

Those who study midlife, such as developmental psychologists, tend to avoid loaded emotional descriptions, preferring to speak of a midlife "transition" or "passage." But no matter what word is chosen to describe them, these years are frequently marked by a profound, potentially life-transforming set of challenges.[2]

Many circumstances, such as an individual's profession, marital status, and socioeconomic background, shape the timing and texture of the midlife years. Moreover, because no specific age inaugurates midlife, and because individuals approach it in so many different ways, this transition is significantly different from the other passages discussed in this volume.

Taken together, these factors explain why midlife is not usually included in traditional listings of the life cycle moments celebrated in religious communities.[3] This absence is found within Judaism, too. Perhaps because of its antiquity and the absence of a significant number of midlife years before modern times (a situation resembling that of adolescence), there is no consciously developed midlife rite of passage within traditional Judaism. Even recent attempts to articulate contemporary Jewish outlooks on the human life span make only passing reference to the qualities and tasks that distinguish the adult middle years.[4]

Some older Jewish sources, however, do reflect an understanding that one's character is crystalized in new ways during these decades. This is most readily seen in the words of Judah, son of Tema, as recorded in Pirkei Avot (The Sayings of the Sages):

> 5 years is the age for Scripture
> 10 for Mishnah;
> 13 for the Commandments;
> 18 for marriage;
> 20 for seeking a livelihood;
> 30 for full strength;
> 40 for understanding;
> 50 for counsel;
> 60 for wisdom [or old age];
> 70 for white hair;
> 80 for the strength of age;
> 90 for being weighed down by the years;
> 100 as if already dead and gone from the world.

This passage suggests that in ancient Jewish sources, the human life span was not seen as a continuous, undifferentiated stream of months and years, but was marked by expectations distinctive to each decade of life. Moreover, Judah's words acknowledge that the qualities gained during the middle years—understanding, counsel, and wisdom—are of particular significance.

Midlife in Contemporary American Culture

How does one know that the middle years have arrived? Consider the messages delivered by two astute social commentators, cartoonists Charles Schulz and Jules Feiffer. In a typical encounter, Charlie Brown's "psychiatrist," Lucy, is listening to him describe how anxious he is about his dad, who "every night sits in the kitchen eating cold cereal, looking at the pictures in his high school year book."

"How old is your father?" asks Lucy.

"I think he just turned forty," responds Charlie Brown.

"Nothing to worry about," counsels Lucy. "He's right on schedule!"

That "Peanuts" strip suggests that turning forty necessarily leads to nostalgia for one's youth and anxiety about one's alimentary canal. Alongside nostalgia and anxiety, a Feiffer cartoon adds a third emotion: self-awareness. Feiffer presents this message in a set of pictures showing a young boy who gradually ages.

"Ever since I was little," says the lad, "I was looking for *the answer*." The next frames then depict the growing man as he searches for the solution to life's puzzle, asking the same question—"Are you the answer?"—of religion, his therapist, his creative impulse, drugs, and finally, sex.

"Then," says the man, "on my fortieth birthday, I woke up and I knew—the answer lies inside me!"

The final sketch shows the man, his disheveled pajamas hanging loosely on his shoulders, peering into his bathroom mirror and asking mournfully: "You're the answer?"

Taken together, these cartoons illustrate the popular American belief that turning "forty" (as *the* symbolic age of midlife) is marked by personal tumult, which pushes the individual to accept that not only has his or her youth come to an end, but with it any hope of ever uncovering "the" answer to the meaning of life.

Judith Viorst, in her best-seller *Necessary Losses*, addresses both these perspectives when she notes,

> As our past realities start to collapse, we challenge the self definitions that have sustained us, finding that everything seems up for grabs, questioning who we are and what it is we are trying to be, and whether, in this life of ours, the only life we have, our achievements

and our goals hold any value. . . . We know that the meter is running and that our choices are steadily narrowing and that, although there is still much to want and to give, some precious parts of our life are over forever. Our childhood and youth are gone and we must pause to mourn our losses before we move on.[5]

Viorst's use of the phrase "mourn our losses" to characterize midlife carries forward what she believes to be the operant metaphor of all human life: the need to accept the successive "necessary losses" of life. During midlife, such losses may include the abandonment of remaining childhood dependencies and adolescent fantasies, as well as the ultimately unrealizable expectations of adulthood. There are also more tangible losses to contend with, such as the illness and deaths of friends and family members.

Many adults do experience midlife as a "working through" of such losses, which can lend these years a somber, even melancholy, quality. After passing through these years and rethinking one's accomplishments and values—as, in other words, one becomes reconciled to the "necessary losses" of midlife—most people feel themselves more purposefully reoriented as they approach the second half of life.

While many speak of experiencing such a midlife transition, there is not unanimity either about the inevitability of a midlife "crisis" or about the factors that explain its seeming ubiquity in American culture. Bernice Neugarten, a distinguished psychologist, speculates that much of what passes for "midlife crisis" is characterized as such precisely because it is written and spoken of so insistently that many people feel compelled to experience turmoil so as to be *au courant*.[6]

Anthropologist Stanley Brandes has extended this line of thought, insisting that the routinely accepted "midlife crisis" derives, not from any particular physical and psychological changes within the person, but rather from a set of cultural assumptions unique to Western society. Brandes notes that many cultures do not recognize "milestone" birthdays as being significant and, indeed, appear quite unaware of the notion of age itself, whereas in Western society age often figures prominently in assessing one's accomplishments and stature. While not denying that many people do experience the midlife years as a time of trauma and personal reassessments, Brandes, like Neugarten, concludes that these years are often tumultuous because Americans are "pre-programmed" by the culture to expect them to be.[7]

Views from the Jewish Tradition

Jewish society, sharing in as well as shaping Western culture, is a tradition highly sensitive to the qualities and prerogatives of age. The Bible routinely notes the ages of both the patriarchs and matriarchs, and the standard rabbinic commentaries frequently amplify the import of a biblical character's age. One striking example is seen in the commentary of the medieval sage Rashi on the biblical verse "The life of Sarah was a hundred years and twenty years and seven years" (Genesis 23:1). Rashi explains that the seemingly awkward repetition of *years* in this verse is meant to teach that Sarah was as "morally upright at one hundred as most others are at twenty, and as wholly beautiful at twenty as others are at seven."[8] This comment in fact reveals a common rabbinic tendency to ascribe certain personal qualities to specific ages within the life span.

Throughout the Bible, we read that the goal of life is to attain "length of days." The author of Psalm 90 dreams of reaching the golden age of "seventy, or by reason of strength, eighty years." To live as long as Moses—120 years—is the basis of the traditional Yiddish blessing offered at many joyous occasions: "Biz hundredt unt tzvantzik!" ("May you live to reach 120!") Both in the Ten Commandments and in the Holiness Code of Leviticus, chapter 19, those who attain "hoary old age" are saluted as worthy of special attention. It is natural that the rabbinic codes took cues from the Bible in specifying the privileges the elderly should expect, as well as in elaborating the special qualities that age was said to confer.[9]

Although most of the classic Jewish texts extolling maturity refer exclusively to the "elderly," in the passage from Pirkei'Avot quoted earlier we see that every age of life carries its own unique assignment. The central years of adulthood—ages forty through sixty—are to be directed, asserts Judah, toward achieving the qualities of "understanding, counsel, and wisdom."

In their Hebrew original, these words evoke unique meanings. *Binah,* "understanding," is generally associated with the intellectual prowess necessary to make sophisticated connections and penetrate to the deeper meanings of life. That is why, according to the tradition, it is only after age forty that one is permitted to engage in the study of mystical literature without risking potentially dire consequences. *Eitzah*, "counsel," comes from having "experienced" enough successes and failures that one has the ability to respond to others with equanimity and to provide consistently thoughtful guidance. In Yiddish such a person is said to possess *sechel*, or common sense. *Ḥokhmah*, "wisdom," the third quality that distinguishes midlife, connotes a special love of discernment, acuity, and insight.[10]

Judah's appraisal of the achievements of adulthood gives us a Judaic framework of values within which the midlife passage can be viewed today. For the qualities that he specifies—understanding, counsel, and wisdom—find echoes in current literature on adult development as well as in our own lives.

"Working Through" Midlife

One of the more intriguing designations for midlife is the one used in German: *Torschlusspanik*, a "fear of closing gates."[11] This term has an evocative ring to those familiar with the Jewish liturgy. At the conclusion of the High Holy Days, as Yom Kippur (the Day of Atonement) draws to a close, the congregation joins in a service called *Neilah*, a Hebrew word meaning "bolting," its original reference being to the closing of the Temple gates in Jerusalem at the end of the holy day.[12]

After Jerusalem's destruction, when the Yom Kippur service was shifted from the Temple to the synagogue, the "bolting" was symbolically continued by leaving open the synagogue ark containing the Torah scrolls throughout the *Neilah* service, closing the ark doors only after the last words of that day's liturgy were sung by the entire congregation. Over time, the liturgy elaborated on this theme, most notably in the following medieval poem, known as a *piyyut:*

> Open for us the gates, even as they are closing.
> The day is waning, the sun is low.
> The hour is late, a year has slipped away.
> Come, let us enter the gates at last.[13]

This theme of "open and closed gates" has been expanded in several modern prayer books into a metaphor for the closing gates in each individual's journey through life:

> As a man begins life, it spreads before him like a corridor with many doors. But as he walks down this corridor the doors close behind him, one by one, year by year. . . . The corridor of life stretches before us. Each one of us must perforce walk down its stately length. The gates do not stand open forever; as we walk down the corridor they shut behind us. And at the end they are all closed, except that dark door that leads to the ultimate chamber of God. . . . Let us open the gates to those things in life which abide eternally—before the gates swing shut, before the doors are closed. [14]

This contemporary meditation on the *Neilah* service articulates a central theme of midlife. According to students of adult development, the need to come to grips both with the symbolic doors that have been sealed forever and with the decision about which of the remaining openings one will move through now illustrates the fundamental midlife challenge.

One scholar, Elliot Jacques, argues that the reality of "closing doors" is, in fact, *the* issue that defines the midlife passage. As he studied how a number of artists advanced into these years, he became convinced that as individuals grappled, in a new and profound way, with the inevitability of their own death and came to terms (or not) with the choices they had made up to that point, they were transformed in a way that seemed to shape their remaining years. [15]

Daniel Levinson, who directed the famed Yale studies that led to the book *The Seasons of a Man's Life*, found that the middle years generate a substantial shift in the thinking of many people. Levinson notes that while his subjects, in approaching their middle years, at first emphasized their past and the choices they had made, as the midlife years proceeded their focus shifted almost exclusively to the future. They then asked some potent questions:

> What have I done with my life? What do I really get from and give to my wife [or husband], children, friends, work, community—and self? What is it I truly want for myself and others? What are my central values and how are they reflected in my life? What are my greatest

talents and how am I using (or wasting) them? What have I done with my early Dream and what do I want with it now?[16]

Such questions reflect a new awareness of the movement of time, the passing of the generations, and the shifting strengths and weaknesses of the body and mind. Most people shuttle back and forth, Levinson found, through a young/old polarity, one moment feeling as though they were twenty-five, and the next, as though seventy-five. During this process, each person comes to terms with a self that, though perhaps less limber, is not necessarily less responsive. Led to a fresh perspective, the individual comes to realize that youth has gone forever and understands, often for the first time, the inevitability of his or her death—though again, this realization need not be an occasion for despair.[17]

Alongside a growing acceptance of personal mortality, the individual at midlife becomes deeply concerned with the ultimate *meaning* of his or her own life. He or she considers not only how much time is left, but whether his or her life will have made an enduring contribution to those who survive. This concern propels the individual toward an orientation that the famed psychologist Erik Erikson called "generativity."[18]

At midlife, Erikson says, the choice the individual faces is between "generativity versus stagnation." Acquiring the mode of generativity— learning how to establish, reach out to, and guide the next generation— is the essential challenge of midlife. If one is successful in this, one develops the virtue of care: "Care is a quality essential for psychosocial evolution, for we are the teaching species . . . only man can and must extend his solicitude over the long, parallel, and overlapping childhoods of numerous offspring united in households and communities. As he transmits the rudiments of hope, purpose and competence, he imparts meaning."[19] It is not only, says Erikson, that human beings are driven to care for successive generations; it is also that, in so doing, "generative" individuals more clearly discover the essential meaning of their own lives.

For Carol Gilligan, who has sought to show the ways women's development diverges from, as well as is similar to, that of men, this generative quality is also a central theme of women at midlife. Indeed, it is an attribute that she believes girls acquire more "naturally" than boys, for girls are more often raised to consider interpersonal relationships a critical measure of life's worth. This developmental emphasis significantly shapes girls' and women's values. Gilligan argues that "since the reality of connection is experienced by women as given rather than as freely contracted, they arrive at an understanding of life that reflects the limits of autonomy and control . . . [a] path not only to less violent life but also to a maturity realized through interdependence and taking care."[20]

Caring for others does not mean, however, that the individual ceases to be concerned about legitimate self-interest. To be sure, one of the central tasks of midlife is to decide how to stand up to a sometimes hostile world and how to come to terms with the pettiness and injustices that can plague everyday life. Accepting the imperfections of the world, seeking to change those aspects that will yield while standing firm against those that will not, is a vital duty of these middle years. By so doing, the individual demonstrates the capacity to take increased responsibility for the shape of his or her own life.[21]

Researchers speak of one additional impetus of midlife: an overarching drive for integration. Men and women search with a special urgency for the means and symbols by which they can bring the diverse strands of their lives into meaningful coherence.

Making peace with personal mortality, accepting the call to reach out and nurture a new generation, reaffirming one's deepest principles while defending oneself against a frequently anarchic and unfriendly world, and striving toward an ultimate unity that integrates one's beliefs and values—these, according to the premier students of adult development, are the primary tasks at midlife. They are, as well, the primary responsibilities of a meaningful Jewish life.

Jewish Theology and Midlife

The Jewish tradition, centered on life inside community, calls for the upholding of the mitzvot (commandments) as *the* means for ennobling the Jewish people and enhancing the world. Such an emphasis on the active life may have precluded the formulation of the sort of personal meditations and spiritual manuals that typify other religious traditions of both the East and West, especially Roman Catholicism with its heritage of individual spiritual direction. However, the Jewish tradition does contain some notable efforts to chart the course of inner spiritual development. One famous medieval example of this genre is Bahya ibn Paquda's *Ḥovot ha-levavot* (*Duties of the Heart*), once a widely read guide to the personal religious life. Both the mystical and hasidic traditions also dwell on aspects of personal development and its relationship to the spiritual life.[22]

Martin Buber and Harold Kushner are two twentieth-century Jewish theologians who have sought to uncover the richness of the Jewish sources in guiding individual growth, especially in midlife. Buber was not only an innovative philosopher and a vigorous critic of secular thought; he was also a highly original interpreter of the hasidic tradition. Among his efforts to unlock that heritage for the modern person is an essay entitled "The Way of Man According to the Teachings of the Hasidim."[23] Weaving beguiling stories from the hasidic masters into his singular vision of religious humanism, Buber offers a moving meditation on personal meaning as it can be found within a Jewish setting. One example offers a fitting illustration.

Buber notes that according to the hasidic tradition the self needs to be directed toward fulfillment, yet still remain focused on caring for the world outside. He approvingly cites Rabbi Eliezer, who once upbraided a family member who was bemoaning his lack of religious piety with these words: "O my friend! You are thinking only of yourself. How about forgetting yourself and thinking of the world?" These words, says Buber, point to the appropriate attitude for every individual. In life, he writes,

> One need only ask one question. What for? What am I to choose my particular way for? What am I to unify my being for? The answer is: Not for my own sake alone. To begin with oneself, but not to end with oneself; to start from oneself, but not to aim at oneself; to comprehend oneself, but not to be preoccupied with oneself.[24]

The quest for personal fulfillment, in the end, is most meaningfully realized when an individual focuses on what Buber called "the life of dialogue," that is, relationships with other human beings and with God—commitments that social scientists identify as central to the midlife agenda.

A more recent attempt at relating Jewish tradition and psychology can be found in the work of Rabbi Harold Kushner. Best known for a meditation on personal tragedy, *When Bad Things Happen to Good People*, Kushner, in a second best-seller, *When All You've Ever Wanted Isn't Enough*, explores the search for meaning through analysis of the biblical book of Ecclesiastes. Confessing that he used to read that work as if it were written by a cynical young man determined to combat all the sham of life, Kushner concedes that such a reading misconstrues the book's pathos. He no longer sees Ecclesiastes as an idealistic youth, but as a man who is "desperately afraid of dying before he has learned how to live. Nothing he has ever done, nothing he will ever do, makes any difference, he feels, because one day he will die and then it will be as if he had never lived. And he cannot handle that fear of dying and leaving no trace behind."[25]

Writing within the shadow of life's "closing gates," Ecclesiastes offers his readers ways to conquer the terror prompted both by the physical end of life and, more important, by the specter of never having left any imprint on the world. Kushner calls attention to some innocent-sounding words, taken from the closing chapters of the book:

Go, eat your bread in gladness and drink your wine in joy, for your action was long ago approved by God. Let your clothes be freshly washed and your head never lack ointment. Enjoy happiness with a woman you love all the fleeting days of life that have been granted you under the sun. Whatever it is in your power to do, do with all your might. (Ecclesiastes 9:7–9)

These verses point to a central attitude of living, especially as one enters maturity: the call to enjoy everyday encounters and their simple gifts rather than to run after some grand solution to life's riddles or to defer gratification to future retirement. By ceasing to pursue The Answer to life, the individual is freed to discover the multiple *answers* that life provides within the daily acts related to work, play, and home. Then the individual will come to a renewed appreciation of the everyday, realizing that the seemingly mundane sides of life are themselves ultimately meaningful.[26]

Religious writers speak of this orientation as the "hallowing of the everyday." Modern psychology affirms that this perspective is one of the hallmarks of maturity. Daniel Levinson, for example, notes that nearly all of his subjects had a "Dream," a central, driving aspiration that seemed to grab hold and lend an indelible shape to each individual's existence. One of the jobs of midlife, however, is to escape from the tyranny of that dream:

> The task is not to get rid of the "Dream" altogether, but to reduce its excessive power; to make its demands less absolute; to make success less essential and failure less disastrous. . . . Later, a man may continue to seek excellence, but he gains more intrinsic enjoyment from the process and product of his efforts, and he is less concerned with recognition and power.[27]

Other Jewish voices, modern and classical alike, illustrate meaningful correspondence between authentic Jewish teachings and modern psychology on the critical midlife issues.[28] There is also one embracing Jewish source that illuminates the themes of the adult years; it is a composite voice: that of the *maḥzor*, the High Holy Day prayer book. In many ways, the *maḥzor* can be considered *the* manual for guiding the Jew through the puzzles of midlife. Two examples drawn from the High Holy Day season—one the manner of dress associated with Rosh Hashanah (the Jewish New Year) and Yom Kippur, the other a special passage that occupies a pivotal place in the liturgy for those days—exemplify how ancient teachings powerfully illuminate personal midlife issues.

Among the customs associated with observing both holy days is that the worshiper wear a *kittel*, the Yiddish term for an unadorned white linen robe. Although in many congregations only those who officiate at these services adhere to the practice, among more traditional Jews it is still customary for many congregants to wear a *kittel*. White has traditionally been associated with purity, which explains why the custom arose to wear a *kittel* on these special days. Jews are also traditionally buried in a similar simple white shroud. The entire High Holy Day liturgy, moreover, is punctuated with the Hebrew refrain *Zokhreinu le-ḥayim*—"Remember us for Life!" Thus the worshiper, enveloped in a garment that underscores life's frailty and finiteness, is asked to affirm his or her own life and to make positive choices that will enhance the years ahead. The worshiper embraces a religious paradox, concurrently praying for life while dressed in the clothes of death—a powerful liturgical reenactment of what the social scientists call the "young-old" polarity of midlife.[29]

This prayer, among many in the *maḥzor*, emphasizes that the High Holy Days are *the* time when the Jew confronts his or her mortality and resolves to remold the days that are left in a way that will be personally transforming, socially responsible, and ultimately significant. This annual rite of atonement can be seen as an ongoing effort at midcourse correction. The tradition urges each Jew to reach in and reshape the inner self, so that he or she can then reach out to others and to "the Other." Thus the Jewish calendar itself provides a structure within which some find help in resolving the tensions of midlife.

"Observing" Midlife

Throughout the ages, Jews have sought not only to derive meaning from the traditional formulas but to transform and enhance their inheritance. Contemporary American Jews are particularly attracted to the refashioning of old rituals, as well as to the creation of new ones. For many, the deeply personal and liturgically rich ritual of the High Holy Days may suffice as a sort of midlife or aging ceremony, a means for regularly reassessing their lives and refocusing themselves. Other contemporary Jews, however, have expanded traditional formulas and created new ones to mark midlife.

One elaboration of a traditional rite of passage is the "adult Bar/Bat Mitzvah." While the precise content of study varies, those who celebrate this rite as adults frequently learn Hebrew for the first time, master Torah reading or the chanting of the haftarah (the prophetic reading assigned for a given Shabbat or festival), become familiar with the structure and meaning of Jewish prayer, and otherwise immerse themselves in Jewish textual study on a more serious level than ever before.

The goal of many who participate in these courses is to be able more fully to express their Jewish identity in the classic setting of synagogue life. This is especially true for Jewish women, who earlier were denied the opportunity for formal Jewish training and hence full ritual participation in the synagogue.[30] For them, adult Bat Mitzvah is related to being part of a transition generation. For this ceremony to become a true midlife rite for women and men, however, it will need to have its own name and character; for this reason, in many synagogues it is termed Bar or Bat Torah, to distinguish it from the adolescent version.

For some Jews, events in their children's lives reflect a "working through" of their own midlife transition. Two examples, one a recent phenomenon, the other a ceremony imported from Eastern Europe, exemplify this fact. Many parents first experience feelings associated with midlife when their children leave home, either to begin college residence or to create their own home. This potentially traumatic time, when both parents and children wrestle with many issues and concerns, has stimulated the rise of "leaving home" ceremonies, centered around a regular Jewish home ceremony such as *havdalah*, the Saturday evening observance that "separates" Shabbat from the other days of the week.[31] A more traditional Jewish ceremony associated with midlife has long been performed at the wedding reception of the last child in the household to be married, when the parents are toasted at having reached such a joyous moment. The most common custom is a wedding dance, during which the parents are seated with boughs of greenery arranged as crowns upon their heads. All assembled circle around them, singing Yiddish and Hebrew melodies, praising their merit and extolling their good fortune.

Some contemporary Jews mark midlife by adopting a more intense pattern of Jewish study and practice. For some, this return to Judaism is so all-encompassing that they are called by a unique name: *ba'alei teshuvah*. *Teshuvah* means "to return," and historically has referred to the act of deliberate *return* to an observant Jewish life, fully studying and practicing the mitzvot. Today, the term is not necessarily reserved for those who were once observant and then strayed, but refers also to those who grew up in nontraditional homes and have chosen to adopt a Jewish life pattern at odds with their previously nonobservant life.

Ba'alei teshuvah choose to "return" at many different ages, including midlife. While many motivations prompt a person to become religiously observant, the author of a recent study gives a reason that has a particularly midlife "ring" to it. From scores of interviews, this author discovered that the "returning" was frequently set in motion because the *ba'al teshuvah* was overwhelmed by what he or she labeled the "emptiness of success." A consumer-oriented life-style failed to produce the expected personal meaning, leading these "returnees" to seek a way of life that promised greater fulfillment.[32]

For other modern Jews, traditional forms of study and behavior either do not entice or are found wanting. Women especially have felt the need to create rituals that reflect the physical and psychological changes of the middle years. Some women have created rituals that focus on menopause and the profound sense of change and loss that attend the realization that they will no longer be able to bear children. In *Miriam's Well*, a book that explores traditional and contemporary rituals for Jewish women, the springtime Hebrew month of Iyyar, characterized in the religious calendar as a time of communal mourning, has been selected as the time to mark this midlife passage.[33] In the ritual, women are encouraged to offer personal reflections about their feelings as they say farewell to one stage of their physical life. Pertinent texts are offered as a means of encouragement:

[We are ready] to mark the passing of physical fertility and to rededicate ourselves to a greater focus of spiritual, intellectual, and artistic creativity and fertility.

[We are prepared] to say good-bye to the womb, *reḥem*, the center of childbearing.

[We wish] to praise and give thanks for the cycles of life which pulsate through our bodies.

[We want] to say good-bye and good riddance to tampons and sanitary napkins and pads and foams and jellies and diaphragms and pills and anything else I've left out—forever.[34]

More elaborate efforts to mark midlife from a woman's perspective can be found in the work of Irene Fine, who has collected several texts and rites that focus on maturing women. She describes one intricate ceremony, open to both family and friends, in which the celebrant took note of the losses associated with entering this new stage of life, as well as the many new possibilities that awaited her. The celebrant chose to call her midlife ceremony *Ma'aseh Bereshit*—"The Work of Creation"—and she told her community why:

B're-shit means creation or first fruit. I like this symbolism for midlife. It speaks of being fruitful and having new beginnings at a time of life when everyone tells women that the time of bearing fruit, of creating for the world, is past. Although my womb will no longer produce a child, my heart and my mind are full of creation . . . and that is Kadosh, Holy. This is a time of my life when I create anew, with less of the old possibilities, with more wisdom in the ways of the world and my particular place in it.[35]

This ritual, developed by Jewish women in California in the 1980s, brings us back full circle to the words voiced nearly two millennia ago by that other Jew, Judah, son of Tema. He spoke of three decades—the forties through the sixties—as a time when the individual should strive for an increased measure of understanding, counsel, and wisdom. The women who composed the Ma'aseh Bere'shit text have captured the insights of Judah, as well as those uncovered by contemporary specialists, that midlife is paradoxically a time of loss, coupled with an opportunity for new beginnings and growth.

On many levels, the middle years hold out the promise that life will be marked by greater *understanding* of one's inner self, deepening commitment to *counsel* and care for the generations that follow, and growing *wisdom* to appreciate the subtleties and breadth of existence. As individuals seek to embrace these qualities, they exemplify the ways in which midlife is a time both of celebration and renewal.

NOTES

1. Bob Woodward and Scott Armstrong, *The Brethren: Inside the Supreme Court* (New York: Simon & Schuster, 1979), p. 194.

2. Stanley Brandes, *Forty: The Age and the Symbol* (Knoxville: University of Tennessee Press, 1985), p. 4

3. Hayyim Schauss, *The Lifetime of a Jew* (New York: Union of American Hebrew Congregations, 1950).

4. See for example, Sharon Strassfeld and Kathy Green, *The Jewish Family Book* (New York: Bantam Books, 1981), pp. 375–395. In its both thoughtful and whimsical survey of the life cycle of the Jew, *The Second Jewish Catalog*, ed. Sharon Strassfeld and Michael Strassfeld (Philadelphia: Jewish Publication Society, 1976), uses the term *middle years* as its table of contents heading for Bar and Bat Mitzvah, Confirmation, and Leaving Home. See also Simeon Maslin, ed., *Gates of Mitzvah: A Guide to the Jewish Life Cycle* (New York: Central Conference of American Rabbis, 1979).

5. Judith Viorst, *Necessary Losses* (New York: Simon & Schuster, 1986), pp. 270–271.

6. Bernice L. Neugarten, "Time, Age, and the Life Cycle," in *A Life Transitions Reader*, ed. Vivian Rogers McCoy et al. (Lawrence: University of Kansas Press), pp. 8–10.

7. Brandes, *Forty*, pp. 17–33.

8. See the traditional commentary (Hebrew) of Rabbi Shlomo Yitzchaki of Troyes, known as Rashi, on Genesis 23:1.

9. Gerald Blidstein, *Honor Thy Father and Mother: Filial Responsibility on Jewish Law and Ethics* (New York: Ktav, 1975), pp. 37–59.

10. Commentary (Heb.) of Rabbi Pinchas Kehati on *M. Avot* 5:21.

11. This term originated in the Middle Ages, when many cities were walled and danger often lurked outside their protective shelter. Today, that term refers to the fear felt by many in midlife that it may be too late to accomplish those goals one had envisioned. See Carola H. Mann, "Midlife and the Family: Strains, Challenges, and Options of the Middle Years," in *Midlife: Developmental and Clinical Issues*, ed. William H. Norman and Thomas Scaramella (New York: Brunner/Mazel, 1980), p. 132.

12. During the centuries that the Temple was the center of the nation's worship, the gates to the inner Temple were kept open on the day of penance, thereby announcing symbolically that the people would come forward to be forgiven of their sins. As the sun set, however, the gates were shut, signaling that the chance to seek atonement on that day had expired. See Mishnah Taanit 4:1; Talmud Yerushalmi, Taanit, 67C.

13. See traditional text in, for example, *Mahzor for Rosh Hashanah and Yom Kippur: A Prayer Book for the Days of Awe*, ed. Jules Harlow (New York: Rabbinical Assembly, 1972), p. 724.

14. Milton Steinberg, in *Yearnings: Prayer and Meditation for the Days of Awe*, ed. Jules Harlow (New York: Rabbinical Assembly, 1968), p. 29.

15. Elliot Jacques, "Death and the Mid-Life Crisis," *International Journal of Psychoanalysis* 465 (1965): 502–514.

16. Daniel Levinson et al., *The Seasons of a Man's Life* (New York: Ballantine Books, 1978), pp. 241–249.

17. Ibid., pp. 191–259.

18. Erikson theorized that individuals pass through eight stages of growth, each of which he labels by a set of polar terms, for his clinical work convinced him that individuals face the challenge of each time span either by opting for a "positive" mode unique to that age or slipping into a regressive posture with its corresponding "negative" attribute. See Erik Erikson, *Childhood and Society* (New York: W. W. Norton, 1963), pp. 261–268.

19. Erik Erikson, *Insight and Responsibility* (New York: W. W. Norton, 1964), p. 130.

20. Carol Gilligan, *In a Different Voice* (Cambridge, Mass.: Harvard University Press, 1982), p. 172.

21. Levinson et al., *Seasons of a Man's Life*, pp. 242–243.

22. See, for example, Abraham J. Heschel, *A Passion for Truth* (New York: Farrar, Straus & Giroux, 1973); and Arthur Green, *Tormented Master: A Life of Rabbi Nahman of Brastlav* (New York: Schocken Books, 1981).

23. Martin Buber, *The Way of Man According to the Teachings of the Hasidim* (Secaucus, N.J.: Citadel Press, 1966), pp. 9–41.

24. Ibid., pp. 31–32.

25. Harold Kushner, *When All You've Ever Wanted Isn't Enough* (New York: Summit Books, 1986), pp. 37–38.

26. Ibid., pp. 139–152.

27. Levinson et al., *Seasons of a Man's Life*, p. 248.

28. See Sol Landau, "The Needs of the Middle Years—A New Area of Exploration," in *Analysis* (New York: Institute for Jewish Policy Planning and Research of the Synagogue Council of America, 1980), pp. 1–6.

29. I am grateful to Rabbi Jack Riemer, who drew my attention to a sermon by Rabbi Robert Kahn on this theme. Many other prayers in the High Holy Day liturgy reflect the young/old polarity theme.

30. Ruth Manson, "Adult Bat Mitzvah," *Lilith* (Fall 1989): 21–23.

31. Strassfeld and Strassfeld, eds., *Second Jewish Catalog*, pp. 88–89.

32. M. Herbert Danzger, *Returning to Tradition* (New Haven: Yale University Press, 1989), pp. 223–250.

33. Penina V. Adelman, *Miriam's Well: Rituals for Jewish Women Around the Year* (Fresh Meadows, N.Y.: Biblio Press, 1986), pp. 67–70.

34. Ibid., pp. 69–70.

35. Irene Fine, *Midlife: A Rite of Passage* (San Diego: Woman's Institute for Continuing Jewish Education, 1988), p. 32.

SUGGESTIONS FOR FURTHER READING

Midlife, as a unique stage in adult development, has yet to receive the attention of Jewish writers in the way Christian thinkers have addressed it. The sources listed below provide useful models of how religious considerations can be applied to the unique challenges of individuals at midlife.

James W. Fowler, in *Becoming Adult, Becoming Christian: Adult Development and Christian Faith* (San Francisco: Harper & Row, 1984), analyzes prevailing adult development theories (Erikson, Levinson, and Gilligan) and discusses his own work in faith development, as originally presented in his pioneering *Stages of Faith*. He then applies the theories to a central Christian theological theme: vocation.

Harold Kushner, in *When All You've Ever Wanted Isn't Enough* (New York: Summit Books, 1986), turns to the biblical book of Ecclesiastes to outline the path to personal religious meaning at midlife.

Sol Landau, "The Needs of the Middle Years—A New Area of Exploration," *Analysis*, no. 67 (June 1980), is a brief summary of the challenges faced by synagogues in addressing the unique concerns of their congregants at midlife.

John Franklin Roschen, *Baby Boomers Face Midlife: Implications for Faith Communities in the 90's and Beyond* (Minneapolis: Adult Faith Resources, 1991), is a concise review of the current literature, both general and religious, on midlife development and its relationship to faith, originally prepared for a conference for churches and synagogues facing the programmatic task of responding to the baby boomers entering midlife.

Evelyn Eaton Whitehead and James D. Whitehead, in *Christian Life Patterns: The Psychological Challenges and Religious Invitations of Adult Life* (New York, Doubleday, 1982), link current developmental theory to the Christian theological tradition, especially its liturgy and daily ritual.

IRWIN H. HAUT

"The Altar Weeps"

Divorce in Jewish Law

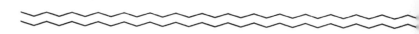

Introduction

In the cycle of life, there are moments of extreme joy and of profound sadness, both of which come into play in connection with marriage and divorce. In this chapter we shall explore Jewish law as it relates to divorce— including the equality of the spouses in initiating divorce proceedings, the particulars of the divorce process itself, modern dilemmas confronting the Jewish community in divorce law, and finally some possible solutions to those dilemmas.

Under Jewish law, a marriage validly entered into can be ended *only* by the death of one of the parties or by a document known as a *get*.[1] The writing, transmission, and acceptance of the *get* are all governed by specific rules. Moreover, *only* the husband has the right to give the *get* to his wife; if he refuses to do so, his wife is unable to remarry. She is then called an *agunah*, or "anchored woman"—that is, one who cannot free herself from the marital bonds. Various approaches have been suggested for the resolution of this problem, including that of a legislative enactment, or *takkanah*, that would permit the wife to sue for divorce.[2] And indeed, some ancient Semitic traditions, evidence of which is reflected in the records of the Jewish community of Elephantine, did permit the wife to initiate divorce proceedings.[3]

The basic rules relating to marriage and divorce are enunciated in the Torah, the five books of Moses. Prior to the performance of a marriage ceremony, the parties enter into an agreement, known as the *ketubbah*,[4] which provides that in the event of divorce or the death of the husband, the husband or his estate is obligated to pay the wife[5] a sum of money somewhat similar to today's alimony.

The biblical rules relating to divorce are set forth in Deuteronomy 24:1, as follows: "A man takes a wife and possesses her. She fails to please him because he finds something obnoxious [literally, a matter involving nakedness—*ervat davar*] about her, and he writes her a bill of divorcement, hands it to her, and sends her away from his house."

Over the centuries, through their explanations of these phrases, the rabbis erected an elaborate legal system, often exhibiting great compassion for the husband and wife. For instance, although bound by the explicit provisions in the Torah giving the husband the right to divorce his wife, they sought both to avoid divorce and to limit the power of the husband.

The rules relating to divorce under Jewish law are elaborated upon at great length in the Mishnah Gittin and in the Talmuds of Babylonia and Palestine, Tractates Gittin, which contain the comments and rulings of the early rabbis. Later, they were codified in various codes of Jewish law—written by Maimonides in the *Mishneh Torah* in the twelfth century; Jacob ben Asher in the thirteenth century; and Joseph Caro in the Shulḥan Arukh in the sixteenth century.

Both Talmuds contain sayings reflecting the sanctity of marriage and the distaste of the rabbis for divorce, best exemplified by the statement of Rabbi Eleazar, that "one who divorces his first wife, even the very altar sheds tears because of him."[6] It is understandable, then, that the rabbis insisted that prior to any divorce proceedings the parties should attempt to resolve their differences and be reconciled with each other in mutual love and respect. As pointed out by a leading writer in the field,

> The reconciliation of persons about to be divorced, or who had already been divorced, afforded a fair field for the application of . . . ethical precepts. Besides the legal safeguards against unreasonable and ill-

advised divorces, moral suasion was a potent factor, and it was the duty of the judges or Rabbis to exercise their influence in checking the unrestrained passions that often prompted men to divorce their wives without cause.[7]

The monetary payment required by the *ketubbah* agreement was instituted by the rabbis to discourage hasty divorces. They reasoned that the fact that the husband is required to make a substantial payment acts as a check on an ill-advised decision to divorce his wife.[8] The detailed procedures established in connection with the writing and transmission of the *get* also were designed to dissuade the husband from acting precipitously.[9] Thus, although the rabbis accepted the Divine ordinance written in the Torah permitting divorce, they did so with reluctance.

The attitudes of the rabbis differed as to the grounds for divorce, with the school of Shammai holding that divorce is appropriate *only* in a case of adultery, by the wife, while the school of Hillel maintained that some fault, however minimal, had to obtain. A third view was that of Rabbi Akiba, who lived a hundred years after them, that divorce is permitted even in the complete absence of fault on the part of the wife. Their disagreement centered on the proper interpretation of the term *ervat davar*. Shammai, the strict constructionist, took this phrase in its literal sense, of involving physical nakedness,[10] whereas both Hillel and Rabbi Akiba understood the term figuratively.[11]

Formal Requirements

Get is the Aramaic term for a legal document. (*Shetar* is the more commonly used Hebrew term.) The *get* is written in Hebrew and contains twelve lines, which is the numerical value of the Hebrew letters *gimel* (three) and *tet* (nine) spelling that term.[12]

The formal requirements for the writing of the *get* include the following:[13]

1. The *get* must be dated. According to custom, it is dated from the year of creation of the world according to the Jewish calendar (thus, 1990 = 5750). If the date is erroneous or if it was omitted, the *get* is not valid.

2. The *get* must be handwritten and include the exact names, including all nicknames of the particular individuals involved in the divorce.
3. The husband must specifically request of the scribe preparing the document that the *get* be written for his wife.
4. The place of residence of the parties must be included specifically.
5. Since the *get* certifies divorce and establishes the end of the marital relationship, it must contain words of complete separation. It must therefore explicitly state that the wife is permitted to remarry at will whomever she chooses. Then the *get* must be signed by two competent witnesses.
6. Finally, a *get* must be physically delivered by the husband (or his agent) to his wife (or her agent), or delivered to a place, such as her residence, that is under her actual and physical control. This rule assures that the wife has actual or presumptive notice of its contents and, thus, of the change in her marital status. At the time of delivery, the husband must inform the wife that a *get* is being delivered. Under Jewish law, either the husband or the wife may appoint an agent to give or to accept a *get*.

Procedure

The *get* procedure, including the formalities of preparing the *get*, are so complex that the Talmud declares: "Rabbi Yehudah said in the name of Shmu'el: those [Rabbis] who are not well versed in the intricacies of marriage and divorce may not participate in divorce proceedings."[14]

Technically under Jewish law, appeal to the Jewish court, the *bet din*, in connection with the preparation and transmission of a *get* is unnecessary, since a *get* properly prepared, even by learned laymen, is valid. The complexities involved have led over time to the custom that the *get* be prepared and transmitted under the supervision of a rabbi learned in the law of divorce. Recourse to a full *bet din* is necessary to compel either spouse to participate in divorce proceedings.

Briefly, the proceedings are as follows:[15]

1. The parties appear before a rabbi learned in the law, a scribe, and two witnesses.

2. The husband orders the scribe to write the *get* for his wife, which the scribe proceeds to do, using a quill pen.
3. The husband declares that he is giving the *get* of his own free will, and a similar declaration is made by the wife concerning its receipt.
4. The *get* is then signed by the two witnesses.
5. The parties are again questioned as to whether they are giving and accepting the *get* voluntarily. The husband must state that he will never in the future cast any aspersion on the validity of the *get*.
6. The husband takes the *get* and drops it directly into his wife's cupped hands, stating: "This is your *get* and you are divorced from me, and are permitted to marry any man."
7. She then places the *get* under her arm and symbolically leaves by turning and moving several steps away.
8. The divorcée then returns, and the *get* is taken from her by the officiating rabbi, who tears the *get* crosswise.
9. Finally, the divorced woman is given a receipt (*petur*) to prove her divorced status.

The Search for Equality

THE TALMUDIC PERIOD (220–500 C.E.)

Although it is a fundamental principle of Jewish divorce law that only the husband is empowered to give a *get*, from early times the wife did have some rights in the matter. The husband's rights to divorce his wife against her will were limited by the Torah in two instances, in which it was explicitly declared that divorce was prohibited (though if she consented, of course, the divorce could proceed).[16]

First, Deuteronomy 22:28–29 states that in the case of the rape of an unmarried woman, the rapist must marry her, if she so chooses, and he is prohibited from ever divorcing her. Second, Deuteronomy 22:13–19 states that a newly married groom who falsely accuses his bride of having committed adultery after their formal betrothal (*erusin*) may never divorce her. As previously noted, there also existed a difference of opinion as to whether fault on the part of the wife was a prerequisite to the husband's right to divorce her. Later, the right of the husband to divorce his wife was curtailed under talmudic law if she was insane or else so mentally incompetent that she could not care for herself.[17]

In fact, according to the Talmud a wife could demand that her husband give her a *get* in the following cases:[18]

1. if the husband became afflicted with a loathsome disease after marriage, or if the existence of the disease was unknown to her prior to the marriage;
2. if the husband was impotent or sterile;
3. if the husband refused to provide her with necessities, or refused to engage in sexual relations with her;
4. if she was subject to physical or verbal abuse by the husband, or to misconduct, as, for example, if he forced her to violate a religious precept;
5. if her husband was engaged in some malodorous occupation, such as gathering dog dung, smelting copper, or tanning hides;
6. if the husband sought to leave the place where the couple resided and move to another country and she refused to go with him;
7. if the husband became an apostate.

In these cases, if the *get* was not forthcoming from the husband, the wife would petition the court (*bet din*), which would then compel the husband to give a *get*, even applying physical coercion if necessary.

Technically, in these circumstances it is not the *bet din* that is granting the *get*, or terminating the marriage, because unlike the situation in Western societies,[19] the giving of the *get* is a personal act between a husband and wife, with the courts and state (in Israel today) playing no role. The aid of the *bet din* is sometimes invoked to force one of the parties—usually the husband—to participate in divorce proceedings. Nevertheless, the role of the *bet din* is that of aiding the enforcement of rights that already exist. It is the husband, and he alone, who gives a *get*, rather than any *bet din*, or, in Israel today, the state.

There is obviously a tension between the halakhic rule that the giving of the *get* must result from the husband's free choice and the notion that the court can force the husband to give a *get*. This tension was resolved in talmudic times by the exotic logic that compulsion is applied until the husband objectively states his consent.[20] At a later period this apparant contradiction was rationalized by Maimonides, who asserted that the husband really wants to follow the decree of the *bet din* which has ordered him to give a *get*,[21] but he is being prevented from doing so by evil inclination, which spurs him to rebelliousness. By applying force, reasoned Maimonides, the court is doing no more than helping the husband to overcome his evil inclination, thereby permitting the husband's goodwill to emerge so that he complies with the court's directive and gives his wife a *get*. Admittedly, this is a legal fiction, designed to reconcile the rigorous requirements of Jewish divorce law with justice for the wife.

Not every court is authorized to use such compulsion, however. Problems have arisen in this area of law, precisely because it is *only* a Jewish *bet din* that can so pressure a man, and then *only* when authorized by Jewish law. Thus, if a particular *get* was not required under Jewish law, it is void, even if given under the compulsion of a *bet din*.

Where, however, a *bet din* has ordered a husband to give a *get* that is required under Jewish law, and a Gentile court, or even Jews or Gentiles acting individually, then performed the act of forcing the husband to give the *get*, the divorce is generally held to be valid because the Gentile court, or the individual Gentiles or Jews, were properly enforcing the directives of the *bet din*.

THE GEONIC PERIOD (600–1200 C.E.)

For solutions in this troubled area of law, one need only review developments in the law during the period of the ascendancy of the Geonim. There existed two ancient and respected legal traditions in Jewish law affording protection to women in connection with divorce. The first of these, dating back to the Jewish community in Elephantine in Egypt and extending through the early medieval period, gave protection by means of an explicit provision in the *ketubbah* granting the wife the right to demand and obtain a *get*.[22] This approach is supported by respectable historical precedents.

After the conclusion of the Babylonian Talmud in approximately 500 C.E., there followed a period of legal efflorescence in the academies of Babylonia under the leadership and direction of their titular heads, called Geonim. This period lasted until the thirteenth century. The Geonim were particularly active in the area of divorce law; their compassion for women embroiled in unhappy marriages is manifested by their rulings. As the direct successors of the talmudic rabbis, they wrote, as it were, on a blank slate. Their jurisprudential genius is clearly manifested by their rulings in this as in other areas of law, *none of which have been ever duplicated* and many of which were later rejected outright by European authorities. Their spectacular achievements in this area of law consisted in the fact that for the first and unfortunately last time in Jewish jurisprudence, almost complete equality was effected between men and women as regards the rules relating to *get*.

Under the Geonic legislation, which lasted approximately five hundred years, it was enacted that a wife, if she desired a divorce, could petition the court for a *get*.[23] As stated by Sherira Gaon, in the tenth century:

When the Rabbanan Savorai [predecessors of the Geonim—successors of the Amoraim, 500–698 C.E.] saw that Jewish women go and attach themselves to the Gentiles, in an attempt to force their husbands to give a *get*, and sometimes the latter give *gittin* [pl. of *get*] under duress and grave questions arose as to whether they are properly being forced to give a *get* or improperly, and dreadful consequences ensue, it was enacted by [earlier Geonim] . . . that the husband is forced to give a *get* where the wife seeks a *get* . . . and we follow this *takanah* [legislative enactment] more than three hundred years later, and you do the same.[24]

In such circumstances, the court would direct the husband to give a *get*, applying compulsion if necessary.[25] Under this approach, the right of the husband to divorce his wife against her will remained inviolate; yet the wife was given a corresponding right to demand a *get*, even against the will of her husband. The wife's rights were thus equalized with the husband's except that it was still necessary for her to apply to the court to compel the giving of the *get* if the husband refused to do so voluntarily. Of course, the husband was under no such disability, since he could direct the preparation of the *get* and transmit it, at his will, as under talmudic law. This practice might be seen as the earliest form of "no-fault" divorce.

Maimonides, although rejecting the Geonic approach in the matter,[26] demonstrated his own lenient approach by ruling as follows: "If she says [she is rebelling] 'because he is repulsive to me, and I am unwilling voluntarily to engage in sexual relationships with him,' we force him to divorce her immediately, for she is not as a slave that she should be forced to have intercourse with one who is hateful to her."[27]

It is indeed unfortunate that the attitudes of both the Geonim and Maimonides in the matter were resoundingly rejected in Spain, France, and elsewhere,[28] owing to the force of the personality and scholarship of Rabbenu Tam, a French authority. Rabbenu Tam ruled that compulsion was *never* again to be exercised, *except* in those cases specifically provided for in the Talmud.

The pressure to interject a measure of equality into divorce law did exist on the European continent. However, it took a different direction under the leadership of Rabbenu Gershom of Mainz, who legislated in the tenth and eleventh centuries that a woman could not be divorced against her will,[29] thus somewhat improving the position of women in countries subject to that decree. As stated by Rabbenu Asher: "When he [Rabbenu Gershom] saw how the generation was abusive of Jewish daughters, insofar as divorcing them under compulsion, *he enacted that the rights of women be equal to those of men,* and just as a man divorces only from his own will, so too a woman might henceforth be divorced only willingly."[30] Although this enactment was a far cry from the liberal rights accorded women by the Geonim, and even under the approach of Maimonides, it was nevertheless a step in the right direction, which unfortunately has not been followed up by appropriate enactments to this day.

Modern Dilemmas and Solutions

The development of the institution of civil divorce in various European states gave rise to problems in Jewish divorce law, the reverberations of which are still being felt.[31] As long as divorce was subject to the authority of the church in Europe, Jewish residents generally retained autonomy over divorce, which was governed and controlled by Jewish courts. With the growth of civil divorce, however, Jewish law had to come to grips with a situation where a Jewish couple seeking divorce would be required to apply to the secular authorities for the civil termination of their marriage, and *then* to end their marriage under Jewish law by means of the *get* process. This duplication of effort was necessary because the state did not recognize a *get* as effecting the legal termination of the marriage, and conversely, Jewish law did not consider the civil divorce valid. Thus has arisen the problem, particularly pressing in Western societies, of the husband or wife refusing to permit the termination of the marriage under Jewish law by agreeing to give or accept a *get*, though a civil divorce has already been pronounced.

The "recalcitrant spouse" is a concern to both the Orthodox and Conservative branches of Judaism, which adhere to the requirement that a *get* is necessary to end a marriage. It poses a less direct and immediate problem in those branches of Judaism that consider civil divorce sufficient for Jewish law, though even here problems can emerge later on. For instance, under Jewish law, any children of a second marriage are deemed illegitimate (*mamzerim*) unless any first marriage of either of the spouses was ended by a *get*. The disabilities of such illegitimacy under Jewish law are considerable. Under Deuteronomy 23:3, an illegitimate person is prohibited from entering into a marital union with another Jew unless he or she is also illegitimate. While this may seem esoteric to many readers, in fact more than one-third of the world's Jews now live in Israel and another substantial proportion in other countries where traditional Jewish law holds sway. Given modern mobility, one cannot know with whom one's children will fall in love. Therefore the lack of a *get*, in an era with a high divorce rate, can cause problems for tens of thousands of children of second marriages.

It is therefore crucial for contemporary Jews to realize that regardless of whether they, or their ancestors, followed the liberal or the more traditional branches of Judaism, they can be affected by the reach of Jewish law. There are certain procedures available to the husband that in many circumstances enable him to evade the application of the enactment of Rabbenu Gershom that a wife has the right to refuse a *get*.[32] No such procedures are available to the wife, however, with the result that it is usually women who suffer most from recalcitrant spouses. Unable to remarry under Jewish law, and unable to obtain *gittin* from their husbands, these women remain "anchored" indefinitely unless they are willing to violate Jewish law.

The preceding survey, of course, relates only to the historical situation that continues today within the Diaspora, in which Jewish courts lack autonomy. In modern Israel, autonomy of Jewish courts exists once again over marriage and divorce. Nonetheless, the day-to-day situation is not much different from that in the Diaspora. The Israeli courts, although empowered to apply compulsion to force a recalcitrant husband to give a *get*, rarely do so, under the residual influence of the views of Rabbenu Tam.[33] Moreover, Israel does not provide an option of civil divorce for those who do not wish to observe halakhah.

Extensive abuses can be found today, both in Israel and in the Diaspora, including documented instances of extortion by one spouse or the other (usually the husband). In these instances, a *get* may be refused unless and until certain demands—often involving child custody or support provisions—are met or acceded to. Therefore, one finds numerous cases of women whose religious convictions have prevented them from ever remarrying.

Men and women from within the traditional Jewish community have been greatly troubled by the difficulties faced by *agunot* who have struggled to obtain a *get*. Within the last decade, a number of grassroots organizations have been organized whose purpose is to alleviate the pain and suffering of these women. For example, the GET (Getting Equitable Treatment) organization was formed to facilitate the giving of a *get*. The Kayama organization is dedicated to educating the Jewish public on the necessity of transmitting and receiving a *get* and helping women obtain one.

The pressing nature of these problems has in the last few years become the focus of activist Orthodox Jewish feminists, who support various approaches to resolution of this problem. Agunah is one such women's group, which applies pressure to recalcitrant husbands by holding public demonstrations at their homes or places of business. It also acts as a pressure group to galvanize public opinion to motivate the Orthodox rabbinate to resolve this festering problem, seriously and in an organized fashion. Agunah's immediate goal is to provide concrete social service assistance and encouragement to individuals involved; its long-range goals are to serve as a catalyst for debate and to seek societal solutions from the organized rabbinate, a swift resolution of this problem being the ultimate wish.

Jewish courts have also attempted to keep pace with the growing dimensions of the problem by intensifying efforts at reconciliation of the spouses. Some Jewish courts will not issue a *get* unless the parties have first undergone a specified period of marital counseling, hoping that such counseling will remove or lessen the discord and obviate the desire for a *get*. However, this approach, though worthwhile before the fact, is useless if the marriage has already been dissolved civilly.

As noted above in the chapter on marriage, the Conservative movement, through its respected leader, the learned late Professor Saul Lieberman, has attempted to prevent the problem of the *agunah* through an amendment to the *ketubbah*[34] (see Daniel H. Gordis, p. 105). In 1954, the Conference on Jewish Law, a joint body created by the Jewish Theological Seminary of America and the Rabbinical Assembly of America (both institutions of the Conservative branch of American Judaism), formulated the following addition to, or modification of, the traditional *ketubbah*:

> And, in solemn assent to their mutual responsibilities and love, the bridegroom and bride have declared: as evidence of our desire to enable each other to live in accordance with the Jewish Law of Marriage throughout our lifetime, we, the bride and bridegroom, attach our signature to this Ketubah, and hereby agree to recognize the Beth Din of the Rabbinical Assembly and the Jewish Theological Seminary of America, or its duly appointed representatives, as having authority to counsel us in the light of Jewish tradition which requires husband and wife to give each other complete love and devotion, and to summon either party at the request of the other, in order to enable the party so requesting to live in accordance with the standards of the Jewish Law of Marriage throughout his or her lifetime. We authorize the Beth Din to impose such terms of compensation as it may see fit for failure to respond to its summons or to carry out its decision.[35]

Under this agreement, where a marriage has been civilly dissolved, and either spouse refuses to participate in *get* procedures, the other one may summon the recalcitrant spouse to appear before the *bet din* of the Jewish Theological Seminary for the purpose of counseling to enable the writing of a *get*. This approach has received civil judicial approval by the New York Court of Appeals in the case of *Avitzur v. Avitzur*.[36] That court, in a divided four-to-three decision, held that the clause was enforceable and that the parties could be directed by the courts to appear before the *bet din* for counseling for that purpose. The Court of Appeals did not, however, decide the ultimate issue of whether it would enforce an order of the *bet din* directing the parties to engage in *get* procedures.

There have also been attempts in Orthodox circles to implement a prenuptial agreement, under which the parties agree, under the threat of monetary sanctions, to participate in *get* proceedings upon the civil termination of their marriage.[37]

Another recent approach has been to resolve this problem directly through the civil legislative process. In two jurisdictions, New York and Canada,[38] legislation has been enacted that gives women equivalent rights to men. In New York, a plaintiff in a divorce proceeding may not obtain a civil divorce without complying with *get* procedures, if the marriage was celebrated in accordance with Jewish law. This rule, however, while sometimes helpful where the husband seeks the civil divorce, is generally ineffective because usually it is the wife who is the plaintiff in civil divorce proceedings.

The Canadian legislature has gone one step further. It has enacted a law in which *neither* party to a civil divorce proceeding may obtain any relief from the court unless he or she complies fully with the *get* procedures. This is a wholesome development and, if implemented elsewhere, would be most helpful in resolving this problem outside of Israel.

The *only* viable and complete solution under Jewish law for the pressing problem of the recalcitrant spouse is that of the reenactment of the type of legislation utilized by the Geonim. That solution involves the enactment of a *takkanah*, limited in scope, through which *the refusal by one spouse or the other to participate in* get *proceedings, after the civil termination of their marriage, would result in the retroactive annulment of that marriage.*[39]

It is to the speedy resolution of this pressing problem that this chapter is hopefully dedicated.

NOTES

1. I. H. Haut, *Divorce in Jewish Law and Life* (New York: Sepher-Hermon Press, 1983), ch. 4. On divorce generally, see *Encyclopedia Judaica*, vol. 6, "Divorce" (Keter Publishing House Ltd., Jerusalem, 1973), p. 122; D. W. Amram, *The Jewish Law of Divorce According to Bible and Talmud*, 2d ed. (New York: Hermon Press, 1968); *Jews and Divorce*, ed. J. Fried, (New York: Ktav Publishing House, 1968); S. Daiches, "Divorce in Jewish Law," in *Studies in*

Jewish Jurisprudence, vol. 2 (New York: Hermon Press, 1974; reprinted from *Publications of the Society of Jewish Jurisprudence* 1, [1929]) p. 215.

2. Haut, supra, n. 1, ch. 3; I. H. Haut, "A Problem in Jewish Divorce Law: An Analysis and Some Suggestions," *Tradition* 16 (1977):29.

3. See generally, E. Lipinski, "The Wife's Right to Divorce in the Light of an Ancient Near Eastern Tradition," *Jewish Law Annual* 4 (1981):9; S. Riskin, *Women and Jewish Divorce* (Hoboken, N.J.: Ktav Publishing House, Ltd., 1989); M. Friedman, "Divorce Upon the Wife's Demand as Reflected in Manuscripts from the Cairo Geniza," *Jewish Law Annual* 4, supra, p. 103.

4. Haut, supra, n. 1, ch. 2; *Encyclopedia Judaica*, vol. 10, "Ketubbah," p. 926.

5. See M. Chigier, *Husband and Wife in Israeli Law* (Jerusalem: Harry Fischel Institute for Research in Talmud and Jurisprudence, 1985) p. 159, n. 15, and by the same author, "The Widow's Rights in Jewish and Israeli Law," *Jewish Law Annual* 5 (1985): 44, 48, n. 34.

6. Rabbi Eleazar was a third generation Palestinian Amora, who flourished in the latter half of the third century C.E. His saying is found at B. Gittin 90b.

7. D. W. Amram, supra, n. 1, ch. 7, p. 79, points out that according to an ancient tradition the greatest glory of Aaron, the high priest, was his work in reconciling discontented husbands and wives, inducing them to live in harmony.

8. See B. Ketubbot 11a: "What is the reason for the *Ketubbah?* So that it shall not appear easy to divorce her." For further discussion see Haut, supra, n. 1, p. 7; Amram, supra, n. 1., p. 114; *Encyclopedia Judaica*, supra, n. 4.

9. Haut, supra, n. 1, pp. 20–21.

10. Shammai was a Tanna who flourished in the second half of the first century B.C.E. and the first half of the first century C.E. Hillel was a Tanna who was a contemporary of Shammai. Their disagreement is found in Mishnah Gittin 9:10. See Amram, supra, n. 1, pp. 32–33:

> The school of Shammai interpreted nearly all the Biblical laws strictly and rigorously. They were, to use a term applied to certain interpreters of the Constitution of the United States, Strict Constructionists; they held that a man cannot divorce his wife unless he has found her guilty of sexual immorality. . . . They held that these words (Hebrew, *ervath dabar;* literally, "the nakedness of the matter") signified immorality; and that the old law recognized this as the only legitimate cause for divorce.

11. For further discussion, see B. Gittin 90a.

12. B. Gittin 2a, Tosafot (beginning with the words, *hamayve get*).

13. Haut, supra, n. 1, ch. 6, pp. 27–30.

14. B. Kiddushin 6a.

15. Haut, supra, n. 1, ch. 7, pp. 31–41.

16. Ibid. ch. 4, pp. 18–19.

17. Ibid. p. 20.

18. Ibid. ch. 5, p. 25.

19. For further discussion, see Haut, supra, n. 1, p. 20, and, particularly, n. 18.

20. See generally, Haut, supra, n. 1, ch. 5, pp. 23–24. See Mishnah Erchin 5:6, "and the same rule applies in the case of divorce, we apply coercion, until he [the husband] says I agree [to give the *get*]."

21. See Maimonides, Mishneh Torah, "Laws of Divorce" 2:20.

22. See generally, J. J. Rabinowitz, *Jewish Law—Its Influence on the Development of Legal Institutions* (New York: Bloch, 1956), pp. 6–7 and chs. 5–6. Lipinski, supra, n. 3, pp. 20–21, suggests that there existed an ancient semitic tradition of law, manifested in the marriage contracts of the Jewish military colony in Elephantine, dating to the 5th century B.C.E., pursuant to which there was equality between the spouses as regards divorce. See Riskin, supra, n. 3, pp. 29–32, who takes the existence of such tradition in Elephantine as reflecting a continuing tradition to the talmudic period in Palestine, pursuant to which the wife was entitled to initiate divorce proceedings, presumably on the basis of a provision in her *ketubbah* to such effect. In such regard, he cites two discussions in the Palestinian Talmud, which appear to approve of such practice, at Ketubbot 5:9. He also points out that such tradition extended to the beginning of the medieval period, as reflected in the findings from the Cairo Genizah. See ibid, ch. 5.

23. See generally, Riskin, supra, n. 3; Haut, supra, n. 1, ch. 9 and, particularly, pp. 51–52; Haut, *Tradition*, supra, n. 2, pp. 36–37.

24. The responsa quoted in the text at this endnote is quoted in full in Haut, supra, n. 1, p. 51, from C. Tykocinski, Tekanot Ha'geonim (New York: Sura, Jerusalem and Yeshiva U., 1960), ch. 1. These "dreadful consequences" consist of the fact that if the wife remarries on the basis of a coerced, and hence, invalid *get*, any children born of that union are deemed illegitimate, with serious disabilities under Jewish law.

25. See Responsa of Rabbenu Asher (Asher ben Yechiel, 1250–1327 C.E.), no. 43, subd. 8, who opposes the subject enactment but acknowledges, nonetheless, that it is properly based on the theory that all who wed do so in accordance with the will of the Rabbis and that the Geonic Rabbis, therefore, acted within their power in annulling a marriage in which the wife wanted a divorce. For further discussion, see, Riskin, supra, n. 3, ch. 4.

26. Maimonides, Mishneh Torah, "Laws of Ishut" 14:14.

27. Id. at 14:8.

28. Haut, supra, n. 1, pp. 51–52; Haut, *Tradition*, supra, n. 2, pp. 37–38.

29. Rabbenu Gershom is also well known for his enactment prohibiting polygamy. It is interesting to note that unlike the prohibition of polygamy, which

was not accepted by Oriental communities, the prohibition of divorce against the will of the wife was universally accepted. See B. Schereschewsky, *Family Law in Israel* (Jerusalem: R. Mass, 1974), p. 323; Y. Epstein, Aruch ha'-shulchan (*even ha'ezer*), vol. 6, 119:14; Haut, supra, n. 1, p. 55, n. 31.

30. Responsa, supra, n. 25, no. 42, subd. 1.

31. Haut, supra, n. 1, ch. 10, pp. 59–61.

32. See Haut, supra, n. 1, p. 56 and n. 33, for discussion of circumstances wherein the husband may avoid the application of the subject rule of Rabbenu Gershom, such as where the wife is declared to be "rebellious," by recourse to the *bet din,* or by means of permission obtained from one hundred rabbis.

33. See Haut, supra, n. 1, p. 13; Haut, supra, n. 2, *Tradition,* Appendix.

34. See Haut, supra, n. 1, ch. 11, pp. 63–65.

35. Quoted from A. Leo Levin and Meyer Kramer, *New Provisions in the Ketubah: A Legal Opinion* (New York: Yeshiva University, 1955), p. 2.

36. 58 N.Y.2d 108, 459 N.Y.S.2d 572, 446 N.E.2d 136 (1983). For further discussion of the decision in that case, see Haut, supra, n. 1, pp. 77–80.

37. On prenuptial agreements generally, see Haut, *ibid,* ch. 15, pp. 98–99.

38. Domestic Relations Law §253, enacted by Laws of 1983, ch. 979, §1, eff. August 8, 1983. For Canadian statute, see R.S., c.3, 27 (2d supp.).

39. Haut, supra, n. 1; Haut, *Tradition,* supra, n. 2. It is unfortunate that in his otherwise fine work of scholarship, Riskin, supra, n. 3, after detailing the brilliant contributions by the Geonim to this area of law, and after fully supporting and justifying their *takkanah,* refrained from advocating reenactment of the like type of *takkanah* called for by this writer. Instead he suggests a prenuptial agreement, which is far less effective. See ibid, p. 140.

SUGGESTIONS FOR FURTHER READING

Encyclopedia Judaica (Jerusalem: Keter Publishing House, Ltd., 1973), 6:136–137 ("Divorce").

E. Lipinski, *The Wife's Right to Divorce in the Light of an Ancient Near Eastern Tradition,* vol. 4, *Jewish Law Annual,* p. 9.

I. H. Haut, *Divorce in Jewish Law and Life* (New York: Sepher-Hermon Press, 1983), App. A and Bibliography.

D. W. Amram, *The Jewish Law of Divorce According to Jewish Law and Talmud,* 2d ed. (New York: Hermon Press, 1968), a pioneering work in English by a noted and respected legal scholar, is a good introduction to the subject.

S. Riskin, *Women and Jewish Divorce* (Hoboken, N.J.: Ktav, 1989), is a scholarly book detailing the brilliant contributions by early rabbis, the Geonim, in this area.

NAHUM M. WALDMAN

Bikkur Ḥolim

Sickness in Jewish Law

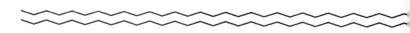

Illness is an ever-present reality at all stages in the human life cycle, from temporary indispositions to chronic
conditions to life-threatening illness. Sickness is only
one of the factors that can shorten life; war, violence,
and accidents are others. While there is no guaranteed
number of years, we do have statistics which indicate
that a certain life expectancy is usual in contemporary
circumstances. We are also the beneficiaries of significant advances in medical science that have increased life
expectancy and give us grounds for optimism. Still, diseases remain that afflict young and old and for which no
cure is currently known. Under these circumstances,
advanced medical technology may add years of active
and meaningful life, may maintain the status quo, or
may prolong the agony of dying.

Understanding the appropriate response to these complex situations in the light of Jewish law and ethics is the
goal of this chapter. Jewish law, halakhah, contains
teachings that deal with the sanctity-of-life obligations
of the physician, the right to take risks, and the length of
treatment. Some of these questions are answered directly, while the answers to others must be deduced and
inferred. Although Jewish law relating to the bioethical
sphere (and many other areas) is not binding, the moral
values embodied in it provide an illuminating guide to
our personal conscience and actions.

Illness and Death in Classical Jewish Sources

The Bible views illness as something sent by God, either as punishment for sin or as a trial of one who has not sinned. Thus, terminal illness may be the result of God's anger. On the other hand, when the righteous die, illness and death are viewed as unavoidable aspects of natural human life. Thus Jacob (Genesis 48:1) and Elisha (2 Kings 13:14) arrive at their final illness, and no sin is attributed to them. Against Rav Ammi's pronouncement that there is no death or suffering without sin as a cause, the Talmud cites several cases of the death of righteous individuals and concludes that death and suffering may occur without personal sin. These righteous people are said to have died because of the "counsel of the serpent," that is, because of the condition of mortality imposed on human beings as a result of the sin of Adam and Eve, which was instigated by the serpent (B. Shabbat 55a–b). Yet God does promise illness as a punishment for violation of the covenant (Deuteronomy 28:59–61), and the removal of illness (but not of death) as a reward for obedience (Exodus 15:26; Deuteronomy 7:15).

In biblical times an afflicted person would seek out God to inquire if he or she would live. For example, the wife of Jeroboam came in disguise to the prophet Ahiyah of Shilo to inquire if her son, Abiyah, would live. She was told that because of the sins of his father, Jeroboam, Abiyah was doomed by God to die. Ahaziah, the son of Ahab, sought out the pagan god Ba'al Zebub in Ekron (Philistia), to the wrath of Elijah and to his own detriment.

How relevant are these biblical and talmudic views to the modern person? The idea that illness and death are punishments for one's own sins or those of others is still held by many people. However, when an attempt is made to match the suffering with the alleged sin, there is often a great discrepancy, raising the painful question of theodicy—the attempt to justify God's ways. A most eloquent ancient rejection of the correlation between sin and illness is found in the book of Job. Rabbi Harold Kushner, in *When Bad Things Happen to Good People*, has written movingly about the distortions that arise when people begin to blame themselves for the death of a loved one. We cannot offer any conclusive statement here. Humans are themselves responsible for illnesses that come about through self-destructive eating, drinking, and substance abuse. On the other hand, there is no way to connect congenital heart defects and cancer with sin. We have to take into account human frailty and vulnerability, the fact that our bodies, remarkable as they are, are subject to attacks by viruses and germs, to hereditary conditions, and to systemic malfunctions. This is part of the human condition, as is the inadequacy of our knowledge.

Visiting the Sick

The custom of visiting the sick is portrayed explicitly in the Bible. The Psalmist laments that his friends do not reciprocate the concern he showed for them in their illness: "Yet, when they were ill, my dress was sackcloth; I kept a fast—may what I prayed for happen to me. I walked about as if it were my friend or my brother; I was bowed with gloom, like one mourning for his mother" (Psalm 35:13–14). The terminally ill Aramean king Ben-Hadad, apprised that Elisha the prophet has come to Damascus, sends his general Ḥazael to inquire of the Lord if he will live. The very contemporary issue of telling the whole truth to the patient is raised in this story. When the king's question is transmitted by Ḥazael, Elisha responds: "Go and say to him 'You will recover.' However, the Lord has revealed to me that he will die" (2 Kings 8:7–10). Elisha chose to spare the dying patient the grim truth. Various views on the question of full disclosure will be considered later in this chapter.

In the Bible there is an example of a visit to one both ill and a mourner when Job's three friends come to console him after he has lost his wealth and his family and has been afflicted with boils all over his body. The friends are not overly supportive, because they and Job become involved in a theological dispute. They answer Job's protestations about his righteousness (and God's injustice) by accusing him or his dead children of wrongdoing. They expound and defend the traditional connection between human suffering and Divine punishment, while Job denies this connection. The friends' insensitivity is recognized by the rabbis of a later generation, who condemn them for waving Job's alleged sins in his face. They are guilty of oppression by words, which includes saying to one who is suffering illness or bereavement what Eliphaz, Job's friend, said to him: "Think now, what innocent man ever perished; where have the upright been destroyed?" (Job 4:7; B. Bava Metziah 58b).

Rabbinic literature reflects an expansion of these concerns and precepts. Visiting the sick is declared a positive commandment, or mitzvah. It is one of the acts of love and mercy called *gemilut ḥasadim*, said to be practiced by God Himself, who visited Abraham when he was ill, recuperating from his circumcision (B. Sotah 14a). Yet because the feelings of the patient must be considered, they place limitations on this commandment. The patient may be embarrassed if people, not as close as family and intimate friends, see him or her in pain, discomfort, or disarray. Thus, it is suggested that those closest come to visit on the first day of the illness, while those who are distant wait until the third day. If, however, the progress of the illness is swift—"jumped upon him" (*kafatz 'alaw*)—they all may visit on the first day (J. Pe'ah, 3.7). In this connection the dignity of the patient is further considered. The text states that we do not enter the room of a patient who has intestinal problems, lest it cause embarrassment, or one who has pain in the eye or severe headaches, because the exertion of trying to speak may affect his or her condition. In the case of one who is confused and finds speech difficult, the visitors should remain in the outer room and inquire what services are needed. They should also be supportive, listening to the patient's expressions of distress and praying on his or her behalf. Visiting the sick is described as an awesome experience, perhaps because of the potential danger, but also, as the Talmud puts it, because the *Shekhinah* (the Divine presence) hovers over the patient's head, supporting him or her on the sickbed (B. Shabbat 12b; Yoreh De'ah 335; B. Nedarim 48a; Naḥmanides, *Torat Ha-'Adam*).[1]

Differences in social status between the visitor and the patient must not interfere with the visit: no one is too important to visit, and no one so unimportant as to justify not being visited (Yoreh De'ah 335:2). It is told of Rabbi Akiba that the sages neglected to visit one of his ill students. Akiba thereupon went himself and attended to the details of cleaning the house. The grateful student said to him, "My master, you have given me life." On the basis of this experience Akiba taught publicly that whoever does not visit the sick is one who sheds blood (B. Nedarim 40a). But what if visiting the sick might be dangerous for the visitor?

Contagious Diseases and Self-Preservation

The issue of visiting people with contagious diseases is raised in the halakhah, along with the physician's fear of being infected and the question of withdrawal from the case. These issues are relevant in the current atmosphere of heightened apprehension about contracting AIDS, a concern very strong among the medical profession. One survey of medical school graduates found that 25 percent did not want to treat AIDS patients because of the risks involved. (HIV-positive blood can, for instance, spurt out against the broken skin or mucous membranes of the eyes of the medical personnel.) Another nationwide study of internists and family care physicians revealed that 32 percent did not agree that they had a responsibility to treat people with AIDS, and 50 percent said they would not work with AIDS patients if given a choice. One doctor, who recently resigned her position as chief of orthopedic surgery at San Francisco General Hospital, equipped her surgical team with protective gear that included double shoe covers, knee-high boots, disposable reinforced gowns, additional sleeve covers, double or triple latex gloves, and a "spacesuit" helmet complete with its own filter system. AIDS activists and other physicians, however, consider this position extreme. (The fear of contamination, moreover, is not limited to the medical profession. The death of Kimberly Bergalis, who contracted AIDS from her dentist, has led to the controversial demand that physicians and dentists who have tested HIV-positive be required by law to disclose their condition.)[2]

In view of this controversy within the medical profession, whose members are morally and professionally committed to help the sick, what is a reasonable way for visitors and medical personnel to balance two halakhic concerns: self-preservation and helping the patient? Do visitors dressed in a kind of "spacesuit" armor increase the pain of isolation and rejection that the dying AIDS patient feels? A doctor's visit and the method of medical care must never ignore the dimension of psychological support, which is essential to the patient's will to recover. Moreover, halakhah does not allow the physician to be indifferent, ruling that any physician who has the requisite knowledge must accept the case. One who abstains is a shedder of blood (Naḥmanides, *Torat Ha-Adam*).[3] But then there is the question of how much danger we are obligated or permitted to expose ourselves to and—an emotionally charged subject—how much objective danger in fact exists in visiting and treating an AIDS patient.

The extent to which one *must* (obligation) or *may* (option) put oneself into a dangerous situation in order to save another has not been fully resolved in halakhic sources. One view is that if there is any chance of healing the patient, who will die if not attended to, one must expose him- or herself to a possible (but not certain) risk and provide proper care. This is a classic instance of the rabbinic principle *bari ve-shemma*, "certain versus uncertain": it is certain that the patient will die if left without care, though it is not certain that the caretaker will contract the disease. This idea is justified by a passage in the Jerusalem Talmud, which states that one must bring oneself into possible danger to counteract the certain death of one's neighbor. The codes of law, however, lead to an opposite conclusion.[4] Thus it is conceivable that the halakhah can justify a doctor's refusal to treat a patient with a severely contagious disease; at least, he may claim this right if there is no hope for the patient's recovery. Joseph Caro, however, in a responsum, states that if one refuses to visit the sick, using contagion as the reason, one is only reflecting one's own fear, not the attitude of the halakhah, for "God is the healer." This attitude of fear, says Caro, would break down the entire distinction between contagious and noncontagious diseases with regard to the obligation of visiting. If this is so for the visitor, it is must be no less so for the physician, who is commanded to heal (*ve-rappo' yerappe'*: Exodus 21:19; Yoreh De'ah 336:1). In the case of AIDS, then, where contagion is possible only under limited, specific conditions that can be avoided when all precautions have been taken (in a way that does not humiliate the patient), health care and visitation should take place.[5]

Prayer as a Life Support

Jewish tradition views it as natural and appropriate that sick persons and those who love them pray on their behalf. One reason for visiting, apart from the invaluable psychological and physical assistance that it gives ("Whoever visits the sick takes away one-sixtieth of his pain": B. Nedarim 39b), is so that prayers will be offered. A talmudic story emphasizes that prayer always serves a purpose. King Hezekiah, after being told by the prophet Isaiah that he would die, prayed with fervor to God and was then told he would live (2 Kings 20:1–6; Isaiah 38:1–5). His healing was the result of his sincere prayer. Because Hezekiah was afflicted, it was the prophet's duty to visit him. Isaiah, however, was rebuked by Hezekiah for unequivocally predicting his death, for prayer is always appropriate: "Even if a sword is raised over one's neck he must not refrain from asking for God's mercy" (B. Berakhot 10a). We are also told in the Talmud that the timing of visits has a relationship to prayer. Visits should not take place in the first three hours of the day, for the patient's temperature is down in the morning and the visitor may think that he or she is not sick enough to require prayers. Visits should also not take place during the last three hours of the day, the late afternoon, because then the patient's temperature and discomfort increase and the visitor may become alarmed and think the patient beyond all prayer (Yoreh De'ah 335:4).

The role of prayer with regard to the terminally ill is seen as consisting of two options: praying for life and praying for death. A talmudic source states: "Whoever does not visit the sick fails to pray for God's mercy that the patient live or die" (B. Nedarim 40a). This strange statement, implying that it might be a positive good to pray that the patient die, is clarified by Rabbenu Nissim Gerondi, who flourished between 1340 and 1380 and who says, "There are times when one must pray for the mercy of the patient's death, as when he is in great pain and cannot go on living" (B. Nedarim 40a). Rabbi Ḥaim Palaggi of Smyrna (ca. 1800), in his book *Hikekei Lev* (vol. 1, no. 50), ruled that family members may pray for the death of one who is dying and in great pain. Palaggi makes a further, very astute observation—that there may be selfishness in their prayer, in that they may be seeking to be relieved of the burden of caring for the patient. Generally, he states, it is preferable that non–family members pray for the sufferer's death.

A classic passage concerning a conflict between prayer for life on behalf of the dying and an act meant to hasten death is found in the story of Rabbi Judah the Patriarch (B. Ketubbot 104a). On the day of his death, the sages decreed a fast and engaged in continuous prayer. His maid went up to the roof and said, "The angels above and humans on earth are contending for Rabbi's soul. May it be God's wish that those on earth prevail." However, when she saw how much pain he suffered, so frequently having to remove his tefillin (phylacteries) to enter the lavatory, she said, "May it be God's will that the angels above overcome the humans below." The rabbis, however, did not stop praying. The maid then took a jar and threw it down from the roof. The noise it made upon impact startled the rabbis and they momentarily stopped praying. Rabbi Judah then died. This story implies that prayer, by the appropriate people, can support life.

What does all this mean to a modern person? There is certainly an important role for prayer, whether one conceives of God in personal or impersonal terms. Prayer can bring about an emotional release and the regrouping of energies needed to face a crisis. It puts the entire situation in a broader perspective, enabling one to relate a personal nightmare to the human condition, shared by so many others. Prayer not only asks for healing but prepares one for the possibility that the request may not be granted. When the patient knows that prayers are being offered on her or his behalf, the very knowledge that other people care affords strength. While many people today, as in ancient times, believe in the unfailing objective efficacy of the prayers of their spiritual leaders or healers, we offer the opinion that prayer is a life-uplifting plea and a powerful statement of one's deepest values and concerns. We do not expect that prayer will act as an autonomous force guaranteeing recovery.

The Role of the Physician

The role of the physician is alluded to in Exodus 21:19, where one who has committed assault and battery upon an individual must pay for his forced idleness from work and his cure (ve-rappo' yerappe').[6] In the Bible the prophet Isaiah prescribes a treatment for Hezekiah's boils (Isaiah 38:21). However, there is an opposing view. King Asa is condemned for seeking out the physician rather than God in his illness (2 Chronicles 16:12). Rabbinic interpretation broadened the discussion of the role of the physician. The Mishnah informs us that Hezekiah concealed the Book of Healing (Sefer Refu'ot) and that the sages agreed with his action (Mishnah Pesaḥim 4:9). Rashi explains that Hezekiah feared that the people would consult the Book of Healing, be immediately cursed, and therefore would not be humbled before God. On the other hand, Maimonides disagrees, in view of the tradition that the services of the physician in no way contradict trust in and gratitude to God. He argues that just as when one is cured of hunger by eating food he thanks God for the food, so will he thank God if medicine prescribed in a handbook results in healing.[7] What is significant in Maimonides' attitude is that in his view scientific medical practice in no way diminishes a person's faith in God (Maimonides, Commentary on the Mishnah, Pesahim 4:9).

The laws of the physician were collected by Naḥmanides (*Torat Ha-Adam*)[8] and summarized in the Shulḥan Arukh (Yoreh De'ah, 336). It is understood by these classic texts that not only is permission given to the doctor to heal but that he or she is obligated to do so. The physician who refuses to deal with a patient is guilty of violating the principle that "you shall not stand idly by the blood of your fellow" (Leviticus 19:16) and is one who "sheds blood." Even if there is another doctor already on the case, a physician should not refuse to provide services because "one does not become healed from everyone," meaning that one physician may not have the cure but another might. The "permission" implied by *ve-rappo' yerappe'* is intended to protect from prosecution the physician who makes an honest, unintentional mistake. The obligation extracted from that verse prevents him or her from abandoning the case (or medicine itself) because of fear of being accused of malpractice. The contemporary situation of physicians in America might fruitfully be viewed in this light, with the physician compared to a judge (*dayyan*), who "has only what his eyes can see": that is, he cannot be held guilty for judging erroneously on the basis of the best information available to him.

The physician must be competent, must defer to a medical authority higher than him- or herself, and may function only with the permission of the *bet din*, the court. If the physician did not obtain such authorization and harmed the patient, he or she must pay damages, but if the physician did obtain such authorization and erred, no damages are imposed by a human court, but he or she "is guilty under the laws of heaven." If, however, while working under authorization, a doctor willfully hurts the patient, he or she is responsible for all damages. Finally, if a physician unintentionally caused a patient's death, he or she must, like an unintentional killer, flee to a city of refuge, there to be safe from harm.[9]

From these regulations it is evident that in Jewish law the physician is regarded as important, a kind of community leader, but one who is subject to the authority of the community and the law. This position, in which the extremes of low status and unquestioned authority are eschewed, is important for establishing norms regarding the physician's role in society. After all, the physician will have to deal with the difficult questions of whether or not to treat, whether to fight aggressively for an extension of life or to decide not to interfere with the natural process of dying.

The concept of respect for the physician and the concomitant limitation of his or her authority is exemplified by the discussion of whether a sick person may eat on Yom Kippur. According to Jewish law, if an expert physician states that, by not eating, a patient's condition may worsen, but the patient claims that she does not need to eat, the physician's view prevails and the sick person must eat. On the other hand, if the sick person insists that she must eat and even one hundred doctors say that she need not, or even that the food may harm her, the patient must eat. If two doctors say that the patient must eat, while the patient herself and one hundred doctors say that she does not need to, she must eat (Oraḥ Ḥayyim 618 and Ba'er Hetev).

Does it matter if a physician is Jewish or not? The Talmud recognizes situations where the services of a pagan, even hostile physician must be used if the patient will die without this help, though in other situations such services are to be avoided (Avodah Zarah 27b; Yoreh De'ah 155). These laws reflect the intercommunal hostilities before and after the Jewish revolt against the Romans, in 66 and 131 C.E. They do not apply in modern times and to enlightened nations. Certainly today one may turn to a physician of any origin when there is harmony and trust.

When Parents Are Patients

In many cases the patients with whose rights and well-being we are concerned are our parents. What additional halakhic guidance is offered in this case? One question concerns the behavior of a son or daughter who is a physician. Since there is a halakhic prohibition against wounding or bruising a parent, may the physician draw blood from or operate on a parent? In fact, one who performs such an operation is not liable for punishment; nevertheless, it is forbidden to do so, even if only to remove a thorn from the parent, unless there is no one else to perform the procedure and the parent is in pain (Maimonides, *Hilkhot Mamrim* 5:7).

Another issue concerns how much of the burden of caring physically and financially for a parent a grown child must take on. The general law of honoring one's father or mother ordains that one's parents must be provided with food, drink, clothing, and shelter, though from the resources of the parents. If they have no resources but the son or unmarried or divorced daughter (who is not subject to the will of her husband) does, these children can be compelled by the court to pay for the parent's care. If the child does not have resources, he or she is not obligated to become impoverished ("to beg at the doors") to support the parent. Such a child is, however, still obligated to honor the parent with physical services, even if this means absence from work, financial loss, and begging. (This demand is imposed only if the child has food for one day or more. In extreme poverty children have no obligation to honor their parents by missing work or having to beg.) Further opinions allow sons or daughters to limit their support of the parent to the amount of their standard charity contribution (treating the parent as the recipient of that charity), but if the child does have the resources it is said, "May a curse be imposed for limiting support for the parents to the standard charity allocation." A further ruling is that if there are both rich and poor children, only the rich ones are obligated to contribute to the parent's support. Even an illegitimate child (born from incest or adultery) is subject to these obligations toward the parent (Maimonides, *Hilkhot Mamrim* 6:3, 11; Yoreh De'ah 240:5; Isserles gloss, ibid.; Pithei Teshuvah and Ba'er Hetev, ibid.).

One may ask what the halakhah would require today of children if their parents did not have medical insurance. Would they be obligated to pay the high costs of hospitalization or mortgage their home for this purpose? Or would such an action mean impoverishment for them, which might exempt them? How does one define "poverty level" amid the confusions and contradictions of our society? Would it have to be as severe as going begging in the streets? Must one be homeless, on welfare or food stamps, or would a less stringent definition of economic hardship suffice to relieve the child of obligation? Of course, since in our social and political milieu there are no *batei din* (courts) with the authority to impose halakhic obligations and no common agreement on the authority of the halakhah, we are considering the Jewish legal norms as a voluntarily accepted guide to our consciences.[10]

Limits on the child's ability to cope with certain situations should also be considered. The halakhah demands great honor and patience from the child toward the parent. One talmudic example states that if the parent took a bag of cold coins and threw them into the sea, the child must not rebuke or embarrass him or her. A gloss by Moses Isserles introduces a limitation, somewhat strengthening the child's position: it states that the child may prevent the parent from throwing money away if it belongs to the child, and if it cannot be prevented, he or she may sue the parent in court for that sum of money. Throwing money away is a sign of dementia; if the parent becomes insane, the child must try to cope with the situation until "mercy is shown from heaven." If, however, the child cannot cope, he or she may leave and charge others to take proper care of the parent.[11] This ruling has yielded a framework for dealing with a variety of mental dysfunctions, such as dementia and Alzheimer's disease. Maimonides is not referring necessarily to actual physical flight from a parent. His ruling could be interpreted as justifying a certain measure of responsible detachment. Children may turn over the care of the parent to others, letting go of that burden and, it is hoped, of their guilt feelings. By appointing others to take charge of their parents and perform certain services, however, the children do not remove themselves from visiting and helping their parents and from supervising the care being provided.

The Terminal Patient: To Tell or Not to Tell

Rabbinic sources deal with the question of how to relate to the terminal patient. This involves (1) the patient and family members accepting the reality and finality of approaching death and (2) the question of whether to tell the patient the full truth. These sources have also been invoked for guidance in making a decision on terminating treatment. Prayers for recovery, discussed above, have been equated by some with modern life support systems. Praying that one should die involves the recognition that continued life under severe pain is not always the best thing for the patient. In certain situations death is a welcome release, and the patient's family and friends, together with the health professionals, must revise their normal commitment to healing and survival.

Different views exist on the degree of honesty that is demanded in the terminal situation. These are located on a spectrum which runs from the idea that truth is a supreme value and that openly sharing it with the patient acknowledges his or her dignity and autonomy, to a more paternalistic approach in which the doctor seeks to protect the patient from life-destroying depression and despair. Well-known proponents of the view favoring full disclosure are Elisabeth Kübler-Ross and Sissela Bok.[12]

Kübler-Ross, basing her conclusions on interviews with dying patients and on seminars with health personnel, recognizes five stages in the attitudes of the terminally ill: denial, anger, bargaining, depression, and acceptance. These stages should be understood by the caring professional, who should strive to keep avenues of communication open. Denial, for example, may result in part from inadequately prepared and abruptly given information. In the harried and impersonal world of hospitals, the loneliness, fear, and frustration of terminally ill patients often goes unrecognized. The medical profession is itself uncomfortable in the face of death. The refusal of many doctors to reveal the truth about an incurable disease to a patient they consider emotionally unstable and "unable to face it" is not only a paternalistic approach ("we know better than you what is good for you"); it also reflects their own anxiety about death.

Kübler-Ross states that the right question is never "Should we tell?" but rather "How do I share this with my patient?" The doctor should never present the reality as hopeless and should never give a concrete timetable ("You have six months to live") or fail to offer the hope of new drugs or treatments. Of course, some patients will practice denial anyway, but the doctor will have done her or his duty by telling the truth. Very often, patients sense the truth anyway, and they must be able to progress through the various stages and make arrangements for their last days. By making these arrangements they regain some control over their lives.

Sissela Bok approaches the question of telling the truth in various life-threatening situations from a moral point of view. With respect to the doctor-patient relationship, she notes that the Hippocratic oath and various declarations of principles by medical associations obligate physicians to do all they can for their patients, but telling the full truth remains within the physician's discretion. Paternalistic attitudes, justified on grounds of concern for what is best for the patient, may easily turn into attitudes of contempt for the patient's alleged lack of comprehension. Then patients are deprived of the opportunity to face death, to consider its ramifications for themselves, and for them and their family to make plans. Today there is more emphasis on a patient's "Bill of Rights" and less tolerance of the old paternalism. Civil law now requires that any inroads made on the patient's body be preceded by full disclosure and informed consent.

The halakhic view is located somewhere between full disclosure and paternalistic protection. Jewish law recognizes the importance of settling one's affairs, and the sick person is told to do so—to call in loans or repay them, to make an ethical will, and not to fear that death is imminent merely because final preparations are being made (Yoreh De'ah 335:7). When the patient does take a turn for the worse (*natah lamut:* "inclines toward death")—or simply, as Ma'avar Yabbok, a collection of prayers for before and after death, puts it, "there is a great change"—she or he is told to make confession (*viddui*). As this directive can be very frightening and depressing, reassurance is given that many people have confessed and not died, while many have died before they had a chance to confess.

The minimum prescribed confession is "May my death be atonement for all my sins"; the recommended text, however, is "I thank You, O Lord my God and God of my ancestors, that my healing and death are in Your hands. May it be Your will to give me a full recovery. But if I die may my death be atonement for unintentional sins, transgressions, and rebellious acts which I have sinned, transgressed, and rebelled before You. May my rest be in the Garden of Eden, and may I be worthy of the world to come, which is hidden for the righteous" (Yoreh De'ah 338: 1–2). Another suggestion for a minimum is "The Lord God is true, His Torah is truth, and Moses His prophet is true. Blessed be the name of His glorious kingdom forever" (Y. Greenwald, *Kol Bo 'Al 'Avelut*, 22). These deathbed confessionals can be expanded in various ways, by drawing upon the Yom Kippur liturgy.

Clearly, instructions to set affairs in order and to confess are a means of providing disclosure without inducing hopelessness. They are not consistent with a paternalistic concealment of the truth from those who "can't handle it." On the other hand, there must be consideration for the sensitivity and frail condition of a patient. We noted above that the prophets Elisha and Isaiah used two different approaches, the first not telling the dying king that he would die and the second saying it so bluntly and abruptly that later sages took him to task. Support for the former approach is the halakhic position that a patient who has suffered the loss of a family member not be informed lest his or her mind become unhinged (*shemma' tittaref da'ato*) and recovery undermined (B. Mo'ed Katan 26b). Rabbi J. David Bleich, a leading Orthodox decisor, offers a paraphrase that is really an extension: "lest it hasten the patient's own demise." He rejects Kübler-Ross's advocacy of total disclosure, being concerned for the vulnerability of certain patients. He cites examples of "voodoo death," when individuals have died because they believed themselves doomed, as well as the experiences of soldiers under battle conditions, who die from no apparent cause. Bleich also advocates that the physician always hold out hope for the patient and never present him or her with an absolute, hopeless diagnosis.

We have a historical example of such sensitivity in the practice of one Jewish community: that in nineteenth-century Berlin. The officers of the *hevra kadisha,* the burial society, made it their practice to call on all sick people on the third day of their illness. Knowing that their visit could easily frighten patients into believing that the end was imminent, society members would tell the patients that they visited each sick person as a matter of routine, no matter how serious the illness; then they would hold a discussion of all the relevant items in the Shulḥan Arukh, the code of Jewish law. [13]

The difference between the partly paternalistic halakhic position of Bleich and the views of the autonomists, Bok and Kübler-Ross, rests in the authority given or denied the physician to make the final judgment about full disclosure. To Bleich authority really resides not in the physician but in the Torah. All these scholars agree, however, that the patient must never be denied a ray of hope and should have the opportunity to take control of personal affairs. Here the Jewish tradition of writing or delivering an ethical will to one's family becomes relevant, and indeed, many beautiful and moving modern examples have taken their places alongside the historic legacy.[14]

Experimental Treatments and Taking Risks

Precisely when treatment, in the sense of pursuit of a cure or of more time to live, ends and maintenance care for the dying begins is a difficult and hotly debated issue. The answers offered often reflect emotional responses to death and personal philosophy or theology. There is, for example, the matter of who should have the final say about the person: do we humans have the right of choice and control over our final days, or are our lives and bodies lent to us by God, who owns them and has the ultimate say (mediated by the Torah or the church)? The first position would endorse living wills and the right of the patient to stop treatment. The second view would reject the living will and insist on treatment until it is no longer possible, rejecting even passive euthanasia.

Taking a risk with an experimental treatment is relevant both to the terminal patient and to a person who is impaired in function. The halakhah develops its position on risky procedures through consideration of *ḥayye sha'ah*, life that is available at the moment. The classic discussion concerns a person who has been buried under a fallen building. Rescuers must dig and get the person out, even on a sacred day such as Sabbath or Yom Kippur, which is ruled to be of secondary importance. Even if there is a doubt about whether the person is alive or dead, or if the person has only a brief time to live (*ḥayye sha'ah*), the rescue efforts must continue (B. Yoma 85a). In short, everything must be done to preserve what brief life is present. This conclusion is also used to justify the maximalist position of not stopping treatment before the irreversible turn toward death has begun. However, the Talmud also articulates the position that a patient has the right to risk his *ḥayye sha'ah*, the brief life at hand, by trying a treatment or medication that may lengthen his life, but may cut it even shorter (Avodah Zarah 27b).

The element of risk in experimental procedures is recognized as ever-present. Nachmanides (Torat Ha-Adam) says: "With regard to cures there is naught but danger; what heals one kills another."[15] Taking medical risks generally has been liberally interpreted, but as an option, not an obligation.[16]

Is there an optimal ration of benefit and risk, a necessary probability of success? Generally, a sick person is permitted to submit even to serious surgery or dangerous medication in the hope of a cure.[17] The critical factor limiting the autonomy of the patient in a risky procedure is the concept of *refu'ah bedukah*, or "proven cure"—that is, a therapeutic procedure of "known efficiency." This concept was introduced into the discussion by Rabbi Jacob Emden (1697–1776), and, following his lead, J. David Bleich goes to an extreme in insisting that no one has the right to refuse a "proven cure." He equates such a refusal not only with passive euthanasia, which others allow but he rejects, but also with active euthanasia, which all halakhic authorities reject.[18] Another contemporary quasi-paternalistic view is that of Rabbi Moshe Feinstein. Dangerous therapy, in his opinion, may be undertaken if the chances for success are 50 percent, but if they are over 50 percent it is obligatory for a physician to administer the treatment or medication and for the patient (or, if incompetent, his or her family) to accept it. Rabbis Feinstein and Bleich not only seek to set certain limits to the risk and benefit factors; they also seek to make the "certain cure" obligatory upon the patient, family, and doctor. When there is uncertainty, however, the patient's choice again becomes operative. Rabbi Feinstein states that if the physicians are not sure what the chances are, the decision must be left up to the patient.[19]

Other contemporary approaches to this issue are those of Rabbis Elliot N. Dorff and Avram Israel Reisner, who follow the Conservative ideology. The first states that a high-risk procedure may be used, but the decision to employ it must be justified in terms of the benefit the patient may be expected to gain if it works. Neither the doctor nor the patient may elect the procedure on the basis of "one chance in a million" or "What do I have to lose?" reasoning.[20] Reisner's position is similar, but with some limitation of autonomy. No patient is required to undergo significant risk if an alternative treatment exists or if the efficacy of the proposed treatment is in doubt. The patient's own judgment whether to undergo risk is determinative unless medical certainty regarding the efficacy and low risk of a treatment is exceedingly high and the patient's objection is clearly irrational or suicidal. Patient autonomy, says Reisner, does not reach as far as the secular ethicists have proposed, but in

Jewish law it does control most of the significant decisions that must be made when treating the critically ill.[21]

While the difference among these approaches—one stressing aggressive treatment, another attempting to define the obligations of the patient in terms of percentages for success, and still others allowing for a high measure of patient autonomy—are clear, there are also similarities among them. For example, in the case of heart bypass surgery, which is common and has a high rate of success, all the different halakhists would reject a patient's right to refuse the procedure if it were judged to be promising. On the other hand, in the case of cancer, where the drugs are experimental and can damage healthy tissue, even Bleich, the advocate of aggressive treatment, concedes the patient's right of choice.[22] Because there is no structure or process for voting on halakhic measures, if one does not subscribe to a particular halakhic position, the different avenues may be considered options available for guidance and support in these difficult matters.

Limits on the Power and Authority of the Physician

What encouragements or restraints does halakhah impose on the physician in the face of terminal illness, when his or her healing capacity is limited and uncertain? Two opposing attitudes might emerge through exegesis of the biblical passage that justifies the work of the physician, *ve-rappo' yerappe'* (Exodus 21:19). This construction, where the infinitive absolute precedes the verb, is emphatic and intensive. It could mean "he [the physician] must at all times heal"—that is, he must pursue healing until the last possible moment. He may not withhold treatment, nor may he follow a DNR (do not resuscitate) policy with any terminal patient until that patient enters the phase of *gesisah*, "dying," which some interpreters consider to be no earlier than seventy-two hours before death is expected.[23] This kind of exegesis would support the maximalist-treatment approach of Bleich. On the other hand, one might interpret *ve-rappo' yerappe'* as "he [the physician] must heal as long as there is the possibility of a cure"; in other words, when that hope fails he should stop aggressive treatment and provide maintenance care and relieve the pain. This interpretation would support the choice of the patient or family, together with the physician, to accept the process of dying. It would also support the living will and the hospice concepts. Our biblical verse is ambiguous enough to suggest two diametrically opposed interpretations! Moreover, halakhic decision making does not use the biblical texts as its final authority. We must, therefore, rely on the later rabbinic materials, which provide more specific instruction but still leave room for debate. Our problem is to distinguish between living, which may not be shortened, and the process of dying, an inexorable process of nature, which should not be impeded or prolonged.

Euthanasia in Folklore and Halakhah

In the realm of folklore and popular imagination, certain things were thought to have the power to impede the process of dying. They were thought to cause the patient great distress because they blocked the soul from exiting; therefore, they should be removed. The halakhists recognized these impediments as well. The reason that folklore (some would say superstition) has any voice in this matter is that what seems to us today to be fanciful was deemed by our forebears to be realities in nature. Even though we have discarded the idea that these specific features have any efficacy, halakhic categories remain into which genuine natural and scientific factors can be fitted.

The rabbinic story that told how Rabbi Judah's maid interrupted the prayers of the rabbis so that he might die quickly (B. Ketubbot 104a) is rich in implications for halakhic decisions regarding life support systems. The tale assumes that the prayers had the power to maintain the life of a very sick man, or to interfere with his dying. The maid, who dropped the jug and startled the rabbis, did so because she saw how much pain Rabbi Judah was suffering. This pain was both physical and spiritual, for he was unable to wear his tefillin at all times. Was the maid, then, making a decision on the basis of quality of life, a criterion that Jewish law does not accept? By interrupting the rabbis' prayers, she allowed Rabbi Judah to die, thus performing a humanitarian act; but did she consult Rabbi Judah, his wife, or his sons? May we conclude that the prayers of the rabbis were a spiritual life support system that could be turned off when, in the opinion of a bystander, the suffering became too much?

We must note the differences between this classical story and present-day medical realities. In the story, prayer is assumed to be an effective life-preserving act. Yet its effect is not automatic. Prayer is a petition addressed to God, who may or may not grant it. This differentiates prayer from the life support machine, but even so, modern mechanical and electronic devices also are not guaranteed to succeed. Moreover, the prayers of different people are not equally efficacious. The rabbis who prayed for Rabbi Judah may have been in a unique position owing to their unusual spiritual strength.

The medieval mystical work *Sefer Ḥasidim*, par. 723, states that one must not prevent a speedy death. For instance, the sound of wood being chopped outside the house where the dying person lies prevents the soul from departing and must be removed. What appears to us as mere folklore was accepted by halakhic authorities. Thus in a discussion of proper care for a dying person, the halakhah allows no moving of or trauma to the patient, as it might hasten his or her death. In his gloss, Moses Isserles cites the passage from Sefer Ḥasidim about removing the noise of woodchopping and adds that one may also remove salt from the dying patient's tongue. His explanation is significant: "This is not a direct act at all but the removal of that which is preventing [dying]" (Yoreh De'ah 339:1).

Active and Passive Euthanasia

Outside the halakhic world one finds many advocates of active euthanasia. Joseph Fletcher, a Christian writer, has argued for human initiatives in dying. To him, this means active or direct euthanasia, in that passive euthanasia is already practiced in many hospitals. The doctrine that we must do everything to preserve a patient's life is discredited. Human function and happiness are the highest goods, and any means necessary to meet those ends are just.[24] The book *Final Exit* by Derek Humphry advocates doctor-assisted suicide for hopelessly ill patients and praises Dr. Jack Kevorkian for his compassion.[25] The euthanasia societies, Humphry reports, are working for a change in the law and are receiving ever more public sympathy.

Halakhah clearly rejects active euthanasia. Maimonides summarizes the law: "One who kills a person in his death agony [*goses*] receives the death penalty. If that person is dying because of human-inflicted wounds, it is forbidden to kill him, but a human court will not impose sentence upon the killer. Similarly, one may not kill a mortally ill person with a terminal condition [*terefah*], but if he does, he is not judged by a human court but by the laws of heaven" (Hilkhot Rotzeaḥ 2:7–8). The reasoning in the last two cases is that the killer is not the sole cause of the victim's death; thus active euthanasia is forbidden, but the penalty is not the same as for premeditated murder.

In a modern application of the distinction between ending life and removing that which lengthens the process of dying, Rabbi Solomon Freehof, a Reform decisor, concludes that the physician may not take any overt action to hasten the patient's death, such as giving him or her an overdose of an opiate, but may refrain from doing that which will postpone dying. This can include giving the order that the bottle containing the nutrient not be refilled when it is empty. In doing this the physician is committing no sin.[26] There are, however, some halakhists who take a very severe stand on passive euthanasia, which is effected by removal of treatment. They disagree not only with Freehof's opinion, but also with the concept, advanced by Catholic bioethicists, of a distinction between ordinary and extraordinary means. This Catholic position is well expressed by Gerard Kelly, S.J.: "Ordinary means are all medicines, treatments and operations which offer reasonable hope of benefit and which can be obtained and used without excessive expense, pain or other inconvenience. Extraordinary means are all medicines, treatments and operations which cannot be obtained or used without excessive expense, pain or other inconvenience, or which, if used, would not offer a reasonable hope of benefit."[27] Terms such as *reasonable* and *excessive* are ambiguous and allow for different subjective interpretations; it is precisely this room for judgment by doctor, patient, or family that maximalist-treatment halakhists object to.

One of these, J. David Bleich, a spokesperson for the most conservative Orthodox approach, rejects the terms *ordinary* and *extraordinary treatment* and *heroic means* as alien to Judaism. He says, "The obligation to preserve and prolong life requires the use of any available mode of therapy." The idea of "death with dignity" is, in his view, misapplied. Any effort to maintain life is an expression of respect for the dignity of life. Even if the patient wants to die, one should not consider this request, for our sages have said, "Against your will you live; against your will you die" (Avot 4:22).

Bleich also supports this position in terms of his understanding of the obligations of the physician. In the Anglo-Saxon common law, the relationship of physician and patient is a contractual one. The doctor has the right to refuse to treat a patient not under his or her care. Under halakhah, however, the physician is God's messenger. The *bet din* (court) must insure that the burdens of providing medical care are evenly distributed among the available physicians. One who does not heal violates the commandment "You shall not stand idly by the blood of your fellow" (Leviticus 19:16). The distinction between an active (forbidden) and a passive (permitted) act applies only to a *goses*, one in the process of dying, where death is expected within seventy-two hours; it does not apply to the patient who is terminally ill but not yet near death. The latter must always be treated actively, says Bleich. He rejects any derivation of halakhic practice from folklore. Fanciful stories about the removal of noise or salt or about the obligation to pray for the patient's death have no relevance to the question of medical treatments, which are based on scientific factors.[28]

Other traditionalist scholars do not share Bleich's extreme views. The *Compendium on Medical Ethics* (6th ed.), a volume produced by the Committee on Medical Ethics of the New York Board of Rabbis, chaired by Rabbi Immanuel Jakobovits and, after him, Rabbi Moshe Tendler, does not advocate extraordinary treatment in every case. However, it states: "Extraordinary or heroic methods that do not cause discomfort or introduce new risks of morbidity or fatality can be offered for patients who have very limited life span." Note that it does not say "must be offered." It continues: "If new procedures, such as radical surgery or chemotherapy with potentially toxic drugs, subject the patient to significant risk, then only specific anticipated benefits would permit the assumption of such risk." The *Compendium* recognizes that, before the actual death process (*gesisah*), there comes a time when a patient or the family have the right to decide that aggressive treatment must stop. It states: "Where the physician cannot effect a cure, his role is limited to palliation. In all circumstances, his primary duty is to avoid causing further injury."[29]

Essential to the arguments of the maximalist-treatment advocates is the traditional definition of the *goses* as one whose death is estimated to occur within seventy-two hours. Thus before that time, no treatment may be withheld. Rabbi Elliot Dorff disagrees, affirming that modern medicine can sustain indefinitely, with heart and lung machines, people who are "on their deathbeds." If, he says, the term *goses* is to be used at all, it must be defined not in terms of the number of hours remaining to the patient but in terms of the attending physician's judgment that the illness is irreversible and terminal. Dorff explores an alternative approach as well in which he follows the suggestion of Daniel Sinclair that instead of *goses* the operative term for the incurably ill should be *terefah*. The *terefah*, who has no hope of survival, is not equated with the dead, meaning that one may not kill him or her, but he or she is analogous to the dead person, in that treatment can be terminated. There is disagreement in the Talmud as to how long the *terefah* will live, one view being a year; the very confusion on this point, Dorff states, reflects our own confusion about the prospects for the terminally ill patient. Thus the term *terefah* is the best analogue for the patient who has no hope of recovery.[30]

The noted Orthodox scholar Rabbi Eliezer Waldenberg of Jerusalem has also redefined the term *gesisah*. He considers a "final-phase *goses*" as a person who has irredeemably lost all capacity for basic physiological functioning. In that state, Waldenberg argues all forms of life support, including mechanical aids to heartbeat and respiration as well as artificial nutrition and hydration, constitute impediments to the person's dying and may be removed. Nevertheless, before the patient reaches that state and the disease is potentially curable, we must make every effort to prolong his or her life.[31]

On the subject of controlling pain, interestingly, the advocate of aggressive treatment, Bleich, also defends aggressive treatment of pain, even beyond currently accepted medical norms. Halakhah, in his view, justifies the administering of morphine, which in high doses depresses the cerebral center responsible for breathing. A respirator, then, may be required to help the patient breathe. This means that in the case of the terminal patient as well as the moribund patient, controlling pain takes precedence, even if it shortens life.[32] Rabbi Solomon Freehof, in a 1975 responsum, agreed that we may risk the *hayye sha'ah*, the limited life left to the terminal patient, in order to relieve pain. He says: "It is true that the medicine to relieve his pain may weaken his heart, but does not the great pain itself weaken his heart?"[33]

There has been much discussion in the halakhic literature about what substances may or may not be taken from the terminal patient in the final stage. Most halakhists insist that no food or medication be denied the patient. Dr. Fred Rosner, for example, objects vehemently on halakhic grounds to a recent decision (1986) of the American Medical Association's Council on Ethical and Judicial Affairs, which affirms that a physician may ethically withdraw artificial feeding and hydration from terminal or permanently comatose patients if certain of the accuracy of the diagnosis, the irreversibility of the coma, and the patient's wishes.[34] There are, however, halakhic positions less stringent. Rabbi Immanuel Jakobovits permits the removal of medication and treatment, but not of food and water. He goes so far as to permit the suspension of insulin in a patient suffering from diabetes who subsequently contracts cancer, causing excruciating pain.[35] Rabbi G. A. Rabinowitz and Dr. M. Koenigsberg, in a 1971 opinion, argued that food and nutrition may be withheld from a comatose patient with no hope of recovery, as these are factors which "delay one's death."[36] Solomon Freehof also endorsed a passive discontinuation of intravenous fluid. Each day the physician should specifically order the fluid; on a particular day, however, he or she may simply refrain from giving the order. This would be a *shev ve-al ta'aseh* situation ("passively sit by and do not take action").[37] We have noted above the view of Rabbi Eliezer Waldenberg, reflecting a change in his earlier thinking, that life support systems and artificial nutrition and hydration impede one's dying and may be removed from the terminal patient.

Further thought in this area is that of Rabbi Moshe Feinstein. According to him, if a patient with a painful, incurable illness develops a curable intercurrent disease, the latter disease must be treated. If, however, the underlying incurable disease is very painful and the patient refuses additional therapy, it is not obligatory to administer medications that will only prolong a life of pain. One need not force-feed a competent adult patient if he or she refuses food. If a patient refuses treatment because of pain or despair, one should try to persuade him or her to accept the treatment. If, however, the persuasion is upsetting and worsens the patient's condition, this effort must stop. We see here a partial application of paternalism, limited by recognition of the pain factor and fear of hastening the patient's death.[38] Rabbi Solomon Freehof, in a 1969 opinion, arrived at the same conclusion, but without the paternalism or attempted persuasion: "If the patient is a hopelessly dying patient, the physician has no duty to keep him alive a little longer. He is entitled to die."[39] Rabbi Elliot Dorff accepts that when the patient has an irreversible, terminal illness, medications and other forms of therapy may be withheld or withdrawn.[40] Where there is no mechanism for resolving contradictions, we have options.

Living Wills

Related to the question of the freedom of the patient to choose to die and to reject extraordinary treatment is the Living Will, recognized by numerous states. The federal Patient Self-Determination Act, which applies to most health providers that accept Medicaid or Medicare, requires that patients admitted to nearly every health care facility in the country must be told of their right to accept or refuse treatment should they become gravely ill. They are entitled by law to state their wishes in documents known as "advanced directives," expressed in living wills or by health care proxies. The Living Will recognizes the right of a competent adult patient to make a written directive to his or her physician to withhold life-sustaining procedures in the event of incompetence following onset of a terminal condition.

Some traditionalist halakhists consider the Living Will to be against the teachings of Judaism. Their reasons are that the Living Will may be activated prematurely; a patient may change his or her mind without rescinding the formal written statement; a procedure considered to be merely death-postponing may turn out to be life-prolonging; the freedom of the medical personnel may be compromised by their acquiescence; critical illness and terminal illness are not always easily distinguishable; and the pain that the patient fears may ultimately be relieved by more modern methods of pain control.[41] Those who argue for aggressive treatment until the onset of *gesisah* (when death is expected within seventy-two hours) must of necessity reject the Living Will.[42] Still, there is a "Halakhic Living Will," designed and published by Agudath Yisrael, which stipulates that all health care decisions made for the patient "be made pursuant to Jewish Law and custom as determined in accordance with strict Orthodox interpretation and tradition." In view of the less stringent halakhic opinions noted above, this gives the person room to choose from among the various options that will be available when and if he or she becomes terminal. Elliot Dorff cites with approval the opinion of the late Rabbi Seymour Siegel: "What the Living Will makes possible is the giving of the privilege to the patient himself to stop those things 'that delay the soul's leaving the body.'"[43] Avram Reisner essentially agrees, but emphasizes that the decision-making power at the final stage rests solely with the patient, who alone is privy to the dialogue of his or her soul with God and knows God's will. This theological formulation places upon the surrogate—or *shaliah*, the messenger of the patient—the obligation to proceed with great caution and humility, since the messenger is not privy to the dialogue between the patient and God, whence derives the patient's autonomy.[44]

Hospices

Hospices provide palliative and supportive care for terminally ill patients and their families, either at home or in a special facility. The whole family is considered the unit of care, and a team of specialists is involved: doctors, nurses, psychologists, social workers, and clergy. Where possible, family members are encouraged to deliver care to the terminally ill patient. The hospice program is a reaction to the impersonality and coldness of the modern hospital and to the abandonment of the patient by a medical staff frustrated by its inability to effect a cure. In hospice care the emphasis is on communication and caring, acceptance of feeling, and counseling. The concept of the hospice is consistent with the values of halakhah. Most of its operations fall under the laws of *bikkur holim*, "visiting the sick." Hospice care, notes Elliot Dorff, is a form of medical care; it is just that the goal of the treatment has changed. As recognized by halakhists and others, the patient autonomously makes the choice to end hopeless aggressive treatment and to face inevitable death, together with his or her loved ones, with caring and dignity.[45]

Definitions of Death

A hotly debated issue at the present time is the definition of death. The traditional Jewish definition is based on the cessation of respiration. A feather or light piece of paper is placed near the nose several times, to be certain, and the patient is pronounced dead when there is no breathing. This definition derives from the talmudic debate over which is decisive, cessation of respiration or of heartbeat. Because it is possible that no breathing can be detected but the heart may still be beating, scholars like Rabbi Tsvi Ashkenazy (Ḥakham Tsvi, no. 77) have established that the absence of cardiac activity is the crucial criterion of death, with respiration simply indicating the presence of a heartbeat.[46] If breathing ceases, therefore, the heart is de facto considered stilled.

In discussing irreversible coma and "brain death," we must first note that three general parts of the brain, separated by evolution and function, have been distinguished: (1) the "reptilian" hindbrain or lower brain stem, which controls autonomic functions; (2) the "old mammalian" or midbrain at the top of the brain stem, where emotional controls are centered; and (3) the cerebral cortex, or "new mammalian" brain, where "mind," or cerebration, is located and which has evolved in *Homo sapiens* over the past one million years. Respiration and heartbeat are controlled by groups of cells in the lower brain stem.[47] Patients in the condition of PVS (persistent vegetative state), with a flat EEG (electroencephalogram) and lack of responsiveness with no change over a period of one month, are in a state of unconsciousness following upon the destruction of the higher brain (cortex), though the brain stem remains intact. These patients may maintain spontaneous reflexes, including heartbeat and respiration, eye movements and gestures, but they are altogether without consciousness and must be nourished artificially. If maintained on machines, such patients can live for years (one lived thirty-seven years). Increasingly, the courts have considered these situations as cases where there is no conceivable life benefit to the patient and therefore have ruled that life-sustaining treatment, including nutrition and hydration, may be removed.

For halakhists, this condition is highly problematic, for although these patients have no hope of recovery, they are not dying, and quality of life is not admitted as a halakhic criterion for its termination. Avram Reisner takes the position: "Facing an evidently living being . . . we are left with the ḥazakah (the legal presumption) of life, and the requirement to treat that life as we would any other life." Elliott Dorff concludes that persistent vegetative state (PVS) patients should be maintained on nutrition and hydration at least for some time, to allow for the possibility that their coma might be reversible.[48]

An even more severe condition is irreversible coma with no reflexes. In 1968, the Ad Hoc Committee of the Harvard Medical School propounded the following definition of universal coma as the criterion for death: the patient, who is examined twice at a twenty-four-hour interval, consistently displays (1) unreceptivity and unresponsiveness to stimuli, even intensely noxious stimuli; (2) no spontaneous muscular movements or spontaneous respiration; (3) no reflexes; and (4) a flat EEG. These factors, however, apply only when drug intoxication can be ruled out.[49]

This definition, now accepted in numerous states of the Union, has been received differently by bioethicists. Joseph Fletcher argues that death means the cessation of "humanhood": the ability to think, to love, to plan, to communicate. When the newest part of the brain on the evolutionary scale, the cortex, is dead, the human being is dead, even if the "reptilian" and "old mammalian" brains still function.[50] Others dissent, one arguing that this definition of life is too narrow, as if cortical activity is akin to the soul, which leaves the body dead when it departs; in like manner, the nonfunctioning cortex apparently leaves behind a "dead" brain, even though certain automatic functions continue. Still another dissenting view accuses the medical profession of taking a shortcut to death in order to facilitate heart transplants.[51]

Jewish scholars are not all comfortable with the Harvard Criteria. Bleich views them merely as a definition of irreversible coma and cortical death, and therefore invalid as a halakhic definition of death. In his view, as long as there is autonomous breathing and a heartbeat, the halakhic definition of death is not satisfied, even if the cortex is dead.[52] The Compendium, however, reflects a different perspective. While maintaining that a comatose patient who breathes independently, responds to pain, and is capable of independent muscular movement is alive, the fact that a brain stem–dead patient may meet the Harvard Criteria for irreversible coma is considered significant. There is, in fact, a certain ambiguity in the Harvard Criteria, for they can be interpreted as describing both cortical and brain stem death. The brain stem–dead patient, if studied in an autopsy, would show evidence of "respirator brain," a cellular destruction presuming an interference with circulation to the medulla, which the *Compendium* equates halakhically with decapitation.

Movement in Orthodox circles toward a new definition of death—namely, the acceptance of the Harvard Criteria to indicate brain stem death and thus denote an absence of circulation (which is equated with "decapitation"; Mishnah Oholot 1:6)—reflects the thought of Rabbi Moses Tendler and his father-in-law, the late Rabbi Moshe Feinstein. The latter, still holding to the traditional indicators of death, was willing to support them with additional ones, such as the Harvard Criteria and a radioisotope procedure that tests for the flow of blood to the brain (perfusion). For example, Rabbi Feinstein rules that the patient who can breathe independently for fifteen minutes, even with difficulty, must be restored to the respirator. If, however, the patient cannot breathe without the respirator and does not react to noxious stimuli, death should not be declared until the radioisotope test for perfusion is performed. If there is flow to the brain, even if independent breathing is absent, the patient is to be restored to the respirator. If there is no flow, and other signs of death are present, the patient is considered dead. In 1987, the Chief Rabbinate Council in Israel cautiously accepted these brain death criteria for the sake of allowing heart transplants.[53]

Treatment of the Terminal Patient: A Consultative Process

What emerges from this confusing catalogue of opinions is that in most situations several options are available and that ultimate decisions must be made in a consultative manner. The participants in the decision-making process will be the autonomous patient, if competent and conscious; family members; the doctor; and, it is hoped, the rabbi. Even such consultative methods have their drawbacks. The patient may have said, earlier in life, "I do not want to be kept alive; no aggressive treatment." But would he or she say this now if conscious? Family members may clash, with a spouse wanting to remove the respirator and a son or daughter vehemently objecting. And what of the rights of a "significant other" in the decision-making process, whether of the same or opposite sex as the patient? The rabbi also has to decide her or his halakhic-ethical norm: whether to look for a consensus among halakhic opinions, to choose one mentor and remain consistent, or to judge each case on its own merit and involve several opposing opinions so that there will be room to maneuver as the case develops. Much more is at stake here than halakhic or medical opinion. Painful emotions, such as love, guilt, and ones arising from intrafamily conflict, have to be dealt with sympathetically. Ideally, the physician and the rabbi should play the role of counselors, who listen and guide but never pontificate. In this way they may help the family grope toward the appropriate solution for their specific set of circumstances.

NOTES

1. Hayyim Dov Chavel, ed., *Kitvei Rabbenu Moshe ben Nahman*, vol. 2 (Jerusalem: Mossad Ha-Rav Kook, 1964), *Torat Ha-'Adam*, pp. 11–311; see esp. p. 18.

2. *Newsweek*, 20 November 1989, pp. 82–83; *Philadelphia Inquirer*, 27 November 1991, pp. 1A–2A.

3. Naḥmanides, *Torat Ha-'Adam*, p. 42.

4. The view that one must expose oneself to possible danger is not incorporated in the *Mishneh Torah* of Maimonides or the Shulḥan Arukh of Joseph Caro, possibly because they and the Bavli disagree with the Yerushalmi on exposing oneself to danger.

5. On the other hand, opinions have been offered that one should flee the city when there is a plague and one should not visit lepers; Ḥoshen Mishpat 426; Y. Gruenwald, *Kol Bo 'Al 'Avelut*, pp. 17–18, nn. 5 and 6. An article by David Novak, "AIDS: The Contemporary Jewish Perspective," in Stephen Katz, ed., *Frontiers of Jewish Thought* (Washington, DC: B'nai B'rith Books, 1992), 141–56, has recently appeared. Novak deals with the moral and halakhic issues of caring for victims of AIDS. He cites Naḥmanides' model of the obligation of the physician as commanding care when cure is impossible and making this care an act of compassion and *imitatio Dei*. However, despite the obligation to give care he considers the active homosexual and the drug user to be in the category of a "provocative sinner" (*mumar le-hakh'is*), whose actions are habitual and willful. We must, he says, heal their souls while we care for their bodies and respect

those of them who repent. Clearly, this view that homosexuals are sinners (or mentally ill or misguided) is strongly rejected by homosexuals and many others in the community. It creates barriers which taint the willingness to give care with self-righteousness. Apart from the obligation to help and support the victims of AIDS and their families, upon which there is increasing consensus, the moral evaluation of homosexual life styles in the Jewish and general communities is still a matter for emotional debate.

6. Earlier references to the physician in ancient law are the *Laws of Hammurapi*, pars. 206, 215–223; and the *Hittite Laws,* par. 10. The *Laws of Hammurapi* regulate the fees of the physician, depending on the social class of the patient and the nature of the injury. There are also severe penalties for malpractice: "If a physician performed a major operation on a seignior with a bronze lancet and has caused the seignior's death, or he opened up the eye socket of a seignior and has destroyed the seignior's eye, they shall cut off his hand" (par. 218).

7. Maimonides suggests that the *Book of Healing* may have been a book of talismanic figures thought to be effective in healing but that did not prescribe any medical procedures. Alternatively, the book may have taught the preparation of poisons and their antidotes. When the times became corrupt and people consulted this book in order to poison their enemies, Hezekiah saw fit to ban it.

8. Naḥmanides, Torat Ha-'Adam, pp. 41–45.

9. Immanuel Jakobovits, *Jewish Medical Ethics* (New York: Bloch, 1959), 201–243; Fred Rosner, *Medicine in the Bible and the Talmud* (New York: Ktav and Yeshiva University, 1977), pp. 101–112; Yoreh De'ah 336. The discussion about the city of refuge is purely academic, for the institutions of private justice through a family blood-redeemer and asylum in cities of refuge were confined to the early biblical period. Rabbinic exegesis of these social institutions was carried on at a time when they no longer existed.

10. There are, in many Jewish communities, functioning *batei din* (rabbinic courts) that can act as boards of arbitration and whose rulings are based on talmudic law. Under the common law, an adult child is not required to support his parent or grandparent. Thus a hospital or nursing home cannot sue the child for payment when care is given to an aging or infirm parent. The child who does more than the law requires is considered a volunteer. Legal agreements, when clear and not the product of fraud and duress, can alter these circumstances. A child may sign a hospital form agreeing to be legally responsible for her or his parent's expenses, and the hospital can enforce the agreement. It can be said, however, that most families care for aging parents without recourse to legal process. See *Reader's Digest Family Legal Guide* (Pleasantville, N.Y.: Reader's Digest, 1981), p. 706.

11. The basis for this ruling by Maimonides is the talmudic story of Rav

Assi's aged mother. When she asked for jewelry, he obtained it for her. When she said she wanted a man, he said, "I will look into the matter." When she said, "I want a man as handsome as you," Rav Assi fled to Eretz Yisra'el. He realized that she had become insane, and he could not cope with the situation. It is also possible that the sexual overtones of her demand created an intolerable conflict for him. Maimonides generalizes from this incident to insanity in general (B. Kiddushin 31b; Mamrim 6:10).

12. Elisabeth Kübler-Ross, *On Death and Dying* (New York: Macmillan, 1969); and Sissela Bok, *Dying: Moral Choice in Public and Private Life* (New York: Pantheon Press, 1978).

13. J. David Bleich, *Judaism and Healing* (New York: Ktav, 1981), pp. 27–33.

14. Elliot N. Dorff, "Hospice and Ethical Wills," *Rabbinical Assembly Homiletics Service*, September 1981, pp. 29–33; idem, "Rabbi, I'm Dying," *Conservative Judaism* 37 (1984): 37–51; Lawrence Troster, "Kayle's Prayer," ibid., pp. 65–69; Israel Abrahams, ed., *Hebrew Ethical Wills*, 2 vols. (Philadelphia, 1926); Jacob Riemer and Nathaniel Stampfer, eds., *Ethical Wills: A Modern Jewish Treasury* (New York: Schocken, 1983).

15. Naḥmanides, *Torat Ha-'Adam*, p. 43.

16. For example, in our own era, Rabbi Ḥayyim David Halevy, the Chief Rabbi of Tel Aviv, would permit a woman to undergo elective plastic surgery though there is no threat to her life if she does not have the surgery. Here the benefit that offsets the risk is her heightened self-esteem by becoming more attractive; see Halevy, *'Asey Lekha Rav* (Tel Aviv, 1971), 4:326–327.

17. In 1968, the then chief rabbi of Israel, Rabbi Unterman, wrote an opinion limiting the amount of risk that may be taken in heart transplants, permitting them only if the chances for success are greater than those for failure. His reasoning was that the heart patient, in the interval between the removal of the old heart and the implantation of the new one, has lost *ḥezkat ḥayyim*, the presumption of life continuance. This means that in surgery there is a great danger that he or she will die suddenly. This is different from the terminal cancer patient, whose life is ebbing away but chances are that death will not occur abruptly. The latter, therefore, retains his *ḥezkat ḥayyim* and may, therefore, take on any degree of risk that may improve his or her condition.

18. Bleich, *Judaism and Healing*, p. 116.

19. Fred Rosner, "Rabbi Moshe Feinstein on the Treatment of the Terminally Ill," *Judaism* 37 (1988): 188–198, esp. p. 194.

20. Elliot N. Dorff, "A Jewish Approach to End-Stage Medical Care," *Conservative Judaism* 43, no. 3 (1991): 17–18.

21. Avram Israel Reisner, "A Halakhic Ethic of Care for the Terminally Ill," *Conservative Judaism* 43, no. 3 (1991): 60–61. This entire issue deals in depth with the issues of the care of the terminally ill.

22. Bleich, *Judaism and Healing*, pp. 116–122.

23. Yoreh De'ah 339:2; B. Gittin 28a.

24. Joseph Fletcher, *Humanhood: Essays in Biomedical Ethics* (Buffalo, N.Y.: Prometheus Books, 1979), pp. 188–203.

25. Derek Humphry, *Final Exit* (Eugene, Oreg.: Hemlock Society, 1991).

26. Solomon B. Freehof, *Modern Reform Responsa* (Cincinnati: Hebrew Union College Press, 1971), pp. 188–203.

27. Gerald Kelly, S.J., *Medico-Moral Problems* (St. Louis: Catholic Hospital Association, 1958), pp. 129ff.

28. Bleich, *Judaism and Healing*, pp. 134–145.

29. David M. Feldman and Fred Rosner, eds., *Compendium on Medical Ethics*, 6th ed. (New York: Federation of Jewish Philanthropies, 1984), pp. 102–103.

30. Elliot Dorff, "Jewish Approach to End-Stage Care," pp. 19–21; idem, "'Choose Life': A Jewish Perspective on Medical Ethics," *University Papers* (Los Angeles, University of Judaism), February 1985, pp. 19–21; cf. Daniel B. Sinclair, *Tradition and the Biological Revolution: The Application of Jewish Law to the Treatment of the Critically Ill* (Edinburgh: Edinburgh University Press, 1989).

31. Eliezer Waldenberg, *Responsa Tzitz Eliezer*, 13, no. 89, and 14, no. 80; cited by Dorff, "Jewish Approach to End-Stage Care," p. 45, no. 32; and Rosner, "Feinstein on the Terminally Ill," pp. 196–197.

32. Bleich, *Judaism and Healing*, pp. 1–19, 134–145.

33. Solomon Freehof, in *American Reform Responsa*, ed. Walter Jacob (New York: Central Conference of American Rabbis, 1983), pp. 256–257. A different view is that of Rabbi Moshe Feinstein, who permits withholding medicines that would extend the life of a patient in severe pain even before that patient is termed a *goses* (moribund), but does not permit pain relief medication that would shorten life even for a moment; in *Bi-Shevilei ha-Refu'ah*, June 1984, p. 35; cited by Reisner, "A Halakhic Ethic of Care," p. 84, n. 51.

34. Rosner, "Feinstein on the Terminally Ill," pp. 188–189.

35. Jakobovits, *Jewish Medical Ethics*, pp. 121–125, 275–276, and notes; *Ha-pardes* 31 (1956): 1:28–31, 3:16–19; *No'am* 6:272–273, cited in Basil F. Hering, *Jewish Ethics and Halakhah for Our Time* (New York: Ktav and Yeshiva University, 1984), pp. 84–86.

36. *Ha-darom*, 1971, p. 75; cited in Hering, *Jewish Ethics and Halakhah*, pp. 84–85.

37. B. Eruvin 100a; Freehof, Modern Reform Responsa, pp. 197–203.

38. Rosner, "Feinstein on the Terminally Ill," pp. 192–95; Moshe Feinstein, *Igrot Moshe, Ḥoshen Mishpat*, pt. 2, 73:2–5; 74:2–5.

39. Jacob (ed.), *American Reform Responsa*, p. 260.

40. Dorff, "Jewish Approach to End-Stage Care," p. 27.

41. Feldman and Rosner (eds.), *Compendium on Medical Ethics*, pp. 115–117.

42. Bleich, *Judaism and Healing*, p. 139.

43. Dorff, "Jewish Approach to End-Stage Care," p. 39.

44. Ibid., p. 67.

45. Ibid., p. 26; Shelley M. Buxbaum, "The Halakhah of the Hospice," *Women's League Outlook* 56, no. 1 (Fall 1985): 8, 22.

46. Bleich, *Judaism and Healing*, p. 149.

47. Fletcher, *Humanhood*, 163–64; *The Brain: A User's Manual* (New York: Berkeley Group, 1982), pp. 28–63, 183–231.

48. Dorff, "Jewish Approach to End-Stage Care," pp. 36–37; Reisner, "A Halakhic Ethic of Care," pp. 68–69. Both scholars reject the bifurcation of the human brain into the subcortical (stem) and the cortex, the latter being seen as the seat of humanness. They also reject an argument for defining death as cortical death based on Maimonides, who (without making any halakhic decision) considers the intellect of the human being as his specifically human form. The vital principle in humans and animals is the drive to eat, drink, and reproduce (*Yesodei ha-Torah* 4:8); Reisner, "A Halakhic Ethic of Care," p. 88.

49. Henry K. Beecher, "A Definition of Irreversible Coma," *Journal of the American Medical Association* 205, no. 6 (August 6, 1968): 337–340.

50. Fletcher, *Humanhood*, 163–165; Robert Berkow, ed., *The Merck Manual of Diagnosis and Therapy*, 13th ed. (Rahway, N.J.; Merck, Sharp & Dohme, 1977), p. 1395.

51. Robert M. Veatch, *Death, Dying, and the Biological Revolution* (New Haven: Yale University Press, 1976); and Hans Jonas, *Philosophical Essays: From Ancient Creed to Technological Man* (1974); both cited in Tom L. Beauchamp and Seymour Perlin, eds., *Ethical Issues in Death and Dying* (Englewood Cliffs, N.J.: Prentice-Hall, 1978), pp. 18–37, 51–58.

52. Bleich, *Judaism and Healing*, p. 154.

53. Feldman and Rosner (eds.), Compendium on Medical Ethics, pp. 118–120; Dorff, "Jewish Approach to End-Stage Care," p. 82; Rosner, "Feinstein on the Terminally Ill," pp. 154–155. Rabbi Bleich vehemently rejects the blood flow test, as he does the Harvard Criteria; see *Judaism and Healing*, pp. 154–156. Interestingly, a committee of Reform rabbis, headed by Walter Jacob, arrived in 1980 at remarkably similar conclusions to those of some Orthodox decisors. After considering various Orthodox reactions to the Harvard Criteria, they concluded that "these criteria include those of the older tradition and comply with our concern that life has ended" (Jacob [ed.], *American Reform Responsa*, pp. 271–274). I suspect that this Reform reading of the materials, which does not dwell on the distinction between cortical and stem death, may

signify a greater readiness to accept cortical brain death than demonstrated by Orthodox or Conservative interpreters.

SUGGESTIONS FOR FURTHER READING

J. David Bleich, *Judaism and Healing* (New York: Ktav, 1981), contains essays on bioethical problems written from a conservative Orthodox perspective. There is great erudition in Bleich's writings, and the relevant talmudic and halakhic sources are cited.

James Childress, *Priorities in Biomedical Ethics* (Philadelphia: Westminster Press, 1981), is a philosophic study of options in bioethics in terms of paternalism and autonomy.

David M. Feldman and Fred Rosner, eds., *Compendium on Medical Ethics*, 6th ed. (New York: Federation of Jewish Philanthropies, 1984), presents a brief guide to information and decision making in a halakhic mode. The sources are generally not given, and the approach is traditional Orthodox; there is, however, recognition of halakhic points of view less rigid than those of Bleich.

Walter Jacob, ed., *American Reform Responsa* (New York: Central Conference of American Rabbis, 1983), is a collection of Reform responsa to inquiries on many issues, including bioethical ones. Many of the responsa were originally written by Rabbi Solomon B. Freehof. They are brief, and all the relevant talmudic and halakhic sources are cited. The final decisions are in the spirit of Liberal Judaism.

Immanuel Jakobovits, *Jewish Medical Ethics* (New York: Bloch, 1959), is a classic study of Jewish sources dealing with the physician, illness, life, and death. General historic, Christian, and halakhic sources are cited in abundance.

Fred Rosner's *Modern Medicine and Jewish Law* (New York: Yeshiva University, 1972) surveys the range of rabbinic responsa, early and modern, on various biomedical questions. The author does not undertake to decide the questions but cites all the relevant Orthodox authorities. Rosner's *Medicine in the Bible and the Talmud* (New York: Ktav and Yeshiva University, 1977) comprises historical studies dealing with biblical and talmudic evidence for diseases and concepts of medicine.

Joel Roth, *The Halakhic Process: A Systemic Analysis* (New York: Jewish Theological Seminary of America, 1986), deals with the process of establishing halakhah, halakhic practice, methods for choosing rabbinic authorities, custom and law, judicial discretion, and extralegal influences upon the halakhah. The treatment is in line with the historical-traditional approach of Conservative Judaism.

DAYLE A. FRIEDMAN

The Crown of Glory
Aging in the Jewish Tradition

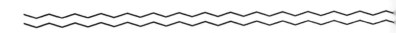

"Gray hair is a crown of glory."
(Proverbs 16:31)

When Jews have birthdays, it is customary to say to them, *'Ad me'ah ve-'esrim:* "May you live to one hundred and twenty!" The wish expresses an important Jewish sensibility, namely, that it is a blessing to live to a ripe old age. One hundred and twenty is the designated ideal age, as we have seen, because Moses lived to that age, and "his eyes were undimmed and his vigor unabated" (Deuteronomy 34:7).

While few Jews manage to attain this extreme longevity in literal terms, both the number of older Jews and the ages to which they are surviving have dramatically increased in recent decades. In 1957, it was estimated that 8.5 percent of the American Jewish population, or about 475,000 individuals, were over the age of 64.[1] In 1970, that figure stood at 12.5 percent and by 1990 the National Jewish Population Survey revealed that the proportion had jumped to 18 percent, or some 975,000 men and women. Not only are there now more older Jews, but there are more extremely old Jews. Among elderly Jews, 33 percent are over 75 years of age, and 10 percent are over 85. The 85-and-over group, in fact, is the fastest-growing segment of the American Jewish community.[2]

Thus, the American Jewish community is "graying" at a rapid and unprecedented rate. Both the increased numbers of elders and the phenomenon of an extended period of old age present tremendous challenges and opportunities to Jewish individuals, families, and communities. This chapter will examine Jewish texts and tradition for models and concepts regarding the process of aging, the treatment of elders, and the meaning of aging. It will conclude with some reflections on directions for future Jewish responses to the new realities of aging.

Images of Aging in the Bible and Rabbinic Literature

Developed over a thousand-year period by a wide variety of authorities, biblical and rabbinic views of aging are naturally diverse, reflecting a mix of idealized and realistic perceptions of the last portion of the life cycle. On the one hand, old age is envisioned as a blessing, a reward for meritorious living, a time when one is deserving of special honor; on the other hand, it is also depicted as a time of loss and incapacity.

While most of the mitzvot (commandments) in the Torah are mandated without assurance of reward, in the few exceptional cases long life is the promised recompense. Length of days is assured for those who honor their parents (Exodus 20:12), for those who do not take away a mother bird's young in her presence (Deuteronomy 22:7), and for those who employ equal measures in commerce (Deuteronomy 25:15). In addition, those who observe "all of the laws and ordinances" (Deuteronomy 6:2) are promised "length of days." According to Proverbs 16:31, one attains old age through *tzedakah*, righteous living.

Many sources portray old age as a blessing. When Abraham dies at 175 years of age, he is described as having reached "a good old age, old and satisfied" (Genesis 25:8). A striking midrash explains how the distinctive signs of old age developed in response to Abraham's request. In his day, no physical characteristics distinguished elders from younger people, so people could not know on sight to pay Abraham the special respect due to the old. Therefore, Abraham asked God to give him, and all older people, distinguishing features (Genesis Rabbah 65:4). In contrast to the contemporary culture, which attaches negative values to the physical features of aging such as gray hair and wrinkles, these sources view them as desirable!

According to other midrashim, old age is a reward for virtuous living, such as faithful attendance at the House of Study (Berakhot 8a), and for a life marked by righteousness and Torah, exemplified by Rav Addah bar Ahaba:

> The disciples of Rav Adda bar Ahaba asked him: To what do you attribute your longevity?—He replied: I have never displayed any impatience in my house, and I have never walked in front of any man greater than myself, nor have I ever meditated (over the words of the Torah) in any dirty alleys, nor have I ever walked four cubits without (musing over) the Torah or without (wearing) phylacteries, nor have I ever fallen asleep in the Beth Hamidrash for any length of time or even momentarily, nor have I rejoiced at the disgrace of my friends, nor have I ever called my neighbor by a nickname given to him by myself or, some say, by the nickname given to him by others (B. Ta'anit 20b).

Here again, longevity is regarded in a positive light.

Old age is strongly associated with wisdom in biblical and rabbinic sources. The old are viewed as leaders with wisdom to impart. The people of Israel are enjoined: "Ask your father and he will tell you, your elders and they shall instruct you" (Deuteronomy 32:7). Or, in the words of the book of Job (12:12): "For wisdom is with the old, and understanding with length of days." The old are accounted wise not only because of learning acquired through study of Torah, but also because of the perspective they have gained through experience. Thus, even uneducated Jewish elders and elderly non-Jews deserve honor because, "In the multitude of [his] years, he has seen and recognized some of the Holy One's actions and wonders" (Kiddushin 32b).

Among the generation in the wilderness, it is the elders (*zekenim*) who are Israel's leaders. While many sources understand *zaken* as a generic term for leaders of any age, the use of a term that also denotes old age surely reflects the general association of wisdom with age. The guidance of elders is seen as critical to the survival of the people of Israel: "When is Israel able to stand? When it has elders. . . . For one who takes advice from elders never stumbles" (Exodus Rabbah 3:8).

Rabbinic doctrine urges acceptance of the elders' opinion when there is a dispute between the generations. Even if the elders seem to be arguing for destruction and the youth for construction, the elders should be heeded, for "the tearing down of the old is building, and the building of the young is tearing down" (Megillah 31b). Thus, the elders' perspective is exemplified as uniquely valuable for the guidance of the community.

Alongside these idealized portrayals of aging in biblical and rabbinic sources exists the stark recognition that aging also brings hardships. Old age is a frightening prospect, as expressed in the renowned lines of Psalms 71:9: "Cast me not off in the time of old age; when my strength fails, forsake me not." Rabbi Jose ben Kisma laments: "Woe for the one thing that goes and does not return," that is, youth (Shabbat 152a). In the same passage, Rav Dimi similarly describes youth as a crown of roses, and old age as a crown of thorns.

Old age is viewed so negatively because of the physical and mental impairments that accompany it, for, "in old age, all powers fail" (Tanhuma Miketz 10). Isaac became blind in his old age (Genesis 27:1), and David was so frail that his body was constantly cold (I Kings 1:1). The physical losses of aging are poignantly described by the eighty-year-old Barzillai the Gileadite in II Samuel 19:35: "I am this day fourscore years old; can I discern between good and bad? Can thy servant taste what I eat or what I drink? Can I hear any more the voice of singing men and singing women?" An exhaustive catalogue of the sorrows and sensory losses of aging is metaphorically described in Ecclesiastes 12:1–7:

So appreciate your vigor in the days of your youth, before those days
    of sorrow come and those years arrive of which you will say, I have
    no pleasure in them; before sun and light and moon and stars grow
    dark, and the clouds come back again after the rain:
When the guards of the house become shaky,
And the men of valor are bent,
And the maids that grind, grown few, are idle,
And the ladies that peer through the windows grow dim,
And the doors to the street are shut—
With the noise of the hand mill growing fainter,
And the song of the bird growing feebler,
And all the strains of music dying down;
When one is afraid of heights
And there is terror on the road. . . .

Before the silver cord snaps
And the golden bowl crashes,
The jar is shattered at the spring,
And the jug is smashed at the cistern.
And the dust returns to the ground
As it was,
And the lifebreath returns to God
Who bestowed it.

The Talmud (B. Shabbat 152a) interprets this woeful passage as a catalogue of all the physical changes and disabilities brought on by aging. The rabbis who cite this passage vie with one another in describing the most horrific visions of old age. Though several authorities apologetically demur, explaining the daunting descriptions as applying only to the wicked, by and large the rabbis see physical debilitation and impairment as a fact of life in old age.

Some rabbinic sources also view mental deterioration as an inevitable concomitant of aging. In a depiction that today would aptly apply to an individual labeled as demented, one source quotes an old man: "I look for that I have not lost" (B. Shabbat 152a). Another old man misinterprets the sound of twittering birds: "Robbers have come to overpower me" (Leviticus Rabbah 8:1). Despite the dominant view that the old are wise, some sources dispute this: "There is no reason in old men and no counsel in children" (Shabbat 89b). Learning from the old is futile, like "writing on blotted out paper" (Avot 4:20).

Because aging so often results in physical and mental deterioration, it is not surprising that older people are sometimes described as defeated and overwhelmed by tasks they had previously accomplished with ease. Thus, Rabbi Simeon ben Halafta, who regularly visited Rabbi Judah ha-Nasi, ceased to do so because "the rocks have grown tall, the near have become distant, two have turned into three and the peacemaker of the home has ceased" (B. Shabbat 152a). He has lost his sense of mastery, his vision, his capacity to ambulate, and his sexual desire. Similarly, Leviticus Rabbah 8:1 states that an old man will not simply set off on a journey to a given place, but will first inquire: "Are there steps to go up there? Are there steps to go down there?" Biblical and rabbinic sources are thus quite realistic about the physical and mental decline that frequently accompanies aging, also recognizing the social isolation and emotional devastation that can result from these impairments.

Notwithstanding these impairments, the elderly are clearly seen as deserving of respect and honor because of their wisdom and life experience. They are in fact essential to the vitality of Israel. "Rabbi Akiba said: why is Israel compared to a bird? Just as a bird can only fly with its wings, so Israel can only survive with the help of its elders" (Exodus Rabbah 5:12). God honors elders by including them in critical moments of the Jewish people's life—the revelation of God's presence at the Burning Bush, the revelation of the Torah at Mount Sinai, the dedication of the Tent of Meeting—and at the future redemption promised in Isaiah 24:23: "For the God of Hosts will reign in Mount Zion and in Jerusalem, and before [God's] elders shall be glory" (Exodus Rabbah 5:12).

Given the high esteem for the elderly, it is not surprising that the Jewish tradition mandates respectful treatment of both parents and other elders. Three specific rubrics in Jewish law address the details of the obligations toward the elderly: honor and reverence for parents, and reverence for elders in general.

Filial Piety: Jewish Tradition's Understanding of Our Obligations Toward the Old

"The prosperity of a society can be judged by the way in which it treats its elderly."
—*Rabbi Nachman of Bratzlav*

In the traditional view, the Jew's obligation toward the elderly emerges from the context of family relations. Two core mitzvot in the Torah set the parameters for this obligation; both concern the relationship of children to their parents. The fifth commandment in the Decalogue enjoins: "Honor your father and mother, that you may long endure on the land which the Eternal your God is giving you" (Exodus 20:12). The Holiness Code (Leviticus 19:3) articulates the responsibility toward parents in a different manner: "You shall each revere his mother and his father, and keep My sabbaths: I the Eternal am your God."[3]

Rabbinic sources suggest that these two mitzvot represent two aspects of filial obligation: one, attitudinal, and the other, behavioral responses to parents. "Our rabbis taught: What is reverence and what is honor? Reverence means that he [the son] must neither stand nor sit in his [the father's] place, nor contradict his words, nor tip the scale against him. Honor means that he must give him food and drink, clothe and cover him, and lead him in and out" (B. Kiddushin 31b). *Mora* (reverence) refers to the obligation to ensure the *dignity* of one's parent. In both public and private settings, one must speak and behave in a way that respects the stature of a parent. Thus, one must not publicly disagree with a parent, unless the disagreement emerges in a discussion of Torah (Shulḥan Arukh, Yoreh De'ah 240:2). One must refrain from judging a parent overly harshly ("tipping the scales against them" (Sefer She'iltot 56), for, indeed, children are sometimes more impatient with parents than are strangers!

These sources do not specifically address the mitzvah or reverence toward *aging* parents. But the emphasis on respect for dignity becomes especially relevant in the relationship between adult children and their aging parents. In particular, the Talmud's injunction that children avoid contradicting their parents' words is pertinent, for it obliges those who care for older relatives to respect their wishes.

The tradition is rich with tales of extraordinary acts performed by children seeking to preserve their parents' dignity. Dama ben Netina, a gentile, had stored valuable jewels beneath his father's pillow (see also Steven M. Brown, p. 40). When rabbis seeking adornments for the priestly vestments offered him a handsome price for the jewels, Dama forfeited the financial opportunity rather than awaken his sleeping father. On another occasion, when Dama was in the presence of the great men of Rome, his mother tore his garment from him, slapped his head, and spat in his face, yet he remained silent rather than rebuking and shaming her (B. Kiddushin 31a). When Rabbi Tarfon's mother's shoe tore, he rushed to place his hands under her feet at each step, until she reached her destination (J. Pe'ah 1:1).

Maimonides later codified this rather extreme interpretation of the filial obligation to revere one's parents:

And how far must one go in their reverence? Even if he is dressed in precious clothes and is sitting in an honored place before many people, and his parents come and tear his clothes, hitting him on the head and spitting in his face, he may not shame them, but he must keep silent, and be in awe and fear of the King of Kings Who commanded him thus. For if a king of flesh and blood had decreed that he do something more painful than this, he could not hesitate in its performance. How much more so, then, when he is commanded by Him Who created the world at His will! (Mamrim 6:7)

Thus, one is obligated to preserve the dignity of parents even if it requires sacrifice and discomfort.

The mitzvah of *kavod*, honoring parents, is interpreted by the rabbis to mandate provision for their concrete needs such as food and drink, clothing and shelter, transportation and companionship. While all sources agree that children are required to provide these services for their parents, there is a lively debate among rabbinic authorities regarding the obligation to assume financial responsibility for parents. Some sources hold that children must financially support their parents (J. Kiddushin 1:7), while others state that they are responsible for the direct provision of services, but not for whatever financial cost is involved (B. Kiddushin 32a). While these duties are not articulated specifically for aging parents, it is obvious that providing basic necessities is most often required when parents are older and less able to provide for themselves.

The obligation to provide for the sustenance and dignity of parents has long been recognized as a very demanding one. Rabbi Simeon bar Yohai called this "the most difficult of mitzvot" (Tanhuma, Ekev 2). While the tradition lionizes those who succeed in discharging this obligation in extreme circumstances, it also recognizes that competing claims may limit the extent of obligations toward parents.

For example, finding a spouse and maintaining a peaceful marital union may sometimes limit the extent of filial responsibility. Thus, Maimonides permits a husband or a wife to exclude the other's parents from the household (though the wife may do so only if she claims that her in-laws are harming or paining her, while the husband need give no justification for his demand) (Ishut 13:14). According to *Sefer Ḥasidim*, a thirteenth-century ethical guide, a son may leave his aged parents to marry a woman in another town if he is able to pay someone else to care for them (sec. 564, p. 371).

The obligation toward one's parents may be limited not only if it affects relationships in the nuclear family, but also if it violates one's personal dignity or well-being. Hence, Maimonides warns parents not to be overly demanding or unreasonable in their expectations of children, lest they "place a stumbling block before the blind" (Mamrim 6:8–9). That is, filial obligation does not give *carte blanche* to unfair parents. Children are not expected to accede to each and every parental request.

Moreover, although children are obligated to provide care for their parents, the tradition acknowledges that there may be times when they need to delegate this task to others. Thus, a son may leave his father if the two are unable to get along without quarreling (*Sefer Ḥasidim*, sec. 343, p. 257). Similarly, "If one's father or mother should become mentally disordered, he should try to treat them as their mental state demands, until God has mercy upon them [i.e., they die] (see also Nahum M. Waldman, p. 178). But if he finds he cannot endure the situation because of their extreme madness, let him leave and go away, and delegate others to care for them properly" (Mamrim 6:8–9).

Significantly, it is the adult child's subjective experiences that determine these limits on filial responsibility. If the child perceives that the presence of a parent in the household leads to conflict, or that the experience of caring for a mentally impaired parent is unendurable, he or she is released from the obligation to provide care directly, or to live in proximity to the parent. Even so, the obligation toward the parent does not cease—the child must ensure that needed care will be provided by others—nor is the emotional connection broken. Still, there is a recognition that the adult child's needs, even emotional ones, may warrant a reordering of the filial obligation.

Applying the Tradition Today

Although these sources concerning filial obligation can be applied to relationships between adult children and their elderly parents, the tradition includes little mention of specific problems of coping with aging parents, particularly of the sort faced today. Just as the realities of aging in today's world are unprecedented, so too are the demands placed on the families of the elderly, particularly on adult daughters. Today's families often need to care for aging parents over prolonged periods of chronic disability and dependency, a situation not encountered by previous generations.[4]

Though the traditional sources do not specifically address contemporary scenarios, one can derive guidance from them. For instance, while the responsibility for care of aged parents is lifelong, we can extrapolate that there are circumstances in which placing a parent in the care of others (professional care givers, nursing homes, and the like) is justified and acceptable. Dementia, the most common reason for institutionalization, is one such circumstance. Adult daughters of the aged, who often suffer physical, mental, and financial hardship as a result of balancing care-giving responsibilities with work and other family demands, might find solace in the tradition's understanding of the balance between obligations toward parents and obligations toward self, spouse, and children.[5]

There is one additional contemporary application of the traditional perspectives on filial piety. Since providing for a parent's dignity includes respecting his or her wishes, Jews may feel called to make special efforts to elicit the values and preferences of elderly parents regarding medical treatment. By discussing and documenting their wishes regarding both the use of specific medical interventions (living wills) and the appointment of someone to act as a surrogate decision maker in the event they are unable to speak for themselves (durable power of attorney for health care), Jews can ensure that they are respecting their parents' dignity and autonomy.

RISING BEFORE THE OLD

Jewish texts offer scant guidance regarding appropriate attitudes and behavior toward older people other than parents. However, one rubric in the tradition does provide a useful perspective on this issue.[6] Like the mitzvah of *mora*, reverence toward parents, it is articulated in the levitical Holiness Code: "You shall rise before the aged (gray-haired) and show deference [*hiddur*] in the presence of the old [*zaken*]; you shall fear your God: I am the Eternal" (Leviticus 19:32). This mitzvah is understood to dictate deferential treatment toward scholars as well as older adults. *Zaken* (old) is taken to refer to people of wisdom, not just those who have attained wisdom through life experience.

The rabbis mandate the same attitude of reverence toward the elderly as that shown for one's parents: "What is the deference [*hiddur*] demanded by the Torah? That you not stand in his [the parent's] place, nor speak in his place, nor contradict his words, but behave toward him with reverence and fear" (Tosefta Megillah 3 [4]). This obligation holds for anyone over a certain age (generally sixty or seventy, according to Ḥayye Adam 69:2). Included in those meriting this deferential treatment are elderly non-Jews and Jews who are neither learned nor particularly righteous, since they are assumed to have acquired understanding of God's ways in the world through life experience (B. Kiddushin 33a). Hence, revering the elderly means recognizing the value of their experience. Even if they have *forgotten* their learning through dementia or other frailty, one still owes them respect: "Take care to honor the old man who has forgotten his learning for reasons beyond his control, as it is said, 'both the [second, unbroken] tablets and the broken tablets [of the Law] were kept in the Ark [of the sanctuary]'" (B. Berakhot 8b). Respect for the elderly is not predicated on their capacity to contribute socially or to benefit those younger than they. They are inherently worthy, even when "broken," and are to be cherished and nurtured, just as Israel treasured the first (broken) set of tablets of the Law.

One must not merely comport oneself so as to give honor to the older person; one must do this in such a way that the older person will know that the honor is meant specifically for him or her. For example, one must rise in the presence of older persons, but should wait to do so until the older person is within four cubits, so that they will recognize that this honor is being accorded them (Ḥayye Adam 69:3). In addition, one must reach out to older persons where they are; thus, if older persons are standing, even if one is sitting and engaged in one's work, one must meet them at their level by rising as well.[7]

Clearly, tradition obligates Jews to behave with reverence for the dignity of every older person, thereby recognizing the value of that person's experience and perspective, though they need not provide personally for the other's basic needs. However, by following the precepts of *gemilut ḥasadim* (acts of loving kindness) and *tzedakah* (righteous behavior), the whole community does share general responsibility for the well-being of older adults among them.

Aging Jewishly: Aging as a Time of Meaning, Celebration, and Connection

Thus far we have examined traditional Jewish attitudes toward aging in general, and the tradition's prescriptions for treatment of elders by their children and by others younger than they. In a graying society, however, another critical set of questions needs to be addressed: How am I to face my own aging? What resources can Judaism provide to those coping with the losses and challenges of aging in their own lives?

These questions are particularly urgent given the negative attitudes toward aging prevalent in contemporary American society. If we attend to the messages implicit in mass media advertisements, for example, we will note that we should look younger, should purchase products to "prevent aging," and that we are to be complimented if we look "ten years younger" than our chronological age. Inherent in these messages is the notion that aging is a plague to be avoided, that looking and feeling "old" is the worst, most undesirable fate imaginable. Not only is the appearance of aging scorned, but older persons' value is often further discounted both because they may not be involved in the world of work and because they are often dependent on others for assistance in the tasks of daily living.

In our society, heavily influenced as it is by the Protestant work ethic, valuations of people are often based on the productive work in which they engage. In any social encounter with a stranger, the typical first question posed is: "What do you do?" People are judged by what they can do or give, not by who they *are*.[8] Those who are no longer working or engaged in active pursuits are seen as drains on society (labeled "greedy geezers" on one notorious magazine cover), or else not seen at all.

American society's attitude toward its retired citizens is that they should fade into oblivion, asking little, content to amuse themselves through recreation, whiling away their final days in sunny resorts in pursuit of golf, bingo, and shopping. Older individuals who were previously respected, active, committed members of the community can suddenly find themselves treated like "wrinkled babies," amused and ignored.[9] Robbed of the means to attain social worth, older people are thus left with lives which may well feel empty and boring.[10] Older Americans thus receive the message that they are superfluous, unappealing, and unwanted. No wonder depression and suicide afflict the old to a degree out of proportion to their numbers![11]

In addition to equating worth with work, Americans have developed negative attitudes toward growing older because dependency is an inexorable feature of aging. If there is any quality that is exalted above all else in American culture, it is independence. From the frontier experience, as well as from America's Protestant founders, comes the ideal of "pulling yourself up by your bootstraps"; and from the popular media comes the still-powerful refrain: "Mother, please, I'd *rather* do it myself." Americans dread having to rely on others for anything.

In a recent cross-cultural study, comparing the experience of aging in rural and suburban American communities to that in Hong Kong, Ireland, and two African cultures, only Americans regarded the prospect of depending on others for assistance as the worst possible thing that might happen to them in growing older.[12] If depending on others is considered a terrible fate, the elderly necessarily face a steady erosion of their self-esteem.

Aging and the Jewish Tradition

What does Jewish tradition have to say about the experience of growing older? What is the role of the elderly and what resources can help them face the last stage of the life cycle with its attendant blessings and burdens? Examination of Jewish tradition and Jewish life demonstrates that aging can be experienced as a time of meaning, celebration, and connection.

The Mitzvah Model: A Life of Meaning

In the concept of mitzvah, or religious obligation, the older Jew can find a way to experience a profound sense of self-worth and social value. Within this traditional framework are models that empower even the physically or mentally incapacitated so that they, too, experience personal significance. From birth, the Jew is part of a community that extends through time and space. Membership in this community involves inclusion in the Brit—the covenant with God established at Sinai, which binds each Jew to mitzvot. Thus, each Jew is *metzuveh* (commanded), bound to the covenant and the commandments, both ritual and ethical. One's fate beyond this world is traditionally seen as dependent on a lifetime record of observing the mitzvot. The redemption of the Jewish people and, indeed, the whole world rests on the collective fulfillment of this ancient covenant through mitzvot.

In this traditional worldview, each Jew's relationship to the mitzvot has cosmic significance. How and whether one observes mitzvot affects one's social as well as religious status. One can gain *kavod* (honor) by exemplary performance of mitzvot—by being faithful, for example, to the mitzvot under difficult or dangerous conditions, or by imbuing observance with particular fervor and intentionality (*kavanah*). Within the social world of the covenantal community, one achieves the highest honor by facilitating others' observance. Thus, it is a special honor to lead others in the recitation of the *Amidah* or other prayers, and to be counted in the quorum for prayer or *birkat ha-mazon* (grace after meals). Theoretically, any Jew can gain importance, success, and honor through the performance of mitzvot.

It is easy to see how valuable this concept and experience can be for older adults. Being conscious of obligation, of being *metzuveh*, gives older adults precisely that which they lack: the opportunity to experience life as meaningful, not empty. In performing mitzvot, older Jews have a chance to participate in valuable activities, to have a meaningful social role in the covenantal community, and to structure their time.

Abraham Joshua Heschel suggests that it is through this experience of being obligated that one truly exists. Older adults who believe that they continue to be obligated, understand themselves as engaged in the central human task of *tikkun olam*—repairing and redeeming the world through observance of the mitzvot. According to Heschel, "What a person lives by is not only a sense of belonging but a sense of *indebtedness*. The need to be needed corresponds to a fact: something is asked of a man, of every man. Advancing in years must not be taken to mean a process of suspending the requirements and commitments under which a person lives. To be is to obey. A person must not cease to be."[13] The state of obligation may provide many older persons with the "sense of significant being," otherwise sorely lacking. To tell older adults that they are as bound to mitzvot as any other Jew is to tell them that something is expected of them, that their actions matter, that they have the means to transcend the narrow confines of their lives' current context along with some of the damning messages communicated by the culture surrounding them.

Halakhah (Jewish law) specifies no special category of obligation for the old. While there is a very clear beginning point of obligation—Bar Mitzvah—there is no endpoint. There is neither retirement from mitzvot, nor a senior-citizen discount. There is also no automatic assumption that an older person is any less competent to perform a mitzvah than anyone else.

Yet the experience of aging may present formidable barriers to observing the mitzvot, such as the inability to ambulate without assistance, sensory deficits, cognitive impairment, and memory loss. The question then arises: How does the mitzvah model apply to those thus hindered? The tradition understands that observance of the mitzvot should be accessible and attainable for Jews. The Torah itself states:

> Surely, this mitzvah which I enjoin upon you this day is not too baffling for you, nor is it beyond reach. It is not in the heavens, that you should say, "Who among us can go up to the heavens and get it for us and impart it to us, that we may observe it?" Neither is it beyond the sea, that you should say, "Who among us can cross to the other side of the sea and get it for us and impart it to us, that we may observe it?" No, the thing is very close to you, in your mouth and in your heart, to observe it. (Deuteronomy 30:11–14)

Models for understanding the obligations of impaired older adults may be found within the halakhic literature regarding the obligations of those who are ill or physically incapacitated. There is a model of adaptive obligation, which might be called "sliding-scale obligation." According to this model, the mitzvot are assumed in principle to apply to each individual, but the authorities use sensitivity and creativity in defining mitzvot so that impaired individuals can fulfill their obligations by simply doing as much as they *can*.

For example, the obligation of daily prayer is considerably altered for the Jew who is physically or mentally incapable of performing it in its complete form. One who is old or weak and unable to stand may recite the *Amidah* (standing) prayers sitting down, or even prone, so long as the person has the capacity to concentrate on the prayers (Orah Hayyim 94:6; Mishnah Berurah 100:20). One who cannot speak may discharge their obligation by mentally reciting the prayers or by meditating upon them (Shulhan Arukh Orah Hayyim 94:6 and gloss). One who does not have the endurance to complete the entire liturgy may abbreviate the *Amidah* (ibid., 100a; and Tur, Orah Hayyim 110). Even the Shema can be abridged to include just the first line if a person cannot concentrate longer (Mishnah Berurah Orah Hayyim 100:21).

What is most significant about this "sliding scale" model of obligation for the old is that, once obligated, one remains so, even in the face of diminished capacity. All of the social and personal benefits of being *metzuveh* continue to accrue, for as long as one performs the mitzvah to the extent of one's ability, one is considered to have fully discharged the obligation.

The mitzvah model has very real implications for today's graying Jewish community. If older adults continue to be obligated to perform all ritual and ethical precepts, then it is the responsibility of the community to facilitate their participation in the full range of mitzvot. Older Jews must be given access to study, prayer, *tzedakah, gemilut hasadim,* and all facets of communal life, not segregated into "Golden Age" clubs whose primary focus is recreation. The elderly can properly be seen as *resources,* not just as recipients of service. Their experience can be used in directing synagogues and communal organizations, as well as in the realm of Jewish education, where there is a dire need for skilled teachers. Their volunteer energy may prove valuable in many different spheres of communal activity.

Access of older adults to mitzvah opportunities requires special sensitivity on the part of the community. The continued obligation of older Jews to participate in worship, for example, may require that synagogues be made more accessible to Jews in wheelchairs or using walkers, provide large-print prayer books, and assure amplification of the sound in sanctuaries. Special transportation efforts, whether carpools or vans, may be necessary to facilitate the participation of older Jews in community activities. The result should be to enrich life, both for the older Jews and for the community, which can benefit from the infusion of energy, commitment, and talent that the elderly have to offer.

A Life of Celebration: Living in Jewish Time

Participation in the rhythm of Jewish life can be especially meaningful for the elderly, for whom time may weigh heavily, seeming routinized and monotonous. Without the schedules of work and family life, there may be little to distinguish one day from another. While earlier in life there was never enough time, now there is all too much time, with too little meaningful activity to fill it. As one older adult said, "You eat, you sleep, and sit around."[14]

Judaism's approach to time speaks powerfully to this experience. In Judaism, time is sacred; we find holiness by living in cycles of significant moments.[15] The Jew lives not from day to day, but from Shabbat to Shabbat, Rosh Ḥodesh (new moon) to Rosh Ḥodesh, and Rosh Hashanah to Rosh Hashanah. Each moment has a *location* in time, characterized by what came before and what will come after. So today is not just Monday, which looks just like Tuesday, and suspiciously like Wednesday, but today is two days after Shabbat, two days before Hanukkah, and a week before Rosh Ḥodesh. Time has rhythm and texture, and great potential for meaning.

In contrast to the way time is experienced in aging, Jewish time continually provides something to look forward to and something to savor. Significant moments are thus stretched out in what has been called the "accordion effect": one feels their power long beforehand and long afterward through the preparation for them and reminiscence in their wake.[16]

Through the rituals that mark significant moments in Jewish time, the older person has the capacity to experience a sense of celebration and affirmation. Ritual connects individuals to their ideals and wishes, values and principles.[17] Ritual may be lighthearted (Purim) or somber (Tisha b'Av), joyous (Simḥat Torah), or solemn (*Yizkor*), but it is always serious, in the sense that it allows older adults to take themselves seriously and to feel a link to those things about which they care most deeply.

A Life of Connection

One universal aspect of aging is loss. As we age, we are forced to part with relationships, roles, and places that have been important in our lives. We have said good-bye to treasured others, and to precious aspects of ourselves. Not surprisingly, these losses often lead older people to feel disconnected from the past, from themselves, and from caring others.

Jewish life offers the older adult many rich dimensions of connection, which may serve to bring solace as well as to provide moorings in a time of confusion. First, Jewish life offers a *vertical* connection, a temporal link to one's personal and communal past and future.

Older Jews relive the past in the present by enacting rituals in which they have participated in the past. When an elderly woman *bentches licht,* recites the blessing over the Shabbat candles, she may say, "I remember my mother doing this." At that moment the past, and her mother, are not lost; they are a part of her present. There is a sense of the "enduring elements of life that do not pass away." Rather than feeling alienated from the past, she may experience her life as a continuum, "a single phenomenological reality."[18] In a larger sense, ritual connects the older Jew to the historical experiences and the ways of life of the Jewish people. In this way, the thread of continuity extends beyond the individual's life span.

Because Jewish time is cyclical, participating in the rituals that mark it also suggests a link to the future, perhaps leading to the hope that one will live to go around the cycle once again. Thus it is that older adults may leave a worship service or holiday celebration with the following wish: "We should all be together and, God willing, do the same thing next year." Furthermore, ritual links the older participant with the future of the Jewish people, affirming that "We have been here and we will continue, despite all of the changes in the world around us."[19] Participating in the rituals of Jewish life affirms that something precious will continue beyond the bounds of one's own life, *le-dor va-dor,* "from generation to generation."

In addition to binding the older person to past and future, Jewish life links the individual *horizontally,* to the Jewish community and the Jewish people. Every time older Jews worship in a minyan, they are not atomized individuals, but part of community. Even performing rituals at home, alone, older adults can feel tied to the Jewish people, for they know that, at that very moment, Jews everywhere are saying kiddush, or reciting the Shema, or lighting Hanukkah candles. Following news of the Jewish world and giving *tzedakah* also reinforce the feeling of belonging to the extended family of the Jewish people. Obviously, joining in communal activities of any sort allows older people to feel their place among their community and people. The importance of this sense of connectedness amid lives of disconnection and discontinuity makes it incumbent upon those involved in the Jewish community to forge connections with older adults in their midst, whether living on their own or in institutional contexts.

A final connection that Judaism offers the older person is a tie to God. Judaism affirms that no matter what and whom we have lost, we retain a connection with the Merciful One. The Healer of broken hearts is with us even in the depths, through whatever shattering experiences will be faced; God will be present until life's end. The older Jew is never truly alone, never cut off, because of the web of connections offered by ritual, community, and belief.

New Challenges for a Graying Jewish Community

The new realities of aging pose fresh challenges for Jewish life. Two are detailed below.

NEW RITUALS

One of the strengths of Jewish tradition is its special way of marking the significant transitions of life. Rituals celebrating life cycle events enable people moving from one phase of life to another to articulate and understand their experience in the context of the ideals of their tradition and with the support of family and community. However, no significant Jewish ritual marks life events between marriage and death, other than those relating to the birth and development of children. Thus, there are no rituals to aid the individual in becoming and being an older adult (see Barry D. Cytron, pp. 146–147).

Aging is now understood as a distinct developmental stage characterized by personal and social change and transition. Therefore, we need to and can create new rituals to mark this life stage.[20] By identifying key moments in the experience of aging, we can marshal the resources of Jewish tradition and community to enrich and sustain aging Jews.

For instance, Marcia Cohn Spiegel created a ceremony for the older woman ascending to wisdom.[21] The ceremony, which marks her own sixtieth birthday, includes recognition of mortality through the donning of burial shrouds, the taking of a new name, and the making of vows marking commitments for this new period of life. Paul Citrin builds on the tradition of ethical wills, in which individuals document the values, ideals, and dreams they wish to pass on to those who will succeed them. He proposes *Av/Em Etzah*, a ceremony in which older adults share with their congregation a written *tzva'at etzah*, a testament of counsel, outlining the lessons life has taught them and the messages they wish to convey to others. Citrin envisions this ceremony as the culmination of a process of study and reflection.[22]

Numerous transitions within the aging process call out for ritual acknowledgment. Retirement is an enormously charged moment, and constitutes one of the most dramatic changes in one's life. Nancy Fuchs-Kreimer has proposed *Bar Yovel*, a ritual that links retirement with covenantal theology; here the commemoration of retirement is modeled on the celebration of the jubilee, the rest given the land after forty-nine years of labor in biblical times. Fuchs-Kreimer's ritual is dense with symbols, including the sounding of a shofar to symbolically expel the demons of boredom, uselessness, loneliness, and despair.[23] Similarly, becoming a grandparent, leaving one's home, and entering a nursing home are other mileposts that may warrant the development of personal or communal ceremonies.

Aging is a time of loss and change, but also of opportunity. The older Jew has time and resources to engage in Jewish life in a new way. Old age may be a time for deepening existing connections to Jewish learning, observance, and community, or it may present a first chance for serious exploration of one's Jewishness.

One way to capitalize on this opportunity might be through a ritual that would allow one to reaffirm the commitment to Judaism. This rededication to the commandments, a *ḥanukkat mitzvah*, would celebrate the culmination of a period of serious study, allowing the older Jew to articulate in the context of the community a commitment to Torah, worship, and loving deeds. Just as the Bar or Bat Mitzvah joins the community of Jewish adults through public ritual, so the older person would reaffirm both commitment and continued connection to the community and tradition.

The "oldest old," those over eighty-five years of age, are the most frail and often the most isolated. It is imperative that the Jewish community develop strategies to support and sustain the frail elderly, not just physically and materially, with housing and health care and social services, but spiritually as well.

The isolation of the old in senior-citizen ghettoes, both through segregated housing and social neglect, impoverishes them as well as the larger Jewish community. Efforts to link young and old through intergenerational study, service, and celebration are promising antidotes to this disconnection and alienation. Older adults in senior adult housing, nursing homes, and senior centers can forge connections with young people in Jewish schools, youth groups, and campus organizations. Intergenerational ties ground the young in the past and provide the old with a sense of significance and connectedness.

The Jewish community today is being called on to grapple with the great challenges of aging. What will the community and the tradition be able to offer the frail elderly hovering at life's edge, whose lives are characterized by physical and mental impairment, loss, and dependency? It may well be that the "mitzvah model" will not address the concerns of those who are no longer able to interact with their environment in any significant way. Perhaps we can regard this last phase of life as Shabbat, the Sabbath of *being* after a life of *doing*.[24] Reflection and meditation, remembering and appreciating, may form the heart of Jewish duty at this last stage of life.

In facing the new realities of extended dependency and compromised living, as in responding to the other new realities of aging, Judaism has the potential to bring comfort, celebration, and meaning, to fulfil the ancient vision of the Psalmist:

> The righteous will flourish like the palm tree;
> They will grow like a cedar in Lebanon.
> Planted in the house of the Eternal,
> They shall flourish in the courts of our God.
> They shall yet yield fruit even in old age;
> Vigorous and fresh they shall be,

To proclaim that the Eternal is just!

God is my Rock, in whom there is no injustice. (Psalm 92)

NOTES

1. Morris Zelkitch, "Trends in the Care of the Aged," *Journal of Jewish Communal Service*, 34:1, Fall, 1957, pp. 126–40.

2. Allen Glicksman, *The New Jewish Elderly: A Literature Review*, (New York: Petschek Jewish Family Center, American Jewish Committee, 1991).

3. For a thorough analysis of the evolution of the Jewish understanding of filial obligations throughout history, see Gerald Blidstein, *Honor Thy Father and Mother: Filial Responsibility in Jewish Law and Ethics* (New York: Ktav Publishing House, Inc., 1975).

4. Elaine M. Brody, "Parent Care as a Normative Family Stress", *Gerontologist*, 25:1, 1985, pp. 19–21.

5. Ibid., pp. 21–26.

6. The halakhic and aggadic treatment of this mitzvah is catalogued in Yitzḥak Schlesinger, *Ve-hadartah penai zaken*, (B'nai Brak: HaMesorah, 1985 [Hebrew]).

7. Responsum of Rabbi Shmuel Ha-Levi Vazner, cited in Schlesinger, *op. cit.*

8. Abraham Joshua Heschel, "To Grow in Wisdom," in *The Insecurity of Freedom* (Philadelphia: Jewish Publication Society, 1966, p. 79).

9. Maggie Kuhn, in a lecture to rabbinic interns at the Philadelphia Geriatric Center, 1990.

10. Heschel, "To Grow in Wisdom," p. 77.

11. B. J. Gurland, "The Comparative Frequency of Depression in Various Age Groups," *Journal of Gerontology*, 131:283–92, 1976.

12. Jennie Keith, Christine L. Fry and Charlotte Ikels, "Community as Context for Successful Aging," in *The Cultural Context of Aging*, Jay Sokolovsky, ed. (New York: Bergin and Garvey Publishers, 1990, pp. 225f).

13. Heschel, "To Grow in Wisdom," p. 78.

14. Jaber Gubrium, *Living and Dying at Murray Manor*, New York: St. Martin's Press, 1975.

15. Abraham Joshua Heschel, *The Sabbath* (New York: Harper & Row, 1966, p. 8).

16. Fred Davis, cited in Kathy Calkins, "Time Perspectives, Marking and Styles of Usage," *Social Problems* 17:487–501.

17. Barbara Myerhoff, "Ritual and Signs of Ripening: The Intertwining of Ritual, Time and Growing Older," in *Age and Anthropological Theory*, P. I. Kertzer and J. Keith, eds. (Ithaca: Cornell University Press, 1984, p. 305).

18. Ibid., p. 306.

19. Myerhoff, "We Don't Wrap Herring in a Printed Page," in Sally F. Moore and Barbara Myerhoff, eds., *Secular Ritual* (The Netherlands: Van Goneim and Co., 1977, p. 218).

20. See Bernice Neugarten, "The Future and the Young Old," *Gerontologist*, Feb., 1975, and Erik Erikson, Joan Erikson and Helen Kivnick, *Vital Involvement in Old Age* (New York: W. W. Norton and Co., 1986).

21. Marcia Cohn Spiegel, "Becoming a Crone: Ceremony at 60," *Lilith*, 21, Fall, 1988.

22. Paul J. Citrin, "*Av/Em Eitza*: Proposal for a New Life-Cycle Ceremony," *Journal of Reform Judaism*, Spring, 1990, pp. 43–46.

23. Nancy Fuchs-Kreimer, "*Bar-Yovel*: Creating a Life-Cycle Ritual for Retirement," *Reconstructionist*, Oct.–Nov., 1987, pp. 21–24.

24. Brian Field, personal communication in the context of his participation in a course on aging that I taught at the Reconstructionist Rabbinical College, 1989.

SUGGESTIONS FOR FURTHER READING

Gerald Blidstein, *Honor Thy Father and Mother: Filial Responsibility in Jewish Law and Ethics* (New York: Ktav, 1975), is an excellent and comprehensive study of the development of the halakhah concerning filial responsibility from the Bible through rabbinic sources.

The landmark paper by Elaine M. Brody, "Parent Care as a Normative Family Stress," *Gerontologist* 25, no. 1 (1985): 19–29, systematically dismantles the myth of abandonment of the elderly by their families and provides a context for understanding the ways in which families care for elderly relatives and the impact of that care upon them.

Allen Glicksman, *The New Jewish Elderly: A Literature Review* (New York: American Jewish Committee, 1991), contains a comprehensive review of data on the American Jewish elderly from demographic studies of American Jewish communities. Glicksman not only provides a sense for the changing numbers of older Jews, but also analyzes the changing characteristics and needs of this new group.

Abraham Joshua Heschel's address to the 1961 White House Conference on Aging, "To Grow in Wisdom" (in *The Insecurity of Freedom* [Philadelphia: Jewish Publication Society, 1966]), is both inspirational and a call to conscience regarding the true meaning and challenges of aging.

Barbara Myerhoff's noted study of the elderly Jews of Venice, California, *Number of Days* (New York: Dutton, 1978), is filled with insight on the meaning of tradition, community, and continuity to older adults struggling with loss and change.

Yitzḥak Schlesinger, in *Ve-hadartah penai zaken* (B'nai Brak: Ha-Mesorah, 1985), provides a comprehensive summary of the development of the law of honoring the elderly throughout halakhah.

JUDITH HAUPTMAN

Death and Mourning
A Time for Weeping,
A Time for Healing

One of the ritual areas about which American Jews are least knowledgeable is death and mourning. Many—perhaps most—Jews celebrate birth, coming of age, and marriage in the context of Jewish tradition. But death is more often observed the American way than the Jewish way. Not only does this abandoning of Jewish practice diminish the dignity and meaning of the rites of closure, it also denies the mourners rich opportunities for consolation.

With hospice care for the terminally ill becoming more common, many people will find themselves present at the moment of death. Overwhelmed by the loss and sorely in need of expressing both grief and love, persons not schooled in Jewish patterns of behavior will not know what to do when death occurs. But those who are familiar with Jewish attitudes toward death and with

I would like to dedicate this chapter to Professor Baruch Bokser, my colleague on the Talmud faculty at the Jewish Theological Seminary, whose death in the prime of life occurred as I was working on this project. My thanks to Rabbi David C. Kogen, Professor Richard Kalmin, and my friends Terri and Jack Lebewohl for their many insightful comments and suggestions.

the rites of mourning do know what initial steps to take to preserve the dignity of the deceased and ease the pain. They would immediately rend their garment and recite the words *barukh dayyan emet*—blessed is the just judge—a brief statement suggesting that as unjust as the death may seem, Judaism asks one to believe that God has reasons for His actions. They would not leave the corpse alone but remain in the room and begin to recite psalms. For a person who feels confused and bereft upon witnessing the death of a loved one, these time-honored structures serve to comfort.

This chapter presents an overview of the laws of mourning, sketching in the general contours and even some details. These laws come to us from the Bible, the Talmud, and more recent Jewish codes of law, in particular the Shulḥan Arukh, first published in 1565. As specific and situation-oriented as the laws of mourning in these works are, anyone who is steeped in this literature begins to notice that a number of principles predominate.

The first is *halakhah ke-divrei ha-mekel be-evel*, that is, in matters of mourning we rule according to the more lenient opinion (Mo'ed Katan 19b) (all references are to the Babylonian Talmud). From the time that an early talmudic master named Samuel formulated this principle, it was invoked whenever there was a conflict of opinion on how to proceed. What it seems to reflect is a sense on the part of the rabbis that dealing with death is so difficult that whatever accommodations can be made to ease the burden of mourning should be made.

A second general principle that emerges from the talmudic material is that death is the great leveler. Whereas elsewhere in Jewish law, particularly in marriage and synagogue ritual, women are treated as subordinate to men, in death they achieve parity. It makes no difference if it was a man or woman, a father or a mother, who died or who mourns: the same rules apply to both sexes. Just as a man is buried, so is a woman buried; in the same way that a man observes rites of mourning, so a woman observes rites of mourning. The final acts of kindness performed for the deceased know no gender differentiation.

The third general principle is that the main concept underlying all Jewish laws of mourning is *kevod ha-met*, preserving the dignity and honor of the deceased. Although *shivah*, the week of mourning, tends to be viewed in contemporary society as affording individuals an opportunity to deal with grief in the communal embrace, the main point of a family observing *shivah* is to make others take notice of the death. Were it not for *shivah*, the world would not miss a beat when someone dies. Putting the family in limbo for an entire week and drawing the community into their lives is a powerful way of making the world mark and mourn the death of their precious relative.

The last general principle to point out about the laws of mourning is that Jewish contact with Gentile society has altered these rules. In a number of instances the medieval commentators say that a particular ancient practice referred to in the Talmud, such as overturning couches in the house of mourning or wrapping the head as a sign of grief, should no longer be followed because it will make Jews a laughingstock in the eyes of the Gentiles or else create the impression that Jews practice magic.[1]

Thus mourning practices, which are in essence a commandment between one person and another person and not between a person and God, are shaped and modified by social standards and occasionally even abandoned with the passage of time. Similarly, new customs can emerge that have no basis in rabbinic or biblical teachings. Because bringing closure to relationships with parents and other close relatives is such a sensitive issue, these added practices, despite their tenuous connection to classical Jewish texts, exert an extraordinarily strong grip on people. The custom of covering mirrors during *shivah*, for example, is obscure in origin and purpose, yet it is scrupulously observed in almost all *shivah* homes. It is rather easy to provide homiletical interpretations for customs like these, as is often done; but it is also important to distinguish between ancient practices rooted in and required by Jewish law and those that somehow attached themselves to the body of Jewish practice over the years.

A final note: Jewish mourning rites have great appeal today because of their ability to meet the emotional needs of mourners, helping them to cope with and adapt to altered life circumstances. Yet one must recognize that the theological approach of those who framed this set of observances differs from that of many people today. The pervasive theme in almost all prayers relating to death is that God decides the length of a person's life and that His decision, always a just one, is determined by the person's moral and religious behavior. As foreign and unacceptable as this idea may be to contemporary sensibilities, it is still possible for the centuries-old prayers and customs to heal the wounds and help the mourner regain balance.

Death

Judaism values greatly acts of loving kindness performed for the dying and the deceased. The Shulḥan Arukh states that one should not leave the room of someone who is about to die so that she not feel abandoned in the very last moments of life (339:4).[2] If possible, when death is imminent, a person should be encouraged to recite the *viddui* (confession), asking God for forgiveness for past misdeeds and a place with Him after death. If the dying person (*goses*)[3] herself is unable to recite this prayer, it may be recited for her by someone else.

Once death has occurred, those sitting with the deceased close her eyes and mouth and pull a sheet over her face (352:4). If they wish to, even if they are not close relatives, they may rend a garment and recite, *Barukh dayyan emet* (340:5).[4] The *shomer*, a family member or hired stranger who has been appointed to stay with the corpse, generally sits nearby reciting psalms. The act of guarding the corpse exempts the *shomer* from all positive rituals, such as praying or donning tefillin. The corpse must not be left alone from the time of death to the time of burial; even so, no one, aside from those appointed to remain with it or prepare it for burial, may view it. No eating or drinking is allowed in the same room as the corpse. Should the death occur in a hospital on the Sabbath, the body is taken to the hospital morgue until the Sabbath is over; in such a case it is impossible for the *shomer* to remain with the corpse. Whether the person died in a hospital, a hospice, or at home, a close relative should call a Jewish funeral home to have the corpse removed and prepared for burial.[5] Most families also call their rabbi at this time.

In preparation for burial, the *ḥevrah kadisha* (holy fellowship), a group of community volunteers or people hired by the funeral home, cleanse the corpse and perform the *taharah*. This process is akin to immersion in a *mikvah* (ritual bath), except that instead of putting the body in the water, the water is poured over the corpse. They then dress the corpse in simple white shrouds and a tallit worn during the deceased's lifetime, place the corpse in the casket, and close it (351:2). Men tend the corpses of men, and women the corpses of women (352:3).

THE CASKET

Jewish law stipulates that a casket is to be simple, preferably made of wooden boards and dowels. The principle is to return the body to the earth from which it came. In Israel, no coffin is used, only a bier, so as to hasten decomposition and mingling with the earth. In the United States, burial in a coffin is standard practice.

The reason for a simple coffin and shrouds is found in the Talmud (Mo'ed Katan 27b). The text tells us that in the mishnaic period, because of the great expense involved in preparing fine shrouds, burying the dead was more difficult than the death itself for the mourning family. As a result, people began abandoning their dead without burying them. To remedy this situation, Rabban Gamliel, a leading rabbinic figure, waived the honor due him and requested that he be buried in a simple shroud of linen. As anticipated, simplicity then became standard Jewish burial practice. The same text also mentions several other enactments made for the sake of the poor, such as burial for all in a plain casket.[7]

TIMING OF THE FUNERAL

A person is to be buried as soon after death as possible. Postponing burial, *halanat ha-emet*, is considered disrespectful to the deceased as well as emotionally trying for the grieving family. Even so, since it is considered an honor for the deceased to have a well-attended funeral, burial usually occurs a day after death, thereby giving sufficient time for the family to make arrangements and notify friends and members of the community of the death (357:1). In certain cases, if family members need to travel from afar, the funeral is held even two days after the death.

A funeral may not be held on the Sabbath, High Holy Days, or the *yom tov* days of Passover, Shavuot, and Sukkot. Although the burial could be performed by non-Jews on the second day of these holidays (*yom tov sheni shel galuyot*), which is of lesser sanctity, this is rarely done. Funerals may take place on the intermediate days of the festival.

ANINUT

The state of deep grief, from the time of death until completion of the burial, is called *aninut*. During this time the mourner, the *onen*, is exempt from fulfilling any of the positive observances of Judaism, such as lighting Hanukkah candles or putting on tefillin, because it is assumed that he or she is distracted by the death and preoccupied with making funeral arrangements (341:1). Yet should a person enter *aninut* on the Sabbath, he or she may attend services, since no funeral arrangements can be made on that day.

Most American Jewish funerals take place in a funeral chapel, generally a privately owned facility that provides all the necessary services to mourners, such as transporting the corpse and preparing it for burial. The funeral of a rabbi, cantor, or communal leader, however, is often held in the synagogue.

While the family members await the start of the funeral, it has become customary for friends to approach them and offer words of condolence. As well established as this custom is, it deviates from the rabbinic teaching "Do not comfort him while his dead still lies unburied before him" (Pirkei Avot 4:18).

KERI'AH

One of the most ancient mourning practices, *keri'ah*, rending one's garment, is referred to in a number of places in the Bible. Jacob, upon hearing news of Joseph's death, rips his clothing in grief (Genesis 37:34). Rending the garment is giving physical expression to one's emotions, showing that the sadness, pain, and perhaps anger are so intense that they lead one to find relief in the destruction of material goods.

Keri'ah became a requirement of the mourning process in the rabbinic period and was supposed to be done immediately upon learning of the death. The Talmud says that "any rending which is not performed at the moment of *hamimut* [wrenching emotion] is not considered rending" (Mo'ed Katan 24a). Today, however, two major changes have occurred in the practice of *keri'ah*. The first is that rending is not usually done upon hearing of the death but either immediately prior to the funeral service or else at the cemetery, just prior to burial. A rabbi or other individual approaches the mourners, asks them to stand up, and, with a blade, cuts the garment the mourner is wearing, such as a tie, shirt, or blouse. The mourner then rends the garment with her own hands, making a rip about three inches long (vertically, over the heart).[7] As she does so she recites the blessing: "Barukh atah adonai elohenu melekh ha-olam dayyan ha-'emet" (Blessed is God, Ruler of the Universe, the Just Judge). The mourners wear the rent garment for the entire *shivah* period. After *shivah*, there is no longer any requirement to wear it.

The second change is that many mourners no longer perform *keri'ah* on a garment they are wearing; instead, the mourner pins on a small black ribbon and then rips the ribbon. This custom probably originated at a time when Jews were embarrassed by public display of their own mourning rituals and felt that it was more dignified to wear a rent black ribbon than a rent garment. Today it seems that such feelings of shame have largely disappeared and a return to traditional practices is called for.

The Funeral Service

A Jewish funeral service is short. It consists of three parts: readings from Psalms, a eulogy, and the Memorial Prayer. A rabbi, relative, or friend recites several appropriate psalms, such as chapters 15, 23, 24, 49, and 90, most of which speak of closeness to God and dwelling with Him as the reward for leading a morally upright life. At the funeral of a woman one often reads chapter 31 of Proverbs, which lauds the accomplishments of the woman of valor. A *hesped* (eulogy) is then delivered, usually by a rabbi but preferably by a son or daughter or other close relative of the deceased. The eulogy, which summarizes the life and achievements of the deceased, is intended to praise him and at the same time express the sadness that is in the hearts of those present (344:1). On certain joyous days of the year, such as Hanukkah, Rosh Ḥodesh (New Moon), and intermediate days of a festival, when burial is permitted but a eulogy is not allowed, a rabbi will find a way to circumvent this ban, such as by interspersing some brief remarks about the deceased between the verses of the psalms.

The funeral service ends with the Memorial Prayer, *El molei rahamim,* which asks a merciful God to care for the soul of the deceased under the sheltering wings of His presence and help it find peace. The centuries-old mournful melody with which these words are chanted is an appropriately somber end to the service.

Several pallbearers, usually friends and relatives, then carry or roll the casket to the hearse, and the assembled group follows for a block or two out of respect for the dead. The Hebrew word for funeral, *levayah,* means to escort; it is this brief act of escorting the body to burial, as was done in ancient times, that is referred to. The casket is then driven to the cemetery, with family and friends following.

THE GRAVESIDE SERVICE

When the hearse reaches the cemetery, the family members and friends again carry or roll the casket to the gravesite, pausing several times on the way, probably as a sign of grief. The rabbi usually walks ahead reciting Psalm 91, which speaks of God's sheltering presence; all others follow the casket. After it is lowered into the ground, friends and relatives help shovel earth, either filling the grave completely or just covering the coffin. At this time, *tzidduk hadin*, a justification of the divine decree, is read. The mourners then recite the "burial kaddish" (376:4). This special kaddish has a long opening paragraph that talks about a time in the future when God will resurrect the dead, rebuild the city of Jerusalem and His Temple, and establish His kingdom in the entire world.

Burial, and particularly the act of shoveling the earth into the grave, brings closure. Up until this point it is hard for a mourner to deal with her feelings because the body has not yet been laid to rest, but from this point on she can confront her emotions. It now becomes possible to extend words of comfort to the bereaved family. Friends form two parallel lines through which the mourners pass and receive condolences as they walk from the gravesite back to the hearse.[8] The family then returns to the place where it will sit *shivah*, usually the home of the deceased. It is customary, before entering the home, to pour water over one's hands (376:4), a practice reminiscent of Temple times when ritual cleanness and uncleanness was a significant factor in Jewish life and water functioned as a cleansing agent for corpse-induced defilement.

Se'udat Havra'ah

While burial is taking place, friends prepare a meal, called *se'udat havra'ah* (meal of consolation), for the mourners to eat upon their return from the cemetery (378:1). The menu usually includes eggs, lentils, and other round foods, which may serve as a reminder of the ongoing cycle of life (378:9). This meal is intended to revive the spirits of the mourners, who now need the care and concern of the community to negotiate the emotional turbulence still ahead of them.

Shivah

Shivah begins upon returning from the cemetery, even if it is already close to sundown, and lasts for seven days. For example, if the burial took place on Thursday at noon, the seventh and last day of *shivah* is the following Wednesday. This last day of *shivah* is abbreviated (see below).

Probably the best known of all Jewish mourning rites, *shivah* (literally, "seven") requires all members of the immediate family to interrupt the normal flow of their lives for an entire week—not go to work, not even go outside—and spend time in the home of the deceased, receiving visits from those who come to comfort them. All their needs are tended to by others, such as preparing and serving meals or answering the doorbell (although the front door is usually left open and visitors enter on their own) and the telephone. It is an old Jewish custom to bring cooked meals to people in mourning. Cut off from the everyday world, the family is given an opportunity to spend all their emotional energy dealing with the death of a person they loved and absorbing the pain, which is deep even if death was expected. Those who come to visit during this week perform the mitzvah of *niḥum avelim*, comforting the mourners and also honoring the dead. The best way of fulfilling this dual goal is to speak of the deceased. An easy way of refocusing a conversation that has strayed far from the topic of death is to ask the mourners a leading question about the deceased.

Anyone who has sat *shivah* knows how comforting and stabilizing—and at the same time grueling—this week is. The gratitude that a mourner feels toward those who take the time to visit during this difficult period is boundless.

RULES OF BEHAVIOR DURING *SHIVAH*

A seven-day period of mourning is a custom that dates back to the Bible, which says, in reference to the death of Jacob (Genesis 50:10), that he was mourned for seven days. It is the Talmud (Mo'ed Katan 21a), though, that presents *shivah* as a full-fledged set of mourning practices, primarily defined in terms of its restrictions:

And these are the things that a mourner is forbidden to do:
(1) go to work,
(2) bathe,
(3) annoint the body with oil,
(4) engage in sexual relations,
(5) wear leather shoes,
(6) read Torah, Prophets, Hagiographa,
(7) and study Mishnah, Midrash, Halakhot, Aggadot.

This set of rules denies the mourner basic physical pleasures as well as spiritual and intellectual pleasure derived from the study of classical texts.[9] In addition, the fact that ordinary labor is forbidden insulates the mourner from the world-at-large and places him at home with little to do other than talk about the deceased and deal with his grief.

Other talmudic statements indicate that a mourner may not don tefillin for the first several days of *shivah* (Mo'ed Katan 21a);[10] that mourners are not allowed to greet others, inquire after their well-being, or respond to a greeting by speaking of their own well-being (Mo'ed Katan 21b). This limitation creates awkward moments at the beginning and end of the *shivah* visit but accomplishes the goal of suppressing levity.

A positive act required during *shivah*, according to the Talmud, is to overturn all couches and beds in the house of mourning (Mo'ed Katan 27a). This practice was transformed, in the course of time, into a requirement to sit lower than is customary. Today, funeral homes supply low stools or stool-shaped cartons for the mourners to sit on. Unfortunately, these boxes are both unattractive and uncomfortable. To solve this problem, many synagogue groups provide an alternative kind of seating: a set of standard folding chairs with part of each leg sawed off is brought for the week to the home of the family sitting *shivah*. In this way the mitzvah of sitting low is fulfilled in a comfortable and even aesthetic manner.

Leather shoes may not be worn during *shivah*, but, as holds true for Yom Kippur, which is also a day of mourning and self-affliction, shoes made of fabric or some other material, such as plastic, are perfectly acceptable (382:1). If a mourner must leave home to go to the synagogue for services, he is permitted to wear leather shoes in the street for purposes of social acceptability.

Although bathing is not permitted during *shivah*, many rabbis interpret this rule as referring to bathing for pleasure.[11] Those who are accustomed and feel a need to shower each day are permitted to do so. The Talmud, and later the Shulḥan Arukh, state that women should not wear cosmetics during *shivah* (Mo'ed Katan 20b; 381:6).

The first three days of *shivah* are considered to be the ones of deepest and bitterest grief, the time it takes to absorb the fact of death and its irrevocability. After this period has passed, but only if absolutely necessary, the mourner is allowed to go to work. Similarly, if he owns a business, such as a restaurant, and would suffer significant financial loss by closing for the week, as would his waiters who are dependent on gratuities, he is permitted to leave the restaurant open, with others managing it, while he sits *shivah* (380:5).

END OF *SHIVAH*

The last day of *shivah* is not observed for a full twenty-four hours. The principle laid down in the Talmud is *Miktzat ha-yom kh-khulo*, meaning that on the final day, observance of a small portion of the day counts for observance of the entire day (Mo'ed Katan 19b). Today, the family in mourning gets up from *shivah* after *shaharit* services on the seventh day, or after *musaf* if the seventh day is Shabbat. As it turns out, *shivah* often consists of only three full days and four abbreviated ones; on the day of burial, *shivah* begins after returning from the cemetery; on Friday, *shivah* ends for the day about two hours before sunset; on Saturday, the mourners sit only at night, after *havdalah* is recited; and on the seventh day only a fraction of the day is observed. However, if *shivah* begins on a Friday or ends on a Sabbath, four full days will be observed.

OTHER *SHIVAH* PRACTICES

It has become common practice for the community to make a *shivah* minyan, to pray daily, morning and evening, in the house of the mourner so that she need not leave her home to go to the synagogue. A *sefer Torah* is even brought in these cases for the Monday- and Thursday-morning readings.[12] Some people light candles during all services held in the home. It is also customary for one of the mourners to serve as *sheliah tzibbur* (prayer leader) for all of the services held in the home. In many homes, during the break between *minhah* and *ma'ariv*, a learned friend is invited to teach Jewish texts, usually Mishnah, in memory of the deceased.

Since mourners sit at home all day, it is a good idea for those who plan to visit them to come at different hours during the day, particularly in the morning, when it is less likely for there to be a crowd. Because *shivah* is not a joyous social occasion, Jewish law frowns on putting out food for the visitors to eat. Baskets of fruit and boxes of candy should not be sent to the mourner or served by them to the visitors. However, as noted above, bringing cooked food for the mourners to eat is encouraged.

Many people believe that it is incorrect to pay a *shivah* visit in the first few days. The unfortunate result of this misconception is that the mourners receive little company at the time when they probably need it the most.

People often wonder whether they should bring their children when going to make a *shivah* call. In most instances the answer is yes, particularly if there are children in the home where *shivah* is being observed. The best way to develop in children a sensitivity toward the importance and kindness of comforting the bereaved, and to demystify mourning for them, is to take them along.

Other customs that have developed over time are to light a candle in the *shivah* home and let it burn for the full seven days, perhaps equating the source of light and warmth with the relationship between the deceased and his family. It has also become standard practice, though not prescribed in the codes of law, to cover all mirrors in the *shivah* home. One explanation is that mirrors encourage one to focus on oneself and mourning should involve attention to the deceased.

When one takes leave of a family in mourning, it is traditional to say to them: "Ha-makom yenahem etkhem be-tokh she'ar avelei tzion ve-yerushalayim" (May God comfort you among all those who mourn for Zion and Jerusalem). Like the reference in the wedding blessings to the joy of Zion, the grieving mother, upon being reunited with her children, this parting statement uses the occasion of an individual's death to express eschatological yearnings for future comfort for the entire bereaved Jewish people.

INTERSECTION OF SABBATH AND SHIVAH

The Sabbath that falls during *shivah* counts for one of the seven days even though it is not publicly observed as a day of mourning. On that Sabbath, the mourners are expected to go to the synagogue for prayers, and no condolences are to be extended to them. When the mourner arrives at the synagogue Friday night, he remains outside until the conclusion of *lekhah dodi*. The congregation then turns to him and greets him with the words, "May God comfort you . . ." A mourner may not serve as prayer leader on that Sabbath, or on any Sabbath in the thirty-day or year-long period of mourning. Otherwise the Sabbath supersedes mourning, suspending all public practices of mourning, such as sitting on low chairs, not wearing leather shoes, and not leaving one's home. Only the private practices of mourning still obtain on the Sabbath during the week of *shivah*, such as the ban on sexual relations and study of classical Jewish texts.

INTERSECTION OF FESTIVALS AND SHIVAH

Even more remarkable are the rules relating to the intersection of *shivah* and a festival. If the burial takes place several days before a festival, or even before sundown on the eve of a festival, the onset of the festival cancels the remaining days of *shivah* or, in the extreme case, cancels *shivah* altogether, provided a symbolic *shivah* was observed for a few moments. In Judaism, public celebration takes precedence over private mourning. No one is expected to mourn, celebrate, then resume mourning again. Nevertheless, as perplexing as it may seem, if someone dies on a festival, and is buried on one of the intermediate days, the family observes the remaining days of the festival and then, upon its conclusion, sits nearly a full, albeit delayed, *shivah* (Mo'ed Katan 20a; 399:1).[13] The logical principle at work here is that a festival can cancel mourning that has already begun, but not mourning that has been postponed.

When the Torah talks about the exacting standards of holiness that apply to *kohanim* (priests) who serve in the Temple, it goes on to say that these rules are relaxed if a *kohen's* close relative dies: he is instructed to defile himself for his mother, father, son, daughter, brother, and unmarried sister (Leviticus 21:2, 3). This short list makes it fairly obvious that the Torah links mourning with flesh-and-blood relatives, what the text calls *she'ero ha-karov*.

The rabbis of the Talmud took the Torah's short list of relatives, expanded it to include one's spouse, married sisters, and half-siblings,[14] and ruled that it is for these relatives and no others that a Jew—*kohen, levi,* or Israelite—sits *shivah* (Mo'ed Katan 20b). That is, the only people for whom one is obligated to sit *shivah* and observe the other rites of mourning are one's immediate family: parents, siblings, spouse, and children.

Today, given the prevalence of complicated family configurations, attributable in many instances to death, divorce, and remarriage, a variety of questions arises. What if a divorced parent's second spouse dies: are step-children required to sit *shivah*? Does one sit *shivah* for step-siblings? The rule seems to be that the obligation for mourning still falls only on blood relatives. As for siblings, only those who are blood relatives, like half-siblings, are included, but not step-siblings. Similarly, one is not required to observe the mourning rites for step-parents or step-children. The question of adoptive parents and adopted children is trickier, given the deep emotional attachment between them, identical to that of natural parents and children. In all of these cases Jewish law holds that although there is no absolute obligation to sit *shivah* and say kaddish, it certainly is permissible and commendable to do so.[15]

If a child dies before it is thirty days old, Jewish law does not prescribe any rites of mourning (Mo'ed Katan 24b; 374:8). As insensitive as this rule may seem, the explanation appears to lie in the fact that *shivah* honors the dead, and the Talmudic rabbis did not deem it appropriate to honor such a young child.

Today, more and more people, in particular women, find it meaningful and emotionally restorative to conduct a rite of mourning for the loss of a fetus. Suggestions have been made to recite a *mi shebeirakh* prayer in the synagogue after the miscarriage and, following her recovery, to invite the mother to recite publicly *birkhat ha-gomel* (a blessing said upon recovery from illness). In this way the community can be called upon to offer the couple emotional support and assistance in coming to terms with their grief.[16]

Mourners Who Live in Different Cities

Since it is not unusual today for brothers and sisters to live in different cities, apart from each other and also apart from their parents, the question of where to sit *shivah* for a parent who dies can be difficult to resolve. It is becoming common to sit the first three days in the home of the deceased parent or one of the siblings, together with the other mourners, and then return to one's own home for the latter part of *shivah*.[17] The logic behind this division is that the most effective and meaningful comforting can be offered by one's own friends and neighbors, who will be able to do so only when the mourner returns home.

Children and Mourning

Although children who have not reached the age of mitzvot—twelve for girls and thirteen for boys—are not obligated by any of the mourning rules, the tendency in most instances of a child suffering a loss of a parent or sibling is to involve her to the extent possible in the rites. Although it used to be common practice to shelter children from death and cemeteries, mental health professionals now consider it far better for a child to attend the funeral, watch the burial, rend her garment, sit *shivah*, and even recite kaddish for her parent or sibling. Children, too, need opportunities to express their love and grief openly, and Jewish mourning rites offer that to them.

Kaddish

Together with sitting *shivah*, saying kaddish is the most familiar and widely observed of all Jewish mourning practices. During *shivah* and afterward, at each of the daily services, mourners recite *kaddish yatom* (mourners' kaddish). Many mourners try to attend *shaharit* services in the morning and *minḥah/ma'ariv* in the late afternoon in order not to miss an opportunity to recite this prayer, but many rabbis rule that attending one service a day fulfills the mourners' obligation. Kaddish may be recited only when a quorum of ten Jews—a minyan—is present.

Kaddish is a prayer that says nothing about death or any event in the life of human beings. It is a doxology, a prayer extolling God, saying that He surpasses our praises, that we are unable, in this world, using our human faculties, to describe Him and His attributes adequately. Kaddish was not composed for mourners but is a set of paragraphs recited many times during every prayer service as a sort of marker or divider between the main sections of the service. For instance, at *ma'ariv* (evening prayer), *kaddish shalem* (full kaddish with an insertion petitioning God to answer our prayers) is recited after the *Amidah* and immediately before *alenu*. *Kaddish yatom* (a slightly shorter version of kaddish) is recited after *alenu*, marking off that last part of the service. That is, in general, each section of the service, be it a section of psalms or hymns, a Torah reading, or a set of petitions, is followed by the recitation of some form of kaddish. The kaddish that has come to be known as *kaddish yatom*, and is now recited only by mourners, was thus originally a fixed part of the service, totally independent of mourning and mourners. Over time, however, it came to be recited only by those present who were in mourning.

No one knows why this change took place. Statements in the Shulḥan Arukh suggest that the reason this particular prayer is reserved for male mourners is to give them an opportunity to honor their deceased fathers (376:4). If the sons recite kaddish and lead services, they show the community that their father properly discharged his obligation to educate them and transmit to them the principles and practices of Judaism.

It is also possible, according to some, to find a message appropriate to mourners in the kaddish prayer. By noting in its opening line that the world was created according to God's will, the prayer suggests that we do not understand why death occurs when it does, particularly when people die young, or why dying in some instances is so painful and prolonged. In a sense, what everyone longs for is *mitah bi-neshikah*, death by a kiss—a fast and painless death, preferably in one's old age. But the kaddish which asserts that the world was created as He wished it to be, meaning that God is in control and has reasons for His actions, may offer comfort to those who challenge God because of the untimely or difficult death of a family member. Kaddish is essentially a prayer that looks to a glorious future, one in which the whole world recognizes one God and, as a result, lives in harmony and peace.

Kaddish derabbanan, recited in the morning service after reading texts from the Talmud, is also reserved for mourners.

ALTERNATIVES TO KADDISH

When a person finds it difficult or impossible to say kaddish in the synagogue at least once a day, certain alternatives are available. A mourner may read each day a chapter from the Torah or the Prophets or study a mishnah or a passage from the Talmud.[18] Such study would also reflect well on the person's Jewish upbringing and hence on her parents. It is unfortunate that most people are unaware of this option, so that if they find it impossible to attend services, thinking there is no legitimate substitute they do nothing at all.

WOMEN AND KADDISH

The recitation of kaddish for nearly a year is traditionally viewed as an obligation upon the sons of the deceased, not upon the daughters. However, since Jewish laws of mourning in every other area obligate women in the same way that they obligate men, it follows that women should feel the same duty men feel and recite kaddish in a synagogue at least once a day. Even in Orthodox synagogues, where women are not counted for the prayer quorum and where they sit separately from men, a woman may recite kaddish along with the men from her own seat, just as she recites other prayers from her place during the course of the service.[19] A daughter who is Jewishly knowledgeable and committed to regular synagogue attendance honors the memory of the deceased parent just as much as a learned and observant son does. It is interesting to note that in the biblical and talmudic period women were actively and even formally involved in the mourning rites as keeners (*mekonenot*), composing dirges and leading the responsive recitation of various kinds of lamentations.

LONG-TERM EFFECTS OF KADDISH

In many ways, reciting kaddish on a regular basis for almost a year, let alone honoring the deceased parent, also gives the son or daughter an opportunity to receive communal sympathy for this entire time and even to channel his or her own bereftness into positive action. The need to attend services regularly often gives a new focus to the mourning child and fills a void left by the death of the parent, the community's attention substituting in a certain way for parental attention no longer available to him or her. Many mourners actually forge new bonds to their Jewish community and synagogue minyan as a result of this yearlong experience.

At the time of mourning a parent, which for many people occurs in their forties and fifties, many rediscover what Judaism has to offer and emerge from the year more committed and observant than before. The loss of a parent makes one at once more vulnerable and more open to new experiences or to changing one's way of doing things. Whereas Judaism up until that time may have been experienced vicariously through a parent, at this time a person comes into direct contact with it and struggles to find a new personal meaning in the Jewish faith and community.

ARRANGING FOR SOMEONE ELSE TO SAY KADDISH

In the past, when a person died leaving no sons or leaving sons who were not observant, a kaddish-sayer was paid to recite kaddish at three synagogue services each day. This person was not related to the deceased but was a Jew whose custom it was to pray three times a day in the synagogue. Many have decried this practice because it engenders disrespect rather than respect. If children of the deceased are not available to say kaddish on a relatively consistent basis for the entire period, rather than hire a kaddish-sayer, some rabbis suggest that relatives and friends divide the responsibility among themselves.

Sheloshim

Following *shivah*, the primary mourning period, there is a secondary period of mourning called *sheloshim*, meaning thirty, because it lasts for thirty days. Like *shivah*, one counts from the day of burial, and also like *shivah*, the last day is not full but ends following *shaḥarit* services.

Although *sheloshim* is a period of mourning, it is far less intense than *shivah*. The mourners resume normal social and professional duties but are still restricted in certain ways. One does not cut one's hair during this time, a custom dating back to the Bible of letting one's hair grow wild when in mourning (Leviticus 10:6); this rule applies to both men and women. In addition, men are not to shave for the duration of *sheloshim* (390:1). Another restriction observed for thirty days is not attending social events or even religious celebrations (391:1). However, a mourner may attend the ceremony itself, such as a circumcision, as long as he does not stay for the festive meal that follows. Wearing new clothes during this period of time is also considered inappropriate.

This thirty-day period eases the mourner back into normal routines by allowing the resumption of many but not all of one's regular patterns of social behavior. At the conclusion of the thirty days, a *sheloshim* memorial service is often held, at which time various Jewish texts are taught in memory of the deceased.

The end of *sheloshim* marks the end of the period of mourning for all relatives except parents. Although many people believe and even behave otherwise, after *sheloshim* kaddish is no longer recited for a spouse, sibling, or child. All mourning restrictions are lifted.

Twelve-Month Period of Mourning

The only relatives for whom one observes rites of mourning for twelve months are parents, both father and mother. A text from the Talmud drives home the point that mourning rites for parents are more demanding than those for other relatives. It lists nine ways in which the two sets of practices differ (Mo'ed Katan 22b). The four that are still relevant today are:

> [When mourning] for all the others (siblings, spouse, children), he may cut his hair or shave after thirty days have passed; [when mourning] for his parents, he may not do so until his friends scold him [about his appearance].
> [When mourning] for all others, he may attend a celebration after thirty days have passed; [when mourning] for his mother and father, not until twelve months have passed.
> [When mourning] for all others, he rends [his garment] a *tefah* (handbreadth); [when mourning] for his father and mother, until he bares his heart.

[When mourning] for all others, he bastes the rip after *shivah* and sews it up after thirty days; [when mourning] for his father and mother, he may baste the rip after thirty days, but may never fully mend it.

What is this lengthy rabbinic statement telling us? That parents are in a different category from everyone else; that just as the Torah singles out parents for special honor in their lifetime, promising long life in exchange for proper performance of this mitzvah and threatening death for anyone who curses or strikes parents, similarly the Talmud requires special respect for parents after their death.

I do not think that the Talmud is suggesting that the grief for one's parents is more intense than the grief for a child who dies but, rather, that parents who have given unconditional love to their children, who have given birth to them, raised, educated, and transmitted Jewish and human values to them, and who have established them as functioning and productive human beings, deserve the most prolonged and intensive period of mourning. Children are the continuation of their parents in the most real sense, and therefore they are asked to mourn for the longest period of time.

Following the death of a parent one does not attend *semaḥot* (religious celebrations) or parties for one year, or twelve months on the Jewish calendar.[20] According to the strictest rabbinic ruling, a mourner is not allowed to listen to music, turn on the radio, watch television, or go to a movie or a concert for twelve months. Other halakhic approaches allow most leisure activities as long as they are done in the company of only one or two other people so that the mourner does not experience *simḥat mere'im*, the pleasure of being together with friends.

The key observance for the extended mourning period is saying kaddish each day in the synagogue.[21] Although one would expect the obligation to last for twelve months, it lasts only for eleven. The explanation for this perplexing rule seems to lie in a tradition which states that the most time a person could possibly spend in the netherworld is twelve months. After that, even the blackest soul has atoned for its evil doings and is permitted to make its way to heaven. The recitation of kaddish helps guarantee safe passage from the lower realms to the upper. Therefore, if a child recited kaddish a full twelve months, he might be suggesting that his parents would not leave the netherworld until the end of this period of time—that is, that they were inveterate sinners. The custom thus arose of reciting kaddish for parents for eleven months only (376:4).

Converts and Mourning

A convert to Judaism, according to Jewish law, no longer has kinship ties to her Gentile family. Therefore, if a parent or other relative for whom Jewish law obligates mourning dies, the convert is under no obligation to sit *shivah*. Jewish law, in fact, discourages *shivah* in a case like this but looks benignly upon a convert who wishes to recite kaddish in memory of the deceased relative.

Mourning and Marriage

Should a bride or groom suffer the loss of a close relative within thirty days of a scheduled wedding, it is postponed until the conclusion of *sheloshim* (392:1). Even if it is a parent who died, a marriage may still take place after *sheloshim*—that is, during the twelve-month mourning period. No restrictions are placed on the joyousness of the celebration.

The Kohen and Death

A *kohen*, who in the past was and even today is subject to more demanding laws of ritual purity than other Jews, is not allowed to come into contact with a corpse or even be under the same roof, unless it is one of the seven family members for whom he is obligated to mourn. Because of this holiness code, *kohanim* may not attend funeral ceremonies of anyone other than close family members if the casket is present, nor may they enter a cemetery. Some *kohanim* remain outside the funeral chapel during the funeral service to show their respect for the deceased.[22] These rules apply only to male *kohanim*.

Charity in Memory of the Deceased

Probably the finest way to commemorate the deceased is to make a contribution to charity in his or her name. In many cases the family will indicate what causes were dear to the person's heart, such as social service and educational institutions in the United States or Israel, or a medical research society for a particular disease. Often these donations take the place of flowers, which are not appropriate at Jewish funerals.[23]

Yahrzeit

The *yahrzeit*, a Yiddish word meaning year-day, is the anniversary of the death as determined by the Jewish lunar-solar calendar. Because of differences between the Jewish and general calendrical systems, the secular date of the *yahrzeit* will vary somewhat from year to year. It is customary on this day for the relatives of the deceased—the same ones who observed *shivah*—to attend synagogue services, recite mourners' kaddish, be called for an *aliyah* to the Torah (if the Torah is read on that day), and serve as prayer leader. Many also give charity in memory of the deceased on the *yahrzeit*. A *yahrzeit* candle, which burns for twenty-four hours, is lit at home at sundown, when the *yahrzeit* begins. It is also customary to have an *aliyah* to the Torah on the Shabbat preceding the *yahrzeit*. Some Jews who find it difficult to attend services on the exact day of the *yahrzeit* observe it by saying kaddish on the Sabbath immediately preceding the anniversary.

Tombstone

After about a year has passed it is customary to erect a tombstone at the head of the grave. The Hebrew name and patronym and, more recently, also the matronym, are engraved on the stone, as well as the day of death according to the Jewish calendar. The English name of the deceased and the dates of birth and death according to the secular calendar are usually also engraved.

Unveiling

It is an American (and also Western European) Jewish custom to hold an unveiling of the tombstone about the same time as the date of the first *yahrzeit*. The simple graveside service consists of reading several Psalms and reciting the Memorial Prayer (*El molei rahamim*) and mourners' kaddish. This gathering gives the family an additional opportunity to reminisce about the deceased and thereby honor her. Young children in attendance should be taught to walk around the graves and not on them.

Yizkor

In addition to the yearly remembrance of the deceased on the *yahrzeit*, the ceremony of *hazkharat neshamot*, recalling the souls of the deceased, takes place four times a year in the synagogue—on Yom Kippur, Shemini Azeret (also known as the eighth day of Sukkot), the eighth day of Passover, and the second day of Shavuot. *Yizkor*, the first word of the memorial paragraph and the name by which it is commonly known, means "may God remember [the soul of the deceased and take care of it]." In addition to personal *Yizkor* prayers, in which people name their deceased relatives, collective *Yizkor* prayers are recited for martyrs, victims of the Holocaust and deceased members of the congregation. *Yizkor* is also a call to action: it stipulates that the one who recites the prayer make a donation to charity in memory of the deceased.

It is now almost standard practice that individuals whose parents are still alive and who have not suffered the death of any close relative leave the sanctuary during the recitation of *Yizkor*. Since this custom has no clear rationale and may possibly be rooted in superstition, many rabbis encourage all those present at services to remain in the sanctuary for *Yizkor* and not to separate themselves from the community at its time of remembered, shared grief. In particular, they note, the collective *Yizkor* prayers should be recited by all.

Many people light *yahrzeit* candles on the four days on which *Yizkor* is recited.

Visiting the Cemetery

It is customary to visit the graves of relatives once a year, usually a short time before the High Holy Days (Shulḥan Arukh, Oraḥ Ḥayyim, 581:4). In addition to making sure that the graves are being cared for properly by the cemetery authorities, the reason for this visit is the traditional Jewish belief, called *zekhut avot*, that ancestors intercede on behalf of descendants before the Heavenly tribunal as it decides their fate for the coming year. It is appropriate to recite psalms at the graveside and also the Memorial Prayer (*El molei rahamim*).

Conclusion

Judaism is a life-affirming and joy-affirming religion. At the same time, it recognizes the preciousness of each individual and for this reason prescribes rites of mourning that proclaim to the world the irreparable loss that a single death brings to the family, the community, the Jewish people, and the entire world. The laws of mourning also recognize the difficulty a mourner has in confronting the rupture of a valued relationship, the finality of death, and the emptiness left in its wake. Rites of mourning that take the mourner through the first few days, the first week, the first month, and the first year ease the transition, enabling him or her to come to terms with death and return to life in the real world in a gentle, incremental way.

NOTES

1. Mo'ed Katan 21a, Tosafot, s.v. *Aylu devarim*.

2. All references of this sort are to the Shulhan Arukh, Yoreh De'ah, section, and paragraph.

3. The Hebrew terms will be presented throughout in masculine form, even though the English translation will render them, on occasion, in feminine form.

4. *Keri'ah* (rending the garment) used to be mandatory for all those present at the moment of death. Since fear of loss of valuable garments discouraged people from remaining with the dying, the ritual of *keri'ah* was moved to the day of burial.

5. From this point on, *shomerim* are provided by the funeral home.

6. The Talmud (Mo'ed Katan 27a–b) does not speak of caskets but of plain and fancy biers.

7. For parents the rip is made on the left; for all others on the right.

8. The customary statement of condolence appears below in the section called "Other *Shivah* Practices."

9. Medieval commentators permitted the study of Job, parts of Jeremiah, Kinot, and the laws of mourning (Mo'ed Katan 21a, Tosafot, s.v. *Ve-asur likrot ba-torah*). Therefore, if one wishes to bring the mourner something, a book on the laws of death and mourning is appropriate.

10. According to the Shulḥan Arukh, it is only on the first day of *shivah* that a mourner does not wear tefillin (388:1).

11. See Leopold Greenwald, *Kol bo al avelut* (New York: Phillip Feldheim, 1947), p. 356.

12. Since one may only move a Torah from one place to another if it will be read three times, every effort should be made to do so, for instance by having a Shabbat afternoon *minḥah* service in the *shivah* home, at which time the Torah will be read.

13. The eighth day of the festival counts as the first day of *shivah*, even though the family does not observe that day (399:2).

14. It is more accurate to say that the Torah speaks of both whole and half-siblings on the father's side, and that talmudic rabbis expanded the Torah's list to include even half-siblings on the mother's side.

15. See Isaac Klein, *A Guide to Jewish Religious Practice* (New York: JTSA, 1979), p. 438.

16. See *Women's League Outlook*, Spring 1992, for three fine articles by Conservative rabbis on a ritual response to miscarriage.

17. The first three days are viewed as more intense than the last four. See above discussion on working during *shivah*.

18. I am indebted to Dr. Walter Gadlin for bringing this point to my attention. See Maurice Lamm, *The Jewish Way in Death and Mourning* (New York: Jonathan David, 1969), p. 174.

19. Some Orthodox synagogues will resist such a practice on the part of women.

20. One counts only twelve months even if the Jewish year was intercalated and had thirteen months.

21. R. Moshe Isserles, in his comments in the Shulḥan Arukh, states a preference for the mourner leading services rather than saying kaddish. This reflects better, he says, on the Jewish education given him by his father (376:4).

22. Sometimes special arrangements are made, such as setting up an additional microphone, so that a *kohen* may remain outside yet deliver a eulogy.

23. See Greenwald, *Kol bo al avelut*, pp. 59–60, for a discussion of the rabbinic pronouncements on flowers at a Jewish funeral.

SUGGESTIONS FOR FURTHER READING

The First Jewish Catalog, a do-it-yourself kit compiled and edited by Richard Siegel, Michael Strassfeld, and Sharon Strassfeld (Philadelphia: Jewish Publication Society, 1973), pp. 172–181, provides a lucid survey of the main laws of burial and mourning. The authors encourage readers to become active in their community in order to "re-Judaize" the procedures surrounding death, burial, and mourning. Good annotated bibliography.

Maurice Lamm, *The Jewish Way in Death and Mourning* (New York: Jonathan David, 1969), is a comprehensive, detailed guide to laws, rituals, and customs associated with burial and mourning. Easy-to-read presentation with an attempt to explain many of the practices in psychological terms; complete index for easy reference.

Isaac Klein, *A Guide to Jewish Religious Practice* (New York: JTSA, 1979), provides a wide-ranging and complete look at the laws of mourning and burial, including related topics such as autopsies, cremation, suicide, and exhumation. Fully indexed to the traditional sources.

Hyman E. Goldin, *Hamadrikh: The Rabbi's Guide* (New York: Hebrew Publishing Company, 1939), pp. 95–184, gives a full rendering, in Hebrew and English, of the laws of burial and mourning, with the relevant liturgical texts interspersed among the legal ones. Material is drawn from a wide variety of law codes and treatises on the subject.

Leopold (Yekutiel) Greenwald, *Kol bo al avelut* (New York: Phillip Feldheim, 1947), in Hebrew, gives a detailed, updated compendium of most laws of burial and mourning. The author seeks to bring people back to traditional practice for the sake of honoring the dead. Detailed analysis of each issue with full reference to the sources.

Shulḥan Arukh, Yoreh De'ah, secs. 335–403, in Hebrew, is a complete guide to the rules of burial and mourning. Although first published in the sixteenth century, most rules are still in effect today.

Jules Harlow, ed., *The Bond of Life* (New York: The Rabbinical Assembly, 1975), is a book for mourners. Contains an overview of the rules of mourning, readings from traditional sources, and reflections on death by a variety of authors. Also contains full text, in both Hebrew and English, of all the prayer services that will be recited in the mourner's home.

Jack Riemer, ed., *Jewish Reflections on Death* (New York: Schocken, 1974), is a collection of responses to death written from philosophical, halakhic, and personal perspectives. Fascinating reading.

Glossary

Aggadah – A general designation for nonhalakhic material found in the Talmud and the Midrash.

Agunah – Literally, a "bound" or "anchored" woman who is unable to remarry because her husband will not give her a bill of divorce (*get*), or because there is no certifiable evidence of his death.

Aninut – The state of deep mourning on the part of children, spouses, parents, and siblings of the deceased person prior to the actual burial. One in this status is called an Onen.

Ba'al teshuvah – A remorseful sinner. One who returns to Jewish faith and observance, whether a lapsed believer or one who grew up with little knowledge of Judaism.

Bar Mitzvah, Bat Mitzvah – Literally, a son or daughter of the commandments. Traditionally, boys attain the age of legal responsibility at thirteen, whereas girls reach legal maturity at twelve.

Bedekin – The ceremony just before the wedding at which the groom places the veil over the face of the bride.

Bet din – Rabbinical court (literally, "house of judgment"). A *bet din* is made up of at least three qualified persons. The powers of such courts are limited in the Diaspora; however, in the State of Israel, the Jewish courts have exclusive jurisdiction over the Jewish population in matters of personal status such as marriage and divorce.

Bet Hillel, Bet Shammai – Rival schools of halakhic sages whose debates and controversies greatly influenced the development of the oral law toward the end of the Second Temple period. The views of both were always recorded, although the halakhah most often accords with Hillel the Elder and his followers, who inclined toward leniency.

Bikkur ḥolim – Visiting the sick. An important mitzvah emphasized by the rabbis and included in the category of *gemilut ḥasadim*.

Birkat ha-mazon – The grace after meals. Special sections are added before and after a circumcision and a wedding.

Brit milah – The covenant of circumcision, performed on the eighth day of a Jewish boy's life. Biblical source: Genesis 17.

Derekh eretz – Deference, civility, or respect. A value concept often used with respect to the behavior expected toward parents by children; it also means a worldly occupation and, in some rabbinic passages, sexual intercourse.

Devar Torah – Literally, "a word of Torah," this expression usually refers to a brief talk or lesson related to words of Torah.

Erusin – Literally, "betrothal," this is the first section of the Jewish wedding ceremony, which contains two benedictions.

Gemara – An analysis of and commentary on the Mishnah. Together they comprise the Talmud.

Gemilut ḥasadim – The practice of kindly deeds that help to build the ideal society. Together with Torah and prayer, such deeds of loving kindness (or covenantal love) constitute a central pillar of Judaism—one of the three things upon which the world is based, according to Mishnah Avot 1:2.

Ger – Convert, proselyte, Jew by choice.

Get – A religious divorce document issued by a rabbinical court, in accordance with traditional Jewish law.

Goses/Gesisah – The state that a terminally ill patient is in, according to Jewish law, if his or her death is imminent. Traditionally, this meant that death was anticipated within seventy-two hours.

Halakhah – Jewish law (literally, "the way to walk"). A term denoting the legal portion of the Talmud as well as later codes, in contradistinction to nonlegal, narrative *aggadah*. The term applies to one law and can also be applied to the entire body of Jewish law and particularly to the oral law as determined from the period of the Mishnah onward.

Hatafat dam brit – The extraction of a drop of blood from the remnant of the prepuce as a sign of the covenant. Traditionally required of already circumcised male converts or of children whose circumcision is considered invalid from a religious point of view.

Ḥavurah – A group of Jews who regularly join together for study, prayer, and celebration. These groups, which have flourished in the last two decades, began as a protest against the impersonality of large, modern synagogues but in some cases have been incorporated into the structure of congregations as a means of repersonalizing them from within.

Ḥevrah kadishah – Literally, "holy brotherhood," this Aramaic term describes a voluntary group or society who undertake the performance of last rites and the supervision of arrangements for burial according to Jewish law. Participating in this mitzvah is considered a particularly honorable act. The men and women wash the bodies of the dead of the same gender and dress them in shrouds for burial.

Ḥuppah – The marriage canopy under which the bridegroom and bride are united in the traditional Jewish wedding ceremony.

Kaddish yatom – The word kadosh means "holy," and this prayer of consecration and praise, although it does not mention death, is recited by mourners. Kaddish yatom literally means "the orphan's kaddish."

Keri'ah – The tearing of a garment by a mourner, originally done at the moment that the death was discovered but now done at the funeral or at the cemetery by children, parents, spouse, or siblings of the deceased.

Ketubbah – The written contract of marriage between two Jews, signed by two witnesses before the ceremony and handed to the bride under the ḥuppah or after the wedding. This contract sets forth the husband's obligations toward the wife.

Kevod ha-met – The obligation to do honor to the dead person, which is the main focus of Jewish mourning ceremonials until the burial.

Kiddushin – Literally, "sanctification," kiddushin is the Jewish marriage ceremony that must be conducted in the presence of two proper witnesses.

Kosher/kashrut – Literally, "ritual fitness," kashrut denotes the religious validity of a particular item or commodity (most often, food), according to Jewish law.

Maḥzor – A festival prayerbook.

Mamzer – Legal term to describe the offspring of a forbidden union through incest or adultery involving a married woman. The latter category has increased with the rise in the divorce rate and the drop in the percentage of Jewish marriages terminated by a *get* in addition to a civil divorce.

Midrash – Classical rabbinic biblical interpretation, the purpose of which is to extract and explain the underlying significance of biblical texts.

Mikvah – A pool filled with pure, natural water, which enables the user to attain ritual purity. It is primarily used by observant women who immerse themselves before marriage, following menstruation, and after childbirth. Immersion in the ritual bath is a part of the conversion process for both men and women.

Minhag – Jewish custom that may not have the force of law, but has become established Jewish practice.

Minyan – A quorum for prayer that was traditionally made up of ten Jewish men over the age of thirteen. Today, most Conservative and all Reform and Reconstructionist Jews count women in any minyan.

Mishnah – The first postbiblical compilation of Jewish law, edited by Rabbi Judah HaNasi (Rabbi Judah the Prince). The Mishnah was compiled in the land of Israel around 200 C.E. The commentary on the Mishnah is called the Gemarah, and the two together comprise the Talmud.

Mitzvah – A commandment that Jews are obligated to fulfill. Mitzvot may be explicitly mentioned in the Bible or else deduced from the Torah by the rabbis. According to rabbinic tradition, there are 613 commandments in all. Mitzvot can be broadly categorized as those between human beings and God, and those governing the social relationships between people. Colloquially, the term *mitzvah* is often used to describe any good deed.

Mohel – A ritual circumciser.

Niddah – The technical term for a menstruating woman, with whom marital relations are prohibited in Jewish law.

Niḥum avelim – Comforting of mourners, particularly during *shivah*.

Pidyon ha-ben – Redemption of the firstborn son on the thirty-first day after birth.

Posek (poskim) – Arbiter, decisor, or codifier of Jewish law during the centuries following the completion of the Talmud. Written questions were submitted and written replies were sent after careful expert consideration. These questions and answers came to be known as the *responsa literature*, which was characterized by rendering of halakhic decisions by *poskim*.

Sandak – Literally, "helper," from Greek *sundikos*, "advocate or helper and companion of the child." The *sandak* traditionally assists the *mohel* and holds the baby boy at a brit milah. The *sandak* is often chosen by the parents because he is a religious and ethical role model for the child.

Se'udat havra'ah – The meal prepared for mourners by relatives and friends, to be eaten upon their return from the cemetery.

Se'udat mitzvah – Special celebratory meal held immediately after a circumcision and a wedding. Literally, "commanded meal."

Shadkhan – A marriage broker or matchmaker.

Shalom zakhar – Literally, "peace, male child," a term denoting a ceremony arranged at home by some Ashkenazim on the first Friday evening after the birth of a son.

Sheliah tzibbur – Literally, "representative of the congregation." The technical name for the person who leads the congregation in prayer.

Sheloshim – The first thirty days of mourning after the death of a close relative.

Sheva berakhot – The seven benedictions traditionally found in the wedding ceremony, which are repeated in the "Grace after Meals" of the celebratory meal following the wedding.

Shivah – Seven days of deep mourning observed following the burial of a close relative (parent, spouse, sibling, or child).

Shomer – A guard, especially a person who watches over unburied bodies before the funeral. Leaving such a body alone is considered a mark of disrespect, the opposite of *kevod ha-met*.

Shulḥan Arukh – The "Prepared Table," an authoritative codification of Jewish law written by Rabbi Joseph Caro (1488–1575), one of the later *poskim* and mystics of Safed. The Shulḥan Arukh is a comprehensive presentation of halakhah in four large sections dealing with every aspect of the laws of everyday life in home and synagogue, the laws of kashrut and mourning, marriage, family life, and divorce as well as civil and criminal law.

Simḥat bat – Literally, "joy of a daughter," this is one of the names given to newly developed home and synagogue rituals for welcoming baby girls into the Jewish community.

Taharah – The process of purifying a body before burial. The ritual cleansing performed by the members of the *ḥevrah kaddishah*.

Takkanah – Any rule supplementing Torah legislation and having the force of halakhah. Such enactments usually seek to remedy a particular inequity or problem not covered by existing legal provisions. These often result from changes in economic or social conditions. For example, takkanot of the Chief Rabbinate of Israel have legalized adoption, defined alimony, and prohibited marriage of girls below the age of 16.

Talmud – The major compendium of Jewish law and lore consisting of two parts, the Mishnah and the Gemara. There are two Talmudim: the Bavli (Babylonian Talmud, compiled at the end of the sixth century C.E.) and the Yerushalmi (Jerusalem, or Palestinian, Talmud, compiled at the beginning of the fourth century C.E.).

Tohorat ha-mishpaḥah – The laws of family purity that govern the sexual relationship of Jewish husbands and wives, according to Jewish law.

Tzedakah – Literally, "justice or righteousness," *tzedakah* is used colloquially to refer to charity, especially the obligation to help the poor and underprivileged.

Viddui – The Jewish confessional that is recited on the Day of Atonement, on the day of one's wedding, and on one's deathbed.

Yahrzeit – A Yiddish term meaning the anniversary of the death of a close relative. Observance of yahrzeit on the Hebrew date, primarily for deceased parents, includes burning a twenty-four-hour memorial candle and recitation of the mourner's kaddish.

Yiḥud – The private time set aside for the bride and groom to be alone together just after the wedding ceremony.

Contributors

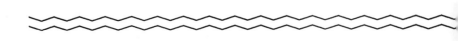

Steven M. Brown received his Ed.D. in curriculum and teaching from Teachers' College at Columbia University. He has served in numerous Jewish education administrative positions and is the author of many articles and books on such subjects as prayer, Conservative Judaism, and Torah study. He presently serves as headmaster of the Solomon Schechter Day School of Greater Philadelphia.

Barry D. Cytron was educated at Columbia University and the Jewish Theological Seminary and holds a Ph.D. from Iowa State University. He is senior rabbi at Adath Jeshurun in Minneapolis and teaches Jewish studies at Macalester College and the University of St. Thomas. He is co-author, with Earl Schwartz, of *When Life Is in the Balance,* an exploration of the Jewish ethical sources on life and death questions. His book for children, *Fire! The Library Is Burning!,* which retells the story of the 1966 fire at the Jewish Theological Seminary, was cited by *Learning* magazine as one of the best children's books of 1988.

Dayle A. Friedman has served as Chaplain of the Philadelphia Geriatric Center since 1985. She was ordained by Hebrew Union College–Jewish Institute of Religion. Rabbi Friedman is an adjunct faculty member of the Reconstructionist Rabbinical College and a founding member of the Governing Council of the Forum on Religion, Spirituality, and Aging of the American Society on Aging.

Rela M. Geffen is Professor of Sociology and former Dean for Academic Affairs at Gratz College. She is also a Fellow of the Jerusalem Center for Public Affairs. She spent the fall of 1992 as a Skirball Fellow at the Oxford Centre for Postgraduate Hebrew Studies. Two of her recent publications are *A Double Bond: Constitu-*

tional Documents of American Jews (co-edited with Daniel J. Elazar and Jonathan Sarna) and "Intersecting Spheres: Feminism and Orthodox Judaism." Dr. Monson is a vice president of the Association for Jewish Studies and a former president of the Association for the Social Scientific Study of Jewry.

Daniel H. Gordis received his B.A. from Columbia College in Political Science. He then attended the Jewish Theological Seminary of America, where he received an M.A. in Judaica and his Rabbinic Ordination. In 1992, he received a Ph.D. from the School of Religion at the University of Southern California. Dr. Gordis has been associated with the University of Judaism since 1986. He now serves as Dean of Administration and Assistant to the President as well as Lecturer in Rabbinic Literature. He is also a Lehman Faculty Fellow at the Brandeis–Bardin Institute and Dean of Faculty at the Brandeis Collegiate Institute. Dr. Gordis is the author of *Am Kadosh: Celebrating Our Uniqueness*, and serves as a senior contributing editor of *The Jewish Spectator*.

Judith Hauptman is Associate Professor of Talmud at the Jewish Theological Seminary of America. Her book, *Development of the Talmudic Sugya: Relationship Between Tannaitic and Amoraic Sources*, analyzes classical Talmudic texts from both traditional and critical perspectives. A popular lecturer on Judaism and feminism, she is currently at work on a volume that examines the legal, social, and religious status of women in rabbinic literature.

Irwin H. Haut is an Orthodox rabbi and a practicing attorney in New York City. He is the author of two books, *Divorce in Jewish Law and Life,* and *The Talmud as Law or Literature.* He has also written numerous articles on secular and Jewish law in American and Israeli law and rabbinical journals.

Stephen C. Lerner is founder and director of The Center for Conversion to Judaism, which has offices in Manhattan and Teaneck, New Jersey. Rabbi Lerner is nationally known for his success in developing programs of outreach and education for potential converts within the framework of Conservative Judaism. He also serves as spiritual leader of Temple Emanuel of Ridgefield Park, New Jersey.

David Novak is the Edgar M. Bronfman Professor of Modern Judaic

Studies at the University of Virginia in Charlottesville. He is the author of six books, most recently, *Jewish-Christian Dialogue: A Jewish Justification.* Dr. Novak is a founder and vice president of the Union for Traditional Judaism and is the coordinator of its panel of inquiry on questions of Jewish law.

Melvin L. Silberman is Professor of Psychoeducational Processes at Temple University. A family therapist in private practice, Dr. Silberman is author of *How to Discipline Without Feeling Guilty* and *Confident Parenting.*

Shoshana R. Silberman is Educational Director at The Jewish Center of Princeton, New Jersey. Jewish teacher, principal, workshop leader, and curriculum writer, Dr. Silberman is the author of *Tiku Shofar: A High Holy Day Mahzor and Sourcebook for Students and Families*, *A Family Haggadah*, and *The Whole Megillah (Almost!).*

Nahum M. Waldman is a native of Boston, Massachusetts, and is a graduate of Hebrew College, Boston, and Harvard College. He was ordained at the Jewish Theological Seminary in 1957 and received an honorary degree from that institution in 1987. He received his doctorate from Dropsie College in 1972 in the field of Assyriology. Dr. Waldman is Professor of Hebrew Literature and Bible at Gratz College, where he also edited the *Gratz College Annual* and *Community and Crisis*, the ninetieth anniversary volume of the College. His publications include a book, *The Recent Study of Hebrew*, a survey of current linguistic research into Hebrew in its various periods, and numerous articles on comparative semitic lexicography, Hebrew literature, and Judaica.

Index

acquainting children with, 49
and acts of loving kindness, 229
agony of, 186–87
American way of, 226
attitudinal stages in face of, 179
brain, 193–95
certain vs. uncertain, 172, 182–84
of children, 239
definitions of, 193–95
family continuity after, 23
fear of, 142, 179
full disclosure on imminence of, 169,
    178–82
as great leveler, 227
hastening process of, 173–74, 186–
    91
Jewish tradition and, 226–27
of parents, 101, 244–46
prayers of, 173–74, 185, 228–29
preparation for, 179–82, 229
prolonging process of, 167, 185–86,
    191
as punishment, 168–70
righteousness and, 168, 170
rituals of, 49, 100, 226–51
"voodoo," 181
as welcome release, 173–74, 178–79
decency, 122
deeds, wedding, 110
dementia, 178, 211, 212
depression, 25, 179
    aging and, 214
    clinical, 18, 19
    prepartum, 18
derekh eretz, 122
destruction, proscription of, 17, 46
Deuteronomy, 95, 99, 152, 155, 160,
    168, 203
devar Torah, 27–28, 106
diabetes, 190
diaphragms, 15, 146
Diaspora, 9, 73, 160–61
divorce, 5, 6, 8–9, 40, 44, 94, 99, 151–66
    children of, 44, 160, 161, 239
    civil, 8, 159–63
    duplication in processes of, 159–60
    financial factors in, 102–3, 152, 153
    grounds for, 116, 152, 153, 155–59

high rates of, 160
husband's obligations in, 102–6, 116,
    152–54, 156–57
ill-advised, 152–53
initiation of, 151–54
modern dilemmas and, 159–63
"no-fault," 158
procedures of, 154–55
recalcitrance in, 160–61, 162, 163
reconciliation attempts and, 152–53,
    161–62
religious, 8, 102–3, 105, 151–59, 160–
    63
reluctant acceptance of, 152, 153
restrictions on, 8, 151, 155
rights of women vs. men in, 151–59,
    160–61, 163
do not resuscitate (DNR) policy, 184
Dorff, Elliot N., 183, 189, 191, 192, 194,
    198*n*, 199*n*
dowries, 39
drugs:
    fertility, 25
    illegal, 55, 57, 169
durable power of attorney, 211
Durkheim, Emile, 3

Ecclesiastes, 93, 142, 205–6
Eden, Garden of, 12, 58–59, 92, 112,
    113, 180
education:
    communal and family programs in,
        63–66, 70*n*
    imperfection and tragedy as part of,
        47–50
    material vs. spiritual values in, 33–36,
        38, 45
    parental responsibility for, 34–39, 42–
        45, 60–61, 63–64, 85–86, 139
    in professions and trades, 38, 59
    religious, 39, 42–44, 45, 51*n*, 58, 65–
        66, 79, 85–86, 87
    see also schools
Eichhorn, David Max, 89
Eisenstein, Judah David, 129*n*
eitzah, 137
elderly people, 8, 9, 202–25
    care of, 37, 47, 55, 207–12

Jeroboam, 168
Jerusalem, 113, 137
Jerusalem (Palestinian) Talmud, 93, 152, 172
Jesus Christ, 73
Jethro, 74
Jewish Campus Life (Monson), 66
Jewish law (halakhah), 5, 10–11, 19, 85, 216
  children in, 23, 35–38
  illness and death in, 167–201, 227–49
  marriage and divorce in, 8–9, 79–80, 92, 97–101, 104–7, 110, 151–66
  procreation in, 15–16, 26–27
  sexual issues in, 26, 115–16, 118
Jewish Theological Seminary of America, 63, 162
Jewish wars, 74, 176
Jews:
  achievement orientation of, 57, 70n
  by choice, *see* conversion
  cultural life of, 82, 87
  emancipation of, 77, 98
  equal rights for, 21
  German-speaking, 21
  historical continuity of, 20, 22, 72–79
  homes of, 83
  oppression of, 65
  other ethnic groups compared with, 56–58
  population statistics on, 14, 202
  see also American Jews; Ashkenazim; Hasidim; Sephardim
Jews in America, The (Hertzberg), 57
Job, 169–70
Jonah, 72
Jose ben Kisma, Rabbi, 205
Joseph, 25, 72, 231
joy, 142, 249
  expressions of, 3
  mixing of, 107
Judah (son of Tema), 133, 136, 137, 147
Judah ben Hai, 115
Judah ha-Nasi (the Prince), Rabbi, 38, 124n, 173–74, 185–86, 206
Judaism, 221
  basic beliefs of, 83
  commitment to growth of, 14, 80

community involvement and, 65–68, 81–82, 87, 140
  comparison of other religions with, 65, 140, 187
  countercultural aspects of, 19
  ethical emphasis in, 33–34, 64, 65, 118
  good life as viewed in, 33–35, 50, 142
  importance of daily life in, 34–35, 37, 142–43
  inheritance of, 25, 76, 82
  periods of calamity in, 13–14, 75
  positive perspective of, 3, 11, 14, 36–38, 47, 64, 74, 115–17, 140–42, 249
  as process of perfecting the world, 33–34, 50, 51, 69, 83, 92, 93, 115, 140
  proselytizing of, 73–78, 81–84, 87
  respect accorded to, 77
  responsibilities of, 81–82
  resurgence of, 31
  return to observance of, 145, 243
  secular culture and, 8, 19, 58, 66, 71, 77–78, 81, 83, 159–63, 228
  studies in, 10, 65, 66, 78, 81–84, 144, 145, 237
  threats to quality of, 71, 77–78, 87–88
  see also specific communities
justice, 50, 157
Juvenal, 73

kabbalat kinyan, 105
kaddish, 4, 23, 239, 240–43, 245–46
  alternatives to, 242
  arranging for sayers of, 243
  burial, 233
  definition of, 241
  long-term effects of, 242–43
  of mourners, 240–43
kaddish derabbanan, 242
kaddish shalem, 241
kaddish yatom, 240–41
kashrut, 37, 42, 43, 49, 82, 83, 87
kavod, 209, 215
Kayama, 161
Kedushah, 91, 92
keeners, 242
Kelly, Gerard, 187
keri'ah, 231–32, 249n

mourning (*cont.*)
communal, 107, 146, 243
consolation and, 9–10, 42, 49, 169,
    231, 234
dignity of deceased in, 9, 227–28, 229,
    230, 234, 242, 246–49
for fetuses, 10, 239
and guarding of corpse, 229
for parents, 244–46
public celebration and, 238
rites of, 227–41
symbolic, 121
twelve-month period of, 244–47
women and, 10, 242
Myerhoff, Barbara, 224–25
mysticism, 141

Nachman of Bratzlav, Rabbi, 207
Naḥmanides, 116–17, 118, 170, 171,
    175, 182–83, 196n, 197n
names, 6
Ashkenazic vs. Sephardic, 20–21
biblical, 20, 22
character and, 19–20
deceased relatives and, 20
grandparents and, 20–21, 22
Hebrew, 6, 21–22, 24, 247
Israeli, 22
phonic linkage of, 21
ritual conferring of, 3, 29–30
secular, 21–22
Yiddish, 21
Naomi, 72
Necessary Losses (Viorst), 134–35, 147n
Neilah, 137–38
Neugarten, Bernice L., 135–36, 148n,
    224n
Neusner, Jacob, 113
New York Board of Rabbis, 188
New York Court of Appeals, 162–63
niddah, 121
niḥum avelim, 234
nisu'in, 108, 109, 112–15
Novak, David, 6, 12–31, 86, 196n,
    259
nuclear destruction, 13
Numbers Rabbah, 76
nursing homes, 65, 222

obscenity, 132
onen, 230
or legoyim, 88
orphans, 22–23
Orthodox community, 7, 104–5, 181
conversion in, 78–79, 85
illness and death in, 187, 195, 242
marriage and divorce in, 81, 98, 99–
    100, 105, 111, 125n, 160, 161, 163
sexual issues in, 118–20
Ovadiah, 74
overpopulation, 14

pain, 170, 173, 178–79, 185, 187, 189–
    90, 191, 227
Palaggi, Ḥaim, 173
Palestinian (Jerusalem) Talmud, 93, 152,
    172
pallbearers, 232
parents, 10, 11
adolescence and, 55–57, 59–61, 63–64,
    68–69
approval sought by, 56
children and, 7, 13, 22–23, 27, 32–52,
    98, 145, 176–78, 207–12
children's care of, 176–78
and commitment to future, 13–14
conflict between, 42, 44
consistency of, 36, 45–47, 56
divorced, 6, 40, 44
frustration of, 49, 56
fundamental goals of, 33, 45
honor and reverence for, 13, 23, 39–
    40, 42–43, 44, 46, 61, 176–78, 203,
    207–11
illness and death of, 101, 176–78,
    244–46
"letting go" by, 58–61, 68–69, 145
love for, 44
mourning for, 10, 244–46
non-Jewish, 10, 23
obligations and responsibilities of, 12–
    52, 59–64, 68–69, 85–86, 119, 139
overindulgence by, 33, 40, 59, 61
as partners with God, 12–15, 23, 32–
    52
as protectors, 33, 47, 49, 55
as role models, 36, 40–41, 50–51, 60

Make books your companion
Let your bookshelf be your garden—
Judah Ibn Tibbon

to become a member –
to present a gift –

call 1 (800) 234-3151
or write:
The Jewish Publication Society
1930 Chestnut Street
Philadelphia, Pennsylvania 19103

A Jewish Tradition